Border Studies
Cultures, Spaces, Orders

Edited by

Prof. Dr. Astrid Fellner, Saarland University

Prof. Dr. Konstanze Jungbluth, European University
Viadrina Frankfurt (Oder)

Prof. Dr. Hannes Krämer, University of Duisburg-Essen

Dr. Christian Wille, University of Luxembourg

Volume 5

Astrid M. Fellner [ed.]

Narratives of Border Crossings

Literary Approaches and Negotiations

The Deutsche Nationalbibliothek lists this publication in the
Deutsche Nationalbibliografie; detailed bibliographic data
are available on the Internet at http://dnb.d-nb.de

ISBN   978-3-8487-8008-2 (Print)
          978-3-7489-2400-5 (ePDF)

British Library Cataloguing-in-Publication Data
A catalogue record for this book is available from the British Library.

ISBN   978-3-8487-8008-2 (Print)
          978-3-7489-2400-5 (ePDF)

Library of Congress Cataloging-in-Publication Data
Fellner, Astrid M.
Narratives of Border Crossings
Literary Approaches and Negotiations
Astrid M. Fellner (ed.)
227 pp.
Includes bibliographic references.

ISBN   978-3-8487-8008-2 (Print)
          978-3-7489-2400-5 (ePDF)

Onlineversion
Nomos eLibrary

1st Edition 2021
© Nomos Verlagsgesellschaft, Baden-Baden, Germany 2021. Overall responsibility
for manufacturing (printing and production) lies with Nomos Verlagsgesellschaft mbH
& Co. KG.

Contents

Contents

Introduction

Narratives of Border Crossings X Border-Crossing Narratives

Astrid M. Fellner

The Proliferation of Borders and the Rise of Cultural Border Studies

Moving into the third decade of the twenty-first century, interdisciplinary border studies have developed a series of approaches that have not only moved beyond the 'borderless' discourses of the post-Cold War era, but that also respond to the most pressing challenges that have characterized the past ten years: the so-called 'migration crisis' and the current health crisis. Following the 9/11 attack in the U.S., the reality of increased border securitization as part of the 'war on terror' has undermined the neo-liberal rhetoric of the 'borderless world.' At the same time, partly as a reaction to globalization and partly as a response to emerging regionalism and ethno-regionalist movements, a number of states have set in motion a process of re-scaling in which they have devolved part of their power in governance to supra-state and sub-state regions (Paasi 2009). Most recently, because of the Covid-19 pandemic the world has witnessed yet another phase in the proliferation of borders. Borders have been closed in many parts of the world, and border securitization has been enforced as part of a larger health politics. As a result, the complex roles of borders and boundaries have become more relevant than ever, necessitating a reconceptualization of boundaries that treats them critically as processes, discourses, practices, even symbols through which power functions.

The emerging field of Cultural Border Studies has responded to this renewed interest in borders by offering theories and methods with which to approach borders from the point of view of literary and cultural studies (Fellner 2020). Concepts such as borderscapes (Brambilla 2015; Brambilla et al. 2015) and bordertextures (Weier et al. 2018; Wille et al. forthcoming) have developed, which critically question the manifold interconnectedness of rules, semantics and other constructions that arise through and around borders. Border imagery in cultural imaginations, representations of borders, imagining and representing in an aesthetic sense (dell'Agnese/

Amilhat Szary 2015; Nyman/Schimanski 2021) all play a central role in Cultural Border Studies. Crucially, b/ordering processes in a categorical sense, such as conceptions of gender, genre boundaries/borders, language borders and linguistic boundaries, urban-rural borders, etc. have become important issues of interests. Indeed, it is not only the territorial borders of the nation-state which divide the world; as becomes especially visible in these pandemic times, it is also social borders which separate and unite people through categories and distinctions and are thus responsible for privileging and marginalizing people. This focus on symbolic and social border dimensions of borders has also led to more elaborate ways of thinking about bordering processes and border crossings. Borders are thereby unmasked as contingent social and cultural productions and as instruments of power, which determine and often also substantiate our perception of the world. This thematic extension, which includes socio-cultural and symbolic-aesthetic questions, goes hand in hand with considerable efforts to conceptually ground the field of research, adding to the manifold empirical case studies a series of theoretical works in the field of Border Studies, which can be mapped onto a progressively developing processual and complex perspective on borders (Wille 2020). The concept of border aesthetics (Schimanski/Wolfe 2017; Schimanski 2019) has emerged in Europe, which, together with the notion of border poetics (Schimanski/Wolfe 2007), investigates the manifold ways in which borders are dealt with within cultural representations. Concomitantly, poetic renditions of borders as well as aesthetic representations of border crossings are inscribed in a rich and well-developed tradition of border literature and border writings in Chicanx[1] Studies, a field of studies which with its focus on the U.S.-Mexican border can be viewed of as constitutive for the field of border studies.

As Jopi Nyman and Johan Schimanski have pointed out, the 2000s have seen both "a 'cultural turn' in border studies and a 'border turn' in cultural studies" (2021, p. 5). Since the spatial turn, questions about cultural and historical constructions and the semantization of spaces and their borders have become important in the humanities (cf. Döring/Thielmann 2008).

---

1   The 'x' is used as a gender-neutral suffix in order to avoid the gendered ending of Chicano/a. The 'x,' as I will show, also has special significance in Chicanx literature (sometimes also written as Xicanx) because of its border-crossing nature. And the 'X' (capital letters), as I want to suggest here, stands for border crossings in general.

As Bachmann-Medick has argued, it is "[t]hrough border transgressions and shifts, through negotiations, migrations, overlaps and the formation of network-like transnational 'imagined communities,'" that "space is virtually becoming a metaphor for cultural dynamism" (Bachman-Medick 2016, p. 221). As a result of this border turn in the humanities, the border has come to figure as a space of difference and cultural encounter which is governed by the laws of the periphery that can be at odds with those at the center (cf. Lamping 2001, p. 12). As a topographical phenomenon but also as a metaphor, borders refer not only to demarcation lines per se, but also to border regions, border areas and so-called borderlands, whereby the border becomes an in-between space, which Gloria Anzaldúa (1987/2012, p. 25) has famously described as "a vague and undetermined place created by the emotional residue of an unnatural boundary" in her field-defining work *Borderlands/La Frontera: Towards a New Mestiza Consciousness*. A *borderland*, as Susan Friedman fleshes out in her spatial reading of intercultural narratives, is a special type of border area, an in-between space, "an indeterminate, potentially shifting and broad terrain across and through which intercultural traffic and transaction circulate" (1998, p. 135).

In this sense, the border, in the humanities and cultural sciences, has become a metaphor for everything that can be dichotomously split up and then interwoven again in different ways (Geulen/Kraft 2010, p. 1). It "may be read as, among other things, a semiotic system, a system of images and imaginations" (Sidaway 2007; p. 163). As identity-formation is unthinkable without bordering processes, the border constitutes a central category of perception: it divides and differentiates; but, at the same time, the border as a site of crossing is also a confluence and a meeting place of exchange that establishes a relation between both sides of the divide. The border, Schimanski and Wolfe explain,

> marks a relation, in both spatial and temporal term, between a limit/horizon and a connection. The border has a performative dimension of border creation and maintenance, as either deed or aesthetic act, which often has unpredictable or strange effects. The border is always presented, marked, represented and medialized. (2007, p. 11f.)

Just like any other concept or object, the meaning of the border can only be grasped through the workings of representation, the process by which people use language as a signifying system to produce meaning.

In the wake of thinkers like Jacques Derrida, Michel Foucault or Homi Bhabha, postmodern and postcolonial ways of thinking, which place the marginal, the liminal and the transgressive in the foreground of scientific debates, have generally been interested in looking for possibilities to

9

transcend binary logic and the defining demarcations that dictate them. Bhabha, for instance, speaks of a "third space" that arises when cultures meet and that forms a zone in which "cultural difference" underlines the constant interaction between cultures and their flexible nature (Bhabha 1990, p. 207ff.; 1994, p. 36ff.). Of particular interest, therefore, are the ways in which theoretical concepts developed by Gloria Anzaldúa, Mary Louise Pratt, Walter Mignolo, and other critics have contributed to an analysis of the hybridities and fluidities that have shaped cultural spaces. The new spatial lexicon of 'contact zones,' 'borderlands,' and 'colonial difference' points to the importance of conceiving borders and border zones as shifting sites of transition and movement, spaces which represent an in-between consciousness as a never-ending process of breaking down binary oppositions. They are heterotopic spaces, spaces of otherness that function in non-conditions. Since the 1990s then, borderlands have become the focus of interest because, as was emphasized in Chicanx criticism, they can represent places of "politically exciting hybridity, intellectual creativity, and moral possibility" (Johnson/Michaelsen 1997, p. 3).

How can we understand the border in terms of aesthetic practice or, for that matter, how can we see cultural border crossings as categories of a borderland poetics? The present volume focuses on the diverse roles that borders play in recent Anglophone literature and film. While the focus in *Narratives of Border Crossings X Border-Crossing Narratives* is on figurative border crossings in the North American context, some articles also look comparatively at other narratives of border crossings or texts which feature a border-crossing narrative. As borders are increasingly moving into the center of aesthetic negotiations, border-cultural productions and narratives of border crossings have also gained prominence beyond Chicanx studies: "The psychological borderlands, the sexual borderlands and the spiritual borderlands have become textualized in the writings of Native Americans, African Americans and Asian Americans, among others" (Benito/Manzanas 2002, p. 5). But not only are narratives of border crossings to be found in ethnic American literatures, postcolonial or intercultural literatures, they have also been moving into the focus of 'mainstream' aesthetic representations in recent years.

Narrative Activity and Border Crossings

While the border has always been an important paradigm in Chicanx literature, border figurations have recently become important in global narratives of migration and cultural crossings. "Border-crossing fiction," as Shameem Black has defined it, displays two criteria:

> First, it foregrounds a dramatic dissonance between the subject and object of representations; second, it seeks to surmount these productions of social difference. Border-crossing fiction therefore embraces the challenge of representation with an intensity that surpasses the general concern with alterity that preoccupies fiction at large. (2009, p. 3f.)

Cultural encounters, intercultural meetings, and representations of alterity can be seen as border crossing movements which generate narrative and structure its progression (cf. Friedman 1998, p. 138). Crucially, questions about the discussion of different understandings of border crossings which embrace the challenge of representation of otherness bring up the question of the poetic and poetological potential of the border and the relation of the border and border crossings to the art of story-telling.

"Stories link human history to place," Julie Cruikshank has argued in *The Social Life of Stories* (1998, p. 18). Narrative functions as a spatial practice as it enables characters to move through time and space. In *The Practice of Everyday Life*, Michel de Certeau discusses the story's function and role as an authorizing and founding principle (1984, p. 123f.). The performative function of a narrative turns narrative activity into a practice which "does not limit itself to telling about a movement. It *makes* it" (1984, p. 81, emphasis original). "Fragmented and disseminated, it is continually concerned with marking out boundaries" (1984, p. 125). This connection between narrative activity and borders also highlights the importance of cultural encounters and crossings, as the border is a paradox, which is "created by contacts, the points of differentiation between two bodies are also their common points. Conjunction and disjunction are inseparable in them" (1984, p. 127). The engendering nature and founding function of narratives has also been stressed by David Newman: "it is at the level of narrative, anecdote and communication that borders come to life" (2007, p. 41). It is through narrative that "we perceive the borders that surround us, which we have to cross on a daily basis and/or are prevented from crossing because we don't 'belong' on the other side" (2007, p. 41). Borders, as Benito and Manzanas have also noted, "link to narrative through literatures which reflect border encounters, as well as the multiple possibilities of crossing and being crossed, silenced and eliminated by the border" (Benito/Manzanas 2002, p. 5).

Border narratives offer a nuanced understanding of the experience of borders and border crossings that are essential for understanding how borders connect to the larger narratives of border formation. Importantly, in its manifestations and effects, the border in cultural productions not only finds its way into a text thematically, but also determines it aesthetically in form and constitution, from its narrative form to the genre tradition. Magic realism, for instance, can be seen as a typical genre of border narratives. Border writings also employ such aesthetic devices as trickster figures or rely on the format of the composite novel (Sadowski-Smith 2008, p. 9): "The common setting of the border as well as common protagonists, themes, and principles of storytelling hold together the individual parts of the short-story cycle or composite novel, a generic convention employed by several border fictions" (2008, p. 9). Because of its defining narrative function, Johanna M. Gelberg describes the possibility of the border as a literary giant which participates in shaping the story as the poetics of the border (Gelberg 2018, p. 21). The belief that the border plays a part in designing literature gives the border a poetic power, which, when transferred to other aesthetic forms, can become effective in all cultural products. This makes the border readable and tangible in cultural texts without necessarily having to be handled as an explicit topic in the text (2018, p. 21). Border narratives, therefore, do not necessarily have to focus on a topographical border in the plot or the setting of the story; the border can be sensed in any narrative which features cultural encounters or zooms in on the intersections of various categories of being, such as race/ethnicity, sexuality, class, etc. that b/order society and define power structures. Consequently, medialized border crossings, or narratives of border crossings, refer not only to depictions of literal acts of the crossing of territorial borders triggered by the movement of people or the experiences of migration and displacement but they also refer to the many meeting points and the multiple crossings that symbolic or conceptual borders constitute. It is these crossings of boundaries or binary oppositions which create conflicts in a narrative and get the story going.

Border crossings engender narratives; they are the site of the X, the crossing, which calls forth "an occasion for story or narration" (Schimanski/Wolfe 2007, p. 10). In his poem "X antecanto: the xicano sign" (1991), Alfred Arteaga has written about the X as sign for border crossings: The X stands for 'ch' in "xicano verse, verse marked with the cross, the border cross [...]," which for Chicanx is "our mark, our cross, our X, our sign of never ceasing being born at the point of two arrows colliding, X, and the gently laying of one line over another line, X" (2020 p. 3). Taking their cue from this poem, Ana Manzanas and Jesús Benito have defined border writing as literature which is situated at "the X, the broad area of the borderlands, the ground which allows space for mestizaje and hybridity" (Manzanas/Benito 2002, p. 14). Narratives of border crossings then not only hinge on this X but flesh out this in-between space, the site of various crossings of territorial, generic, symbolic, temporal or epistemological borders.

The poetological possibility of shaping the border has been theorized as border poetics by the research group Border Poetics/Border Culture. Border poetics analyzes the function of borders in medialized forms of production and examines representations of borders at the "intersection between territorial borders and textual frames."[2] It is defined as "any approach to texts which connect borders on the levels of *histoire*, the word the text presents to the reader, and of *récit*, the text itself, a weave of rhetorical figures and narrative structures" (Schimanski 2006, p. 51, emphasis original). Border poetics looks at both the borders in the world which is presented in texts, and the borders of the text itself (for instance its framings and divisions). It "builds on this proliferation of borders, limits, thresholds and boundaries, positing the interplay of topographical, symbolic, temporal, epistemological and medial borders in any narrative of border-crossing" (Schimanski 2019, p. 2). And it is particularly the multilayered overlays of these various border planes that, as we can see in the following articles, come to the fore in literary analysis.

This collection of articles looks into medialized borders, carving out the various routes that recent narratives of border crossings have taken in staking out the terrain of interstitial spaces. The essays focus on fiction, film, and TV series, which all employ border-crossing narratives which are born from border crossings and then reproduce and dissimulate new crossings. As such, they engage in a narrative poetics of cultural encounter and the multiple border crossings that representations across borders entail. The first section of this book, "Border Crossings in Ethnic North American Literature," groups articles which focus on depictions of textual border crossings in U.S. American literature. Silvia Schultermandl's analysis of Karen Tei Yamashita's novel *Tropic of Orange* shows that border crossings in this text feature both as acts of transgression from the effects of interpel-

---

2   Cf. http://borderpoetics.wikidot.com/border-poetics (04/04/21).

lation on hybridized U.S. subjects and of neo-imperialist transfer of capital and human resources for the benefit of the United States. Through the use of magical realism, Yamashita's novel transgresses various boundaries, ranging from geometrical lines, social borders, national borders to the border between the real and the fantastical. Francesca de Lucia's essay "Between Newark and the West Bank, Crossing Political and Narrative Boundaries in Philip Roth's Israel Fiction" looks at two novels by Philip Roth that negotiate geo-political boundaries, genre boundaries and questions of Jewish diasporic identity as opposed to Israeli-Jewish identity. The author asks about the political and aesthetic implications of the tension between Jewish American and (Zionist) Israeli fiction as exemplified in the narrative techniques and reception of *The Counterlife* (1987) and *Operation Shylock* (1993). Both novels, she argues, stage the crossing of the problematic geopolitical borders between Israel and Palestine while they blur narrative conventions and the metaphorical borders between fact and fiction.

Dorothea Fischer-Hornung's essay "Photography and Mapping: Geronimo and Indigenous Knowledge in Leslie Marmon Silko's *Almanac of the Dead*" looks into the ways in which mapping and photography have constituted forms of visualization of human perception and imagination which have powerfully defined borders and identities. Arguing that Silko uncovers the visual violence of the 'historical' pictures of Indigenous people epitomized by those taken of Geronimo, she shows how Silko portrays Geronimo as both a photographic and historical trickster figure who defies borders as well as literal and photographic capture. Ludmilla Martanovschi's "Cosmopolitan Negotiations: Public and Private Border Crossings in Shirley Geoklin Lim's *Joss and Gold*" reads Geok-Lin Lim's novel in order to analyze cross-border movements and cultural exchanges in their entanglement with female empowerment in a transnational context that encompasses Malaysia, the United States and Singapore. The author argues that the female protagonist of Geok-lin Lim's novel exemplifies the liberating aspects of a cosmopolitan mindset for multiracial and multicultural women in South East Asia. The last article in this section, Bettina Hofmann's "Russian Jewish Emigrant Writers Leaving for the West: David Bezmozgis, Maxim Shrayer, and Vladimir Vertlib," returns to Jewish diasporic fiction, exploring three narratives of literal border crossings, namely two memoirs and a novel, by contemporary Russian Jewish writers who emigrated to Austria, Canada, and the United States. Hofmann focuses on how these narratives activate prior 'American' migration narratives such as that of the Pilgrim Fathers or earlier Jewish émigré writing in order to intertextually write the transition from the USSR to the West, with all three works considered 'sending' their protagonists through Italy. As Hofmann notes: "Some direct their attention not so much to the process of integration upon arrival but rather on the journey itself when crossing different borders, i.e. on the space and time of transition."

In an increasingly globalized world, all cultures can be said to be border cultures, and thus border crossings need not be physical or geographical in order to produce a narrative. What unites the articles in the second section, "Crossing the Boundaries of Class, Gender, Race, and Genre," is that they zoom in on cultural texts which cross symbolic borders. Elke Sturm-Trigonakis, for instance, reads Hari Kunzru's *The Impressionist* from the perspective of a longue durée of globalization and its modes of cultural interaction, from 1800 to the present. In so doing, she specifically wants to engage the entanglement of notions of transgression and liminality in order to think about boundaries of race, class, and gender. This is done through a close reading of selected passages of the novel and their contextualization both with in a historical framework and in the field of postcolonial writing. Nadine M. Knight's "Border-Perforating Catastrophes: The Failure of Border Security in *The City & The City* and *The Bridge*" examines fictional works that investigate how border hyperconsciousness forces a rigid performance of citizen-identity at the expense of physical and mental liberty as well as effective law enforcement. The fictional works engaged are China Miéville's novel *The City & The City* (2009) and the television show *The Bridge* (FX, 2013), both of which belong to the detective/crime genre. Her close readings of border-breaching crimes and their analytical potential, first in the novel, then in the television series allow her to conclude with a comparative assessment lauding the novel for its subversive analysis of borders and security while considering the role of the border in *The Bridge* to be little more than a narrative backdrop. Knight argues that borders fail to enforce justice and in effect lead to increased crime. The next article, Pirjo Ahokas's "Dissecting the Colorblind American Dream in Adichie's *Americanah* and Selasi's *Ghana Must Go*," argues that the African diasporic protagonists of both novels embrace the notion of attaining the 'American Dream' via an alleged colorblindness in contemporary U.S.-American society after the election of President Barack Obama.

Janna Odabas's "A Haunting Controversy. Yamanaka's Fictionalized Melodramatic Ghost Figures" analyzes 'ghost' tropes and techniques in two novels by Lois-Ann Yamanaka that engage post-colonial representations of Hawaii and Asian American experiences more generally as well as the author's handling of the tension between individual aesthetic expression and social responsibility. Page Laws's "Crossing the Borders of Decency? *12 Years a Slave* and the Pornography of Pain" explores the line between desirable historical verisimilitude and potentially titillating sadism—that also bears careful scrutiny and discussion in slavery films. She argues that the film adaptation of *12 Years a Slave* both draws attention to and exploits the complicity of a voyeuristic audience in crimes against humanity, and highlights the tension between the need for an accurate historical depiction of sadistic violence and the danger of yet another sadistic exploitation of its victims.

The final article in this section, Katerina Delikonstantinidou's "Post-Ethnic Virtual Reality in William Gibson's *Burning Chrome*: Savage Hybrids Wandering Cyber-Borderlands," deals with cyberpunk fictions and what she calls a post-ethnic politics of transfiguration that goes beyond the limits of identity and difference. Arguing that *Burning Chrome*'s border-troubling cyberspace is populated by mythobodies/technobodies whose hybrid constitution and character throw into relief the patched and dispersed nature of subjectivity, she shows how inaugurate reconfigurations of identity are characterized by unprecedented mutability and a sense of borderlessness. With its focus on speculative fiction, this article looks into the future, opening up a space for explorative investigations of different approaches to borders. All in all then, this volume aims at further developing the (critical) examination of the symbolic-social dimension of borders by providing a wide range of textual-analytic contributions.

Acknowledgments

This book has been long in the making. Some of the essays in this collection were first presented as papers at the ninth biennial conference of MESEA – the Society for Multi-Ethnic Studies: Europe and the Americas and were then submitted after the call for papers was issued after the conference. Others were commissioned later. The topic of 2014 conference was "Crossing Boundaries in a Post-Ethnic Era—Interdisciplinary Approached and Negotiations." In 2014, during the US presidency of Barack Obama, the terms 'post-ethnic' or 'post-racial' were being discussed by critics and scholars alike. In the last years, it has become clear that the myth of a new post-racial age in U.S. history and the idealism and hopes associated with it have dissipated in the wake of a series of severe ongoing economic and health crises, heavy racial profiling, brutal police violence and continued high incarceration rate of African Americans in North American prisons.

In North American literature, too, some critics have asked themselves whether 'multicultural' or 'ethnic' literature is not in fact experiencing a shift towards a "postethnic" literature. David A. Hollinger's 1995 book *Postethnic America: Beyond Multiculturalism* provocatively argued that recent writings featured protagonists whose feelings of belonging in the attempt to overcome personal and cultural boundaries were strongly connected with notions of longing in terms of affiliation rather than a desire for a culture of descent. The postethnic perspective, according to Hollinger, emphasizes "voluntary affiliations" to a community associated with consent and to a cosmopolitan space while diminishing the importance of the "inherited boundaries" of pluralism (1995, p. 3). While this may be true for some novels in the 1990s, I believe that due to recent social and political developments which have brought about a renewed focus on borders and bordering processes, we have witnessed a rise in the depiction of refugee and migratory experiences that focus on issues of displacement. Published seven years after the conference, the articles in this volume highlight the important role of borders as well as their symbolic-social dimension in cultural productions, showing in which ways the novels, films, and TV series under investigation cross these borders.

My special thanks go to all of the contributors to this volume for their collaboration, their patience, and their willingness to make revisions. The editing of this book has been a long and tedious process, which has involved quite a number of colleagues. I want to thank Simone Puff-Adams for her help during the early stage of this project. Sebastian Weier, Yulia Gordina, Si Whybrew were all kind enough to help review all papers. Special thanks are also due to Marion Rohrleitner for offering her help and expertise with the selection of articles. When it comes to editing this book, I would especially like to thank my research assistant Megan Kelley, who not only carefully proof-read all papers but also helped with the editorial process. Special thanks are also due to Lukas Redemann, who has helped with the format and layout of this book. I could not have done this without you! I am glad that this collection of articles has found a home with NOMOS and the book series "Border Studies. Cultures, Spaces, Orders," and I want to thank my co-editors of this series as well as Beate Bernstein for her kind editorial support. As always, I am grateful toward Eva Nossem for being there for me.

Works Cited

Anzaldúa, Gloria (1987/2012): Borderlands/La Frontera: The New Mestiza. 4th ed. San Francisco: Aunt Lute.

Arteaga, Alfred (2020): Xicancuicatl: Collected Poems. Ed. David Lloyd. Middletown, CT: Wesleyan University Press.

Bachmann-Medick, Doris (2016): Cultural Turns: New Orientations in the Study of Culture. Transl. Adam Blauhut. Berlin: De Gruyter.

Benito, Jesús/Manzanas, Ana Maria (2002): Border(lands) and Border Writing: Introductory Essay. In: Benito, Jesús / Manzanas, Ana Maria (ed.): Literature and Ethnicity in the Cultural Borderlands. Amsterdam: Rodopi, p. 1–22.

Black, Shameem (2009): Fictions Across Borders: Imagining the Lives of Others in Late-Twentieth Century Novels. New York: Columbia Press.

Brambilla, Chiara (2015): Exploring the Critical Potential of the Borderscapes Concept. In: Geopolitics 20, H. 1, p. 14–34.

Brambilla, Chiara/Laine, Jussi/Scott, James W./Bocchi, Gianluca (eds.) (2015): Borderscaping: Imaginations and Practices of Border Making. Farnham: Ashgate.

Cruikshank, Julie (1998): The Social Life of Stories: Narrative and Knowledge in the Yukon Territory. Vancouver: UBC.

de Certeau, Michel (1984): The Practice of Everyday Life. Trans. Steven Rendall. Berkeley: University of California P.

Dell'Agnese, Elena/Amilhat Szary, Anne-Laure (2015): Borderscapes: From Border Landscapes to Border Aesthetics. In: Geopolitics 20, H. 1, p. 4–13.

Fellner, Astrid M. (2020): Grenze und Ästhetik: Repräsentationen von Grenzen in den kulturwissenschaftlichen Border Studies. In: Gerst, Dominic/Klessmann, Maria/ Krämer, Hannes (eds.): Grenzforschung. Handbuch für Wissenschaft und Studium. Baden-Baden: Nomos, p. 436–456.

Friedman, Susan Standford (1998): Mappings. Feminism and the Cultural Geographies of Encounter. Princeton, NJ: Princeton UP.

Geulen, Eva/Kraft, Stephan (eds.) (2010): Vorwort. In: Zeitschrift für Deutsche Philologie, Sonderheft Bd. 129: Grenzen im Raum – Grenzen in der Literatur, p. 1–4.

Hollinger, David A. (1995): Postethnic America: Beyond Multiculturalism. New York: Basic Books.

Johnson, David E./Michaelsen, Scott (1997): Border Secrets: An Introduction. In: Johnson, David E./Michaelsen, Scott (eds.): Border Theory: The Limits of Cultural Politics. Minneapolis: University of Minnesota Press, p. 1–39.

Lamping, Dieter (2001): Über Grenzen: eine literarische Topographie. Göttingen: Vandenhoeck & Ruprecht.

Nyman, Jopi/Schimanski, Johan (2021): Introduction: Images and Narratives on the Border. In: Nyman, Jopi/Schimanski, Johan (eds.): Border Images, Border Narratives: The Political Aesthetics of Boundaries and Crossings. Manchester: Manchester UP, p. 1–20.

Paasi, Anssi (2009): The Resurgence of the 'Region' and 'Regional Identity': Theoretical Perspectives and Empirical Observations on Regional Dynamics in Europe. In: Review of International Studies 35, p. 121–146.

Sadowski-Smith, Claudia (2008): Border Fictions: Globalization, Empire, and Writing at the Boundaries of the United States. Charlottesville: University Press of Virginia.

Schimanski, Johan (2006): Crossing and Reading: Notes Towards a Theory and a Method. In: Nordlit. 19, p. 41–63.

Sidaway, James D. (2007). The Poetry of Boundaries. In: Rajaram, Prem Kumar/ Grundy-Warr, Carl (eds.): Borderscapes: Hidden Geographies and Politics at Territory's Edge. Minneapolis: University of Minnesota Press, p. 161–81.

Weier, Sebastian/Fellner, Astrid M./Frenk, Joachim/Kazmaier, Daniel/Michely, Eva/Vatter, Christoph/Weiershausen, Romana/Wille, Christian (2018): Bordertexturen als transdisziplinärer Ansatz zur Untersuchung von Grenzen. Ein Werkstattbericht. In: Berliner Debatte Initial 29, H. 1, p. 73 – 83.

Wille, Christian (2020): Vom processual shift zum complexity shift: Aktuelle Trends der Grenzforschung. In: Gerst, Dominic/Klessmann, Maria/ Krämer, Hannes (eds.): Grenzforschung. Handbuch für Wissenschaft und Studium. Baden-Baden: Nomos, p. 106–120.

Wille, Christian/Fellner, Astrid M./Nossem, Eva (eds.) (forthcoming): Bordertextures: A Complexity Approach to Cultural Border Studies. Bielefeld: transcript.

Border Crossings in Ethnic American Literature

Moving Borders, Shifting Territories: Border-Polyvalences in Karen Tei Yamashita's *Tropic of Orange*

Silvia Schultermandl

Introduction

When Bobby Ngu in Karen Tei Yamashita's novel *Tropic of Orange* (1997) stands in the Pacific Rim Auditorium, where a wrestling match between the two allegorical figures El Grand Mojado and SUPERNAFTA just ended with the destruction of both contenders, he picks up the two ends of a line that signifies the Tropic of Cancer which, once it got mysteriously dragged North, now runs through the city of Los Angeles. This post-apocalyptic scene closes Yamashita's novel, and Bobby's final thoughts, expressed in figural narrative voice, resonate with the complex border ontologies the previous chapters address: "What are these goddamn lines anyway? What do they connect? What do they divide?" (1997, p. 268). This implicit contradiction of connecting and dividing is characteristic of Yamashita's novel, where neoliberal discourses of free trade and transnational capitalism collide with the lived experiences of illegal immigration, poverty, and the social stigmatization of migrating subjects. Yamashita explicitly positions her protagonists within the recent aftermath of the signing of the North American Free Trade Agreement (NAFTA) and its implication of a new social and economic order along the border between the US and Mexico, between the global North and the global South. Noam Chomsky has been among the first to argue that NAFTA's effect on US-Mexico relations results in "a mixture of liberalization and protection, designed to keep the wealth and power firmly in the hands of the masters of the 'new imperial age'" (1993, n.p.). Chomsky's astute insight that "[c]apital can readily move; people cannot, or are not permitted to" (Chomsky 1993, n.p.), also applies to Yamashita's novel, where the global North and South economically "MERGE, MERGE, MERGE" (1997, p. 206) like traffic on the L.A. freeway system. Meanwhile, migrant workers from the global South are stopped and interrogated by border police and placed under national scrutiny with a mantra-like chant: "Catch 'em and throw 'em back.

Catch 'em and throw 'em back. Catch 'em and throw 'em back" (Yamashita 1997, p. 198).

These border polyvalences occasioned by NAFTA materialize in a neo-imperialist world order which promotes the free flow of capital, goods, and resources on a global scale, while personal mobility remains restricted and policed. As Pamela Thoma rightly observes,

> These contemporary trade agreements between historically unequal partners amount to a new form of colonialism by providing major corporations access to new consumer and labor markets across national borders and, after transnational corporations push out smaller, local businesses and economic production, by providing a vulnerable pool of low-wage labor that migrates (often at great risk) to the United States or Canada in search of employment and to escape agreement-produced poverty. (2010, p. 8)

This global economy results from what Masao Miyoshi calls the "third industrial revolution" (1993, p. 736), a development that began in the 1990s through which transnational corporations take over the precedence of international corporations.[1] This "coexistence of different regimes for the movements of capital and people" (Palumbo-Liu 1999, p. 263) is symptomatic of the 'New World Border,' a concept by Guillermo Gómez-Peña which Yamashita quotes in one of the epigraphs of her novel, and materializes in a border policing in the form of "seismic sensors and thermal imaging, with la pinche migra, colonias of destitute skirmishing at its hard line, with coyotes, pateros, cholos, steel structures, barbed wire, infrared binoculars, INS detention centers, border patrols, rape, robbery, and death" (1997, p. 198).

Yamashita's *Tropic of Orange* depicts the border as a polyvalent and contradictory institution. Border crossings appear as both acts of transgression from the effects of interpellation on hybridized US subjects and of neo-imperialist transfer of capital and human resources for the benefit of the United States. Yamashita's magical realist novel itself transgresses various boundaries—geometrical lines, social borders, national borders, the border between the real and the fantastical, the border between past

---

1   Miyoshi characterizes a transnational corporation as one which is "no longer tied to its nation of origin" but "adrift and mobile, ready to settle anywhere and exploit any state including its own, as long as the affiliation serves its own interest" (1993, p. 736). Multinational corporations, by contrast, are generally "headquartered in a nation" but operate in various countries throughout the world" (1993, p. 736). Miyoshi epitomizes the neo-imperialist effects of transnational corporations when he states that "colonialism is even more active now in the form of transnational corporatism" (1993, p. 728).

and present, the border between the causal and the accidental (especially in the arrangement of plot and narrative patterns), but this does not imply that the world is borderless *per se*. By having a protagonist literally drag the imaginary border constituted by the Tropic of Cancer into the US, thus realigning the cosmic order and re-territorializing what was formerly north or south of the US-Mexican border, Yamashita's novel treats borders as arbitrary yet material manifestations of global power inequalities resulting from the colonial world order. In this new cosmic order, Los Angeles, which David Rieff calls the "capital of the Third World," now is "the second largest city of México" (1992, p. 211). This tour de force of realigning the status quo of contemporary Southern California and, in fact, the rest of the world, frames the novel's depiction of a variety of issues, including urbanism, racial formation, social injustice, environmentalism, migration, and global mobility. All these themes are personified by the seven protagonists who have equal weight in the construction of a multi-layered, interwoven plotline, and, of course, by the eponymous orange itself.

To this end, the novel depicts a persistent disconnect between various social realities and forms of mobility: human mobility; the mobility of trade and exchange; identity politics and body politics. While these instances of mobility occur (literally) simultaneously in the novel—each with their own implications of transnationalism—the transnational means something very different, whether it refers to ecology, human identity and cultural agency, trade, cartography, or history. Each of these themes has been addressed in the present scholarship to varying degrees.[2] What is missing is an analysis of the embedded ambivalence which this tension ultimately produces in the novel. I argue that in raising issues about the polyvalence of the border and the various forms of transnationalism which occur in the border cultures of her novel, Yamashita not only urges the reader to imagine her fictional world in transnational and hemispheric terms, she elaborates how the transnational inadvertently evokes—side by side—discourses of neoliberal and imperialistic practices of globalization in its sanguine call for a borderless world.

---

2   Pamela Thoma's (2010) review essay succinctly summarizes the existing scholarship on Yamashita and transnationalism. See also Lee (2007).

Moving the US-Mexico Border

Yamashita's *Tropic of Orange* depicts two interrelated border ontologies: on the one hand, the geopolitical border separating the US from Mexico, and, by implication, the global North from the global South; on the other hand, internal borders which cut through the social stratum and manifest in racism, poverty, and exclusion from the US social imaginary. With the moving of the Tropic of Cancer into US national territory and the reshaping of the geopolitical and the cosmic world order, her novel brings these two border phenomena into conversation with each other. Yamashita does so through a magical realist intervention that confronts readers with an alternative spatial logic altogether: The tilting of the geographical space of Southern California towards Mexico, which results from the northwards shift of the Tropic of Cancer, is in and of itself a rewriting of existing borders. But what does this do to readers' prevalent understandings of what borders are and how they come into effect?

Recent scholarship in border studies has emphasized both the constructed nature of borders and their mobility. Borders multiply and come into effect every time a person is interpellated as a stranger or foreigner. The border moves from the geopolitical state lines to the many locations inside a country where these moments of interpellation occur. In *Theory of the Border*, Thomas Nail argues that "the border cannot be properly understood in terms of inclusion and exclusion, but only by circulation" (2016, p. 7). Nail introduces the notion of a "kinopolitics" (2016, p. 13) to address the circular dynamics borders generate; he defines the border as a "kinetic structure" (2016, p. 14) sustained by the processes of "expansion and expulsion" (2016, p. 21). Nail's kinopolitics especially applies to migrant labor. In his *The Figure of the Migrant*, Nail contends that the border is the place of labor circuits, "to reproduce an economy of disempowered migrant labor" (2015, p. 32). Yamashita's poignant line "Catch 'em and throw 'em back. Catch 'em and throw 'em back. Catch 'em and throw 'em back" (1997, p. 198) exemplifies the border's function as such an institution, whose purpose is not primarily division but circulation. With this line, Yamashita evokes a secured and militarized border which functions as what Mary Pat Brady's calls an "abjection machine" (2002, p. 52).

Like Nail, Patricia L. Price's Deleuzian notion of the border summarizes the oft-held notion that geopolitical boundaries are "delimiting fixed demarcations of one country from another. This definition of a geopolitical boundary, as that line (or zone) where one nation abuts another, requires spatial contiguity" (2004, p. 118). Instead, she proposes a different border ontology: "Borders no longer function solely laterally, to cordon off states from one another and constitute them as discrete geographic entities. Borders can be discontinuous, fragmented, refracted across space and scale" (Price 2004, p. 118). This refracting of the border implies that the border epitomizes other forms of social exclusion by concentrating their urgency at a specific border line or zone. At the same time, border policing occurs not only within this zone or at this line; its occurrence throughout the country illustrates its ontological complexity as both a line or zone and a ubiquitous institution. In this sense, borders "produce new political subjectivities: this is an almost immediate ideological effect, the wall brings into existence the 'clandestine,' denoting them as such and thus as enemy" (Agier 2016, p. 56), as Michel Agier contends in *Borderlands: Towards an Anthropology of the Cosmopolitan Condition*.

These two border ontologies appear simultaneously in Yamashita's novel. The border's function as an 'abjection machine' and instrument of social exclusion is mirrored in the internal borders Yamashita's multiethnic protagonists experience. *Tropic of Orange* makes sure that readers understand that the border is an institution, or, to use Brady's words, "a system, not merely a site, a place, an image, or a fantasy" (Brady 2002, p. 52). The actual move of the border from the geopolitical boundary into the US establishes this connection on the plot level. Yamashita depicts the border as a site of what Nicholas De Genova terms as 'spectacle of the border.' De Genova argues that "the mere fact of border and immigration enforcement systematically activates the spectacle of 'violations' that lend 'illegality' its fetishistic objectivity" (2013, p. 1183). The above-mentioned long list of border control instruments, incidents, and institutions that produce illegality is overwhelming (to read) and therefore exemplifies the intense fortification of the border to keep out the other. This notion of the spectacle resonates throughout the novel, but it is in the wrestling match among the allegorical figures of labor history and globalization that it becomes most clear. There and in the border patrol mantra-like chant "Catch 'em and throw 'em back. Catch 'em and throw 'em back. Catch 'em and throw 'em back" (Yamashita 1997, p. 198). To be sure, these two examples signify different aspects of the border: its closure towards the other and its openness towards capitalist profit. Yamashita's novel further complicates this distinction between people and profit by juxtaposing free trade with personal mobility.

Signifying the New World B/order

Material object and metaphor, the eponymous orange signifies different forms of transnationalism pitted against each other in the novel's overall treatment of the border. The orange is not a floating signifier but a material representation of the intersection of transnationalism identity politics and global capital. It has a social life of its own[3] and functions as a central protagonist featured in every one of the 49 chapters. By connecting the individual plotlines in the chapters, which are arranged in non-causative ways, the orange simultaneously becomes a synecdochical reference for free trade, labor migration, critical multiculturalism, and nationalism.

So, what happens to this orange in the magical realist setting of Yamashita's fictional world? Yamashita depicts the orange as the novel's most spectacular border crossing agent: it has a significant birthplace, namely the spot which marks the Tropic of Cancer in Gabriel's backyard; it is smuggled into the US at a time when oranges have become an illegal fruit after the surfacing of cocaine-injected oranges in L.A.; it gets chased on the L.A. freeway, tossed around, packaged, stored, and finally peeled and consumed. Its life amidst the capitalist cycle of production, circulation, and consumption is also symbolic of the postmodern condition of the self-in-the-making and represents the innate tensions and contradictions subsequent to its own experience of transnational mobility. For instance, there are moments in the novel when it travels freely and others when it is contained by national security measurements, a fact which alludes to the inherent contradiction of contemporary transnationalism, where goods travel more freely than the people who produce them.

The novel's first chapter, "Midday – Not Too Far from Mazatlán," introduces these contradictions implied in the orange's life. At the chapter's onset, the orange appears as a material marker of the Tropic of Cancer, the imaginary line which marks the northernmost latitude at which the sun reaches its zenith. The setting of the orange evokes an abundance of refer-

---

3   My reason for focusing on the orange itself builds on Arjun Appadurai's project *The Social Life of Things: Commodities in Cultural Perspective* (1986), in which Igor Kopytoff defines commoditization as a process that bears the marks of cultural and ideological construction: "From a cultural perspective, the production of commodities is also a cultural and cognitive process: commodities must be not only produced as material things, but also culturally marked as being a certain kind of thing." (1986, p. 64). Similarly, Molly Wallace contends that "the tracking of metaphor can be a political intervention" (2001, p. 146).

ences to lines, equally connecting and dividing spaces: telephone lines, highways, fences, shadows, etc. (cf. Yamashita 1997, 11ff.). In each of these references, the Tropic of Cancer manifests itself as an alternative celestial border between North and South to the geo-political one drawn by the US-Mexico border. The Tropic of Cancer runs close to the equator and, in the setting of Yamashita's post-NAFTA world, coincides roughly with the geopolitical division between the global North and global South. This special border, "a border made visible by the sun itself, a border one can easily recognize" (1997, p. 71), runs through Gabriel's property, where an orange tree intentionally planted there marks the Tropic of Cancer. As such, the orange tree is one of many symbolic markers of the Tropic of Cancer worldwide. What is special about Yamashita's rendition of the Tropic of Cancer is that it cuts right across one orange, seemingly dividing it into two hemispheres in similar ways as it does the planet. This means that the orange signifies both the globe *and* the line which divides it into two halves.

As a manifestation of an imaginary line, the border in Yamashita's novel equally conjoins and divides people, cultures, and histories. It is a marker which excludes certain groups of people from the national narrative while fortifying the desire to keep the national narrative intact for those members of society it includes and equips with what Claudia Sadowski-Smith calls "territorially-bounded notions of national citizenship" (2011, p. 273). By re-aligning the imaginary border of the Tropic of Cancer to run through the urban geography of Los Angeles, Yamashita's novel connects the biopolitics along the US-Mexico border to the complexly woven social fabric of America's cosmopolis and characterizes the city "as a symbol of the post-national space: it is not a clearly demarcated or homogeneous structure made up of assimilated or assimilating immigrants" (Mermann-Jozwiak 2011, p. 2). In other words, the city and the border function as each other's double in a fictional world where borders themselves can move and, in turn, produce fluid national entities.[4] The border itself, then, becomes a living entity which evokes the palimpsestic space of immigrant and interethnic histories. Moreover, it serves as a reminder of a historically rooted social order which Yamashita's contemporary protagonists struggle with. This is best expressed in the novel's mo-

---

4   Chiyo Crawford's contention that "urban pollution and urban violence are interrelated environmental justice issues" (2013, p. 98) applies to the spatial dimensions of environmental justice, where exploitation of natural resources in the aftermath of NAFTA relates to economic and environmental consequences.

ment when "the line in the dust became again as wide as an entire culture and as deep as the social and economic construct that nobody knew how to change" (Yamashita 1997, p. 254). Setting the novel in L.A. is not only important for the city's geographical proximity of the US-Mexico border, but also for Yamashita's project to "decenter the dominant Anglo Euro-American narratives about Los Angeles, the ones that empower and maintain the dominant image of white and Western superiority" (Hsu 2006, p. 77). Yamashita has acknowledged that she does not "believe that there is any one voice that can represent [L.A.]" (Gier/Tejeda 1998, n.p.); her choice of a poly-perspectival narration of the life of the orange can be seen as an attempt to do justice to the various communities of the city of Los Angeles.

The notion of doing justice is also connected to Yamashita's depiction of the interconnectedness of racial, environmental, and spatial justice to the economic inequalities between the global North and the global South. Readings along these lines investigate how the tensions and contradictions in Yamashita's novel are rooted, literally located, within the spatial and the metaphorical realm of the border. Appropriating Lefevbre's idea of space as production and George Lipsitz's notion of American Studies as a project which grounds cultural phenomena in concrete spaces, Elizabeth Mermann-Jozwiak investigates Yamashita's representation of spatial injustice amid the free flow of transnational exchange of labor and trade. The tension between the mobility of trade and the stasis of prevalent concepts of ethnic identity, so the essay shows, compellingly places the novel at the paradigmatic shift in Asian American Studies. It exemplifies how discussions of Asian American identity were contained within American national discourses of pluralism, diversity, and multiculturalism but did not embrace the contradictions of diaspora, globalization, and transnationalism. Instead, Yamashita's work[5] has challenged scholars of Asian American studies to think beyond interpellation through the nation-state, an appeal which had, as Kandice Chuh proposes, created a level of "anxiety over the consequences of losing focus on the historic and continuing power of the US nation-state in racializing and regulating Asianness within its borders" (2006, p. 618) but which ultimately "exemplifies an Asian Americanist hemispheric practice characterized by a heightened awareness of

---

5   This is true for her *Tropic of Orange*, as well as her earlier work, *Trough the Arc of the Rainforest* (1990) and *Brazil-Maru* (1992). Similar tendencies are also apparent in her later work, *Circle K Cycles* (2001) and *I Hotel* (2010).

the contingent nature of knowledge itself" (Chuh 2006, p. 627). By claiming the US-Mexico border as a site of Asian American histories, Yamashita's novel expands the existing "*frontera* imaginary" (Saldívar 1997, p. xii, emphasis original), which José David Saldívar characterizes as emblematic of "the discursive spaces and the physical places" of the US-Mexico border (1997, p. ix).

If the *frontera* imaginary Saldívar positions is symptomatic of the American border novel, it is most present in Yamashita's *Tropic of Orange* in the metaphoric presence of the geopolitical implications of the US-Mexico border on the social order within the immigrant and migrant lives of the novel's protagonists, no matter their immediate lived experiences of border crossings. It is true that all protagonists, including the eponymous orange, are affected by the literal presence of the US-Mexico border; but more than that, the novel's metaphorical appropriation of the border as a trope of the globalized world resonates throughout the 49 chapters, which evoke transnational capital, mobility, and kinship as some of the themes indicated by the chapter titles. This acknowledgement of the border as a marker of the material realities of living within the geographical realm of the free trade zone is also the steppingstone for identity politics which refute essentialist practices of classification. John Gamber treats the border as a productive space which can allow for subjectivities to come into effect through a productive and creative hybridization he terms 'positive pollutions.' In relation to Yamashita's fictional world, Gamber argues that through "a massive warping of the landscape," "[a]ll boundaries—whether between nations or territories; between past, present, and future; between the self and the other; or between humans and other species—are positively polluted, recognized as porous, and constantly permeated and penetrated" (2012, p. 122). The border in Yamashita's novel relates issues occurring along national borders to the social fabric of urban borders.[6] At the same time, its geographic and conceptual proximity to the Tropic of Cancer extends these connections into the realm of the planetary.

In this specific geographical location, the tree from which the eponymous orange derives serves as a material marker of this "imaginary line" (Yamashita 1997, p. 11). Gabriel, who owns the property that is home to several orange trees, specifically chose this location to commemorate the history of international trade between North and South America: "Gabriel

---

6   See Ana Manzanas and Jesús Benito (2011) on this issue.

had actually brought this tree from Riverside eight years ago. It was a navel orange tree, maybe the descendent of the original trees first brought to California from Brazil in 1873 and planted by L.C. Tibbetts" (Yamashita 1997, p. 11). The eponymous orange of the novel therefore represents the free trade routes of globalization, presently and historically. Gamber, for instance, makes the point that the citrus industry marked the Southern California natural and social landscape by facilitating "agricultural jobs, millionaire landowners, railroads, irrigation, roads in and out of the groves, and travel, investment, and relocation propaganda declaring California to be an Edenic setting of eternal sunshine" (2012, p. 139). Past and present trade routes are implied in the movement of the orange across national borders, a fact which alludes to cyclical exchange patterns of products and ideas both along the North-South and the East-West axes much in the fashion of globalized trade markets. The orange, then, becomes a stand-in for all commodified goods in the global market sphere. Here, the orange stands for consumer goods which seamlessly move between nation-states.

In the same vein, the orange also functions as "the golden avatar of the migrating South" (Rody 2004, p. 135). When Arcangel, who, Yamashita admits, is a "literary interpretation of Peña"[7] (Gier/Tejeda 1998, n.p.), smuggles the orange into the US, "[h]undreds of thousands of the unemployed surged forward—the blessings of monetary devaluation that thankfully wiped out those nasty international trade deficits" (Yamashita 1997, p. 200). In the new world order after the borders between North and South have been realigned, the migrant workers are able to transgress the material border formerly represented by a line of people shuffling across the linoleum floor in the INS detention center.[8] In an era where goods can travel but people cannot, or, in Bobby's street-slang, "Nikes get it. But not the bro" (1997, p. 230), the transnationalism resulting from the shifting of the border implies a re-unification of territories which were one before the annexation of Alta California to the United States through the Treaty of Guadalupe Hidalgo in 1848. When Arcangel introduces himself in one of his performance acts as "Cristobal Colón" (1997, p. 198), the novel's reference to the colonial era acknowledges even earlier instances of global trade and exchange and evokes these 500 years of economic exchange paired with

---

7   Yamashita refers to performance artist Guillermo Gómez-Peña.
8   John Gamber reminds us that the US-Mexico border in Yamashita's novel is not so much a landscape or cultural zone, as border studies scholars tend to see it, but "a sterile administrative place" where lines of people walk on linoleum floors and are administered by border police (2012, p. 131).

cultural cross-pollination between North and South, East and West. This, as Molly Wallace contends, "links the history of colonialism to the politics of contemporary transnationalism" (Wallace 2001, p. 155).

As a representation of the producers and the products of globalized trade routes, the orange experiences different degrees of mobility. In its anthropomorphized form, it becomes a threat to national security like the Mexican immigrants whose homeland got annexed to the US 150 years before NAFTA. At the same time, human bodies, once commodified as trade goods, seamlessly cross national boundaries amidst the flow of transnational money and labor. The novel connects the limitations of personal mobility with free trade by turning the orange into an illegal intruder modeled after the illegal immigrants in the background of the plotline. National paranoia—"See an orange? Call 911" (Yamashita 1997, p. 140)—erupts after the (last) orange, which is suspected to be laced with hallucinogens, was imported illegally. The residents of L.A. are increasingly on edge when facing security warnings moving from "spiked orange alert" (1997, p. 138) to "illegal orange alert" (1997, p. 139) and finally "illegal alien orange alert" (1997, p. 140). In the linguistic conflation of referents of biopolitics and biodiversity, Yamashita implies that the collapse of L.A.'s social order is connected to the disruption of the cosmic order caused by the movement of the orange across the US-Mexico border and the subsequent realignment of the Tropic of Cancer. It also foregrounds the novel's depiction of the multiple and contradictory ideas about mobility and border-crossing. This satiric moment in the novel is countered by the realities of transnational organ trafficking: human bodies cross the US-Mexico border freely when they become commodities, such as the organs harvested from poor Latin American children. This poses a threat to all Hispanic-looking children, like Rafaela's son Sol, to the degree that she abandons her job as Gabriel's housekeeper and flees to L.A. Rafaela's border crossing evokes the mobility of globalized care economies, even in its reversed form, an economy which becomes epitomized in a news story about "Mexican wet nurses" delivering "international breast milk" to the US as one of the "benefits of NAFTA" (1997, p. 91).

It comes as no surprise, then, that the orange, with its multiple and contradictory identities, causes such a frenzy in the US, affecting the governmental level as much as urban subcultures. The overarching issue seems to be that nobody is able to make sense of the events that followed the orange's arrival in the US. Buzzworm, an African American Vietnam Vet and self-appointed mission angel, observes how the "poison orange" incites an "on-site powwow 'tween the gangs" until they agree to "conduct business like a FreeZone" (Yamashita 1997, p. 192). But these agreements are highly improvised and provisional for the duration of time when all systems come to a literal standstill after the car crash and because the orange does not comply with its usual fate as a commodity but takes on a much more active role. Like O.J. Simpson in his white Ford Bronco in 1994, the orange is chased around the L.A. freeway system, where the warping of the Southern California landscape causes a major traffic jam, the only moment of stasis depicted in an otherwise hypermobile setting. In the specific linguistic codes of street culture in which Buzzworm is fluent, the orange even goes by the name 'o.j.' (an abbreviation for orange juice).

Identities Beyond National Borders

The reference to O.J. Simpson roots the novel in an era where multiculturalism as a concept of cultural diversity became seen to be outmoded, in fact, as never practicable to begin with. Multiculturalism's focus on cultural diversity within the US is called into question by many of the novel's characters. Emi, a Japanese American woman so assimilated to white culture that the novel speculates whether she actually has an identity at all, offers the novel's most poignant critique of multiculturalism by postulating that "cultural diversity is bullshit [...] It's a white guy wearing a Nirvana T-shirt and dreads" (1997, p. 128). Not too subtly, Emi exposes "multiculturalism's official rhetoric as superficial, its representation of ethnicity as reductively extolling external manifestations" (Mermann-Jozwiak 2011, p. 4) like the chopsticks a woman wears in her hair to express her hyperbolic affiliation with all things Japanese—"I happen to adore the Japanese culture" (Yamashita 1997, p. 129). In the same vein, chapter two of Yamashita's novel captures the multi-faceted identity of Bobby Ngu, a "Chinese from Singapore with a Vietnam name speaking like a Mexican living in Koreatown" (1997, p. 15), whose staccato speech acts disrupt the illusion of a unified selfhood and gestures towards more complex identity dynamics that can be made sense of using multiculturalism's dominant metaphor of the salad bowl. It separates ethnic identities from national territories and accounts for the problems inscribed into prevalent patterns of racialization in the US. For instance, Bobby Ngu cons American officials in the 1970s, when discourses of multiculturalism were in full swing, into believing that he is a Vietnamese refugee in order to circumvent existing immigration quota for Chinese immigrants. He embodies a Ngu (read: new) sense of self, however, which regards identity as a sequence of performances, all addressing the specific context in which they emerge. The lines he picks up at the end of the novel exemplify his fragmentary personal history and highlight his sense of self-in-the-making. This is also true for the semantic shift in Buzzworm's chapters where the orange appears most often via the reference to o.j., which implies a change from the solid entity of the orange to the fluid quality of the orange juice. This shift in the aggregate states of the orange resonates with the move away from stable concepts of identity to concepts which see identities as always in flux.

On the one hand, Yamashita's novel critiques multiculturalism precisely because it operates with essentialist categories of selfhood unlike most other theories of postmodern identity. On the other hand, the transnationalism which her novel evokes always also implies a history of transnational labor. This becomes visible through Manzanar Murakami, whose name draws attention to the transnational history of Japanese Americans and the encroachment of the nation-state onto the lives of Japanese Americans in the aftermath of World War II. To be sure, the internment of Japanese American citizens during WWII was not so much a response to Pearl Harbor as it was a way of controlling the agricultural market of Southern California, where Japanese American farmers dominated the market. Manzanar, whose name is derived from "his birthplace, Manzanar Concentration Camp in the Owens Valley" (Yamashita 1997, p. 110) and is the Spanish word for apple orchard, thus embodies this convergence of labor history and biopolitics. This connection between the social injustices against Japanese Americans because of their success on the California produce market in the 1940s serves as a historical parallel to the novel's critique of multiculturalism in the references to the racial riots and social turmoil in the aftermath of the King and Simpson trials. Through the figure of Manzanar, Yamashita's novel reminds its readers of the legacy of racial violence against Japanese Americans and that such instances of racial violence go against the discourse of Asian American model minorities, of ethnic pluralism and multicultural diversity. Racial violence in the United States, as the killing of Vincent Chin in 1982 exemplifies, can be linked to economic backlashes on the globalized labor market, which implies that racial politics always also echo transnational economic statuses.[9]

---

9   Helen Zia (2001) discusses these events of racial violence in relation to the economic backlashes to the American auto industry due to the increased import of Japanese cars.

Despite this astute criticism of US border politics in conjunction with transnational trade, Yamashita presents a transnational and anti-essentialist sense of self as desirable identity politics. The protagonist who most explicitly offers a meditation on transnational identity politics is Manzanar, who, like the orange, holds a special place in the novel. He is, in fact, the only protagonist who can make sense of the warping of the L.A. cartography in the aftermath of the geographical and cosmic alteration of the North-South border: "But only Manzanar could see the undulating patterns and the changing geography corrupting the sun's shadows, confusing time, so that all events should happen and end at the same time" (1997, p. 206). His chapters propose a productive way of making sense of transnationalism, not as an ontological category but as a form of aesthetics precisely because he is the only protagonist equipped with the ability to see the city's palimpsestic layers of meaning, history, and culture. He is able to literally see the interconnectedness of the freeway system and the cartographic grid of L.A. with the root system of plumbing underneath the city's surface: "*There are maps and there are maps and there are maps.* The uncanny thing was that he could see all of them at once, filter some, pick them out like transparent windows and place them even delicately and consecutively in a complex grid of pattern, spatial discernment, body politic" (1997, p. 56, emphasis original). The palimpsestic vision that Manzanar professes, a skill which makes him much more prepared to deal with L.A.'s altered landscape, becomes even more intensified by the hemispheric vision he is also able to apply. From his freeway overpass, where he stands day in and day out to listen to and conduct the music of the heavy L.A. traffic, he can see "the great Pacific stretching along its great rim, brimming over long coastal shores from one hemisphere to the other" (1997, p. 170) and sees his own location in L.A. as a node within the North-South, East-West axes. Like the homeless who take over the social organization of L.A., Manzanar, a former surgeon who now spends his days conducting L.A. traffic's music which only he can hear, is not necessarily to be understood as a marginal character, an outcast, or even a freak. He is, in fact, ahead of his time because he already applies his skills to the so-called normal world before it changes in the aftermath of the realigning of the global and cosmic orders with the shifting of the Tropic of Cancer.

Like Manzanar's vision, readers of Yamashita's novel confront this tension between the two interconnected ideas of transnationalism represented by the orange. At the end of the novel, the orange appears in the Pacific Rim Auditorium, where the spectators watch on as the two giants of the North American economy struggle to determine which has the upper hand—the grassroots and subversive El Grand Mojado (The Great Wet-back), whose name evokes the historical linkages between the bracero pro-gram of the 1940s and later forms of international trade, or the neo-liberal SUPERNAFTA. There is something deeply optimistic when Rafaela feeds the peeled orange to El Grand Mojado, but only for a brief moment until the orange and peels are carried out of the Auditorium like Langston Hughes' proverbial "dream deferred." Yamashita's novel confronts the reader with the difficult task to untangle these border polyvalences and literally ends with the imperative "Go Figure. Embrace. That's it." (1997, p. 268).

Border Polyvalences and the Spectacle of Abjection

In her essay, "The Ends of America, the Ends of Postmodernism," Rachel Adams (2007) cites Yamashita's novel as an example of a new kind of postmodernism in Americanist literary history, one which does not realign itself with the dynamics of the Cold War but with newer forms of globali-zation, especially because of its inherent sense of transnationalism, mobili-ty, and migration. In a similar vein, Ruth Hsu suggests that Yamashita's novel evokes a sense of "defamiliarization that allows us to examine the archetypal American figuration of the immigrant more critically so that we might see the individuality rather than the reductive, shared discursive traits that posit a static, essentialist identity category. This process of par-ticularization is a humanizing one; it subverts the homogenizing mytholo-gies of nation and 'the people'" (2006, p. 76). On the plot level, this form of defamiliarization is accomplished through an open-form narrative in which hyper-contexts indicate multiple, simultaneous narrative realities. In Hsu's observation, the "narrative suggests that a complete picture of any-thing is impossible, that there is not a single reality" (2006, p. 90) precise-ly because the "sequential fashion" in which the chapters are arranged does not result from a "causative chain" which drives the plot into a linear direction (2006, p. 93). This irregularity of cause and effect—Hsu em-ploys the term 'emancipation' to highlight Yamashita's authorial agen-cy—"necessitates a reconfiguration of the understandings of perspective, representational politics, and by extension identity politics" (2006, p. 96).

This experimental form is in line with Yamashita's novel's attention to the border's polyvalence as multiple interconnected phenomena. Because the novel refutes a teleological unfolding of migration, identity, and be-longing and because it blurs the parameters of inclusion/exclusion and cir-culation in such a complicated way, it pits different ideas about transnationalism against each other and thereby complicates the very concept of transnationalism. A transnationalism modeled after the free-flowing capital of the global market is at odds with a transnationalism which rejects the nation state as a representational logic of identities, cultures, and communities. But precisely these two ideas meet at the border—in all its various iterations—of Yamashita's novel without solutions or alternatives. On the contrary, it only repeats the above-cited, matter-of-fact quip: "That's it."

Works Cited

Adams, Rachel (2007): The Ends of America, the Ends of Postmodernism. In: Twentieth Century Literature 53, no. 3, p. 248–272, www.jstor.org/stable/20479813, 23/12/2020.

Agier, Michel (2016): Borderlands: Towards an Anthropology of the Cosmopolitan Condition. Malden, MA: Polity Press.

Appadurai, Arjun (ed.): (1986). The Social life of things: Commodities in cultural perspective. Cambridge, MA: Cambridge University Press.

Brady, Mary Pat (2002): Extinct Lands, Temporal Geographies: Chicana Literature and the Urgency of Space. Durham: Duke University Press.

Chomsky, Noam (1993): Notes of NAFTA: 'The Masters of Man'. In: The Nation, www.chomsky.info/articles/199303--.htm, 23/12/2020.

Chuh, Kandice (2006): Of Hemispheres and Other Spheres: Navigating Karen Tei Yamashita's Literary World. In: American Literary History 18, no. 3, p. 618–637.

Crawford, Chiyo (2013): From Desert Dust to City Soot: Environmental Justice and Japanese American Internment in Karen Tei Yamashita's Tropic of Orange. In: MELUS: Multi-Ethnic Literature of the U.S. 38, no. 3, p. 86–106.

De Genova, Nicholas (2013): Spectacles of Migrant 'Illegality': The Scene of Exclusion, The Obscene of Inclusion. In: Ethnic and Racial Studies 36, no. 7, p. 1180–1198, doi.org/10.1080/01419870.2013.783710, 23/12/2020.

Gamber, John Blair (2012): Positive Pollutions and Cultural Toxins: Waste and Contamination in Contemporary U.S. Ethnic Literatures. Lincoln: University of Nebraska Press.

Gier, Jean Vengua/Tejeda, Carla Alicia (1998): An Interview with Karen Tei Yamashita. In: Jouvert 2, no. 2, legacy.chass.ncsu.edu/jouvert/v2i2/YAMASHI.HTM, 23/12/2020.

Hsu, Ruth Y. (2006): The Cartography of Justice and Truthful Refractions in Karen Tei Yamashita's Tropic of Orange. In: Lim, Shirley/Gamber, John/Sohn, Stephen/Valentino, Gina (eds.): Transnational Asian American Literature: Sites and Transits. Philadelphia: Temple University Press, p. 75–99.

Kopytoff, Igor (1986): The Cultural Biography of Things: Commodization as Process In: Appadurai, Arjun (ed.): The Social life of things: Commodities in cultural perspective. Cambridge, MA: Cambridge University Press, p. 64–91.

Lee, Sue-Im (2007): "We Are Not the World": Global Village, Universalism, and Karen Tei Yamashita's Tropic of Orange. In: MFS Modern Fiction Studies 53, no. 3, p. 501–527.

Manzanas, Ana Ma/Benito, Jesús (2011): Cities, Borders and Spaces in Intercultural American Literature. New York: Routledge.

Mermann-Jozwiak, Elisabeth (2011): Yamashita's Post-National Spaces: "It All Comes Together in Los Angeles". In: Canadian Review of American Studies 41, no. 1, p. 1–24, doi.org/10.1353/crv.2011.0007, 23/12/2020.

Miyoshi, Masao (1993): Borderless World?: From Colonialism to Transnationalism and the Decline of the Nationstate. In: Critical Inquiry 19, no. 4, p. 726–751.

Nail, Thomas (2015): The Figure of the Migrant. Stanford, CA: Stanford University Press.

Nail, Thomas (2016): Theory of the Border. Oxford: Oxford University Press.

Palumbo-Liu, David (1999): Asian/American: Historical Crossings of a Racial Frontier. Stanford: Stanford University Press.

Price, Patricia L. (2004): Dry Place: Landscapes of Belonging and Exclusion. Minneapolis: University of Minnesota Press.

Rieff, David (1992): Los Angeles: Capital of the Third World. New York: Touchstone.

Rody, Caroline. (2004): The Transnational Imagination: Karen Tei Yamashita's Tropic of Orange. In: Ty, Eleanor R./Goellnicht, Donald C. (eds.): Asian North American Identities: Beyond the Hyphen. Bloomington: Indiana University Press, p. 130–148.

Sadowski-Smith, Claudia (2011): Introduction: Comparative Border Studies. In: Comparative American Studies 9, no. 4, p. 273–287, DOI:10.1179/147757011X1304521 2814402.

Saldívar, José David (1997): Border Matters: Remapping American Cultural Studies. Berkeley: University of California Press.

Thoma, Pamela (2010): Traveling the Distances of Karen Tei Yamashita's Fiction: A Review Essay on Yamashita Scholarship and Transnational Studies. In: Asian American Literature: Discourses and Pedagogies 1, p. 6–15, scholarworks.sjsu.edu/aaldp/vol1/iss1/3, 23/12/2020.

Wallace, Molly (2001): Tropics of Globalization: Reading the New North America. symplokē 9, no. ½, p. 145–160, www.jstor.org/stable/40550506.

Yamashita, Karen Tei (1997): Tropic of Orange. Minneapolis: Coffee House Press.

Zia, Helen (2001): Asian American Dreams: The Emergence of an American People. New York: Farrar, Straus, and Giroux.

Between Newark and the West Bank: Crossing Political and Narrative Boundaries in Philip Roth's Israel Fiction

Francesca de Lucia

In Arthur Koestler's 1948 novel of pioneer life in Palestine, *Thieves in the Night*, the main character, a young Zionist immigrant taking part in the establishment of a kibbutz, expresses the following thoughts in relation to Jewish identity and the development of a national homeland: "there is this urge in us for the return to earth and normality; and there is that other urge to continue the hunt for a lost Paradise which is not in space. This is our predicament. But it is not a question of race. It is the human predicament carried to its extreme" (1965, p. 335). The Hungarian-born Koestler spent some time during the 1920s in kibbutz Hulda (well-known for having hosted several prominent intellectuals, including the Israeli novelist Amos Oz), before becoming disillusioned with Zionism and eventually settling in England. His cosmopolitan, polyglot background is distant from that of Philip Roth, a third generation American Jew whose personal history is well-rooted in the world of his hometown, and frequent narrative setting, of Newark. In Roth's work, elements of Jewish identity are secular and deeply intertwined with the exploration of a broader American self. It is interesting to observe, however, that even though Roth does not subscribe to Koestler's internationalized perception of Jewish selfhood, he endorses a view of this identity as a writer, as well as possibly of a descendant of immigrants, which seems connected to a notion of instability. Relating his famous encounter with Jewish Italian author, chemist, and Auschwitz survivor Primo Levi, Roth expresses surprise at Levi's rootedness in his hometown of Turin:

> In a large, substantial-looking apartment house built a few years before he was born—and where he was born, for formerly this was the home of his parents—Levi lives with his wife Lucia; except for his year in Auschwitz and the adventurous months immediately after his liberation, he has lived in this same apartment all his life [...]. I don't personally know of another contemporary writer who has voluntarily remained, over so many decades, intimately entangled and in such direct, unbroken contact with his immediate family, his birthplace, his region, the world of his forebears and, particularly, with the local working environment. (1986, n.p.)

Roth's attitude suggests a wider personal perspective in spite of his own attachment to roots and to American identity. Indeed, as pointed out by Emily Budick, Roth's fiction also encloses a more general meditation on Jewish identity, which includes reflections on the state of Israel. Thus, Roth explores the tension identified by Koestler between a desire for normalcy and a permanent sense of restlessness. The two novels I shall focus on in this paper, *The Counterlife* (1987) and *Operation Shylock* (1993), powerfully dramatize a "hunt for a lost Paradise which is not in space" (Koestler 1965, p. 334). The idea of a Jewish homeland, which ultimately resulted in the establishment of the state of Israel in 1948, has been and remains an object of debate amongst intellectuals of the diaspora, and in particular, American Jews. Andrew Furman divides Jewish American attitudes towards Israel in the categories of 'pre-Zionist,' 'Zionist,' and 'post-Zionist.' While the first refers to the outlook of the years preceding the Holocaust, the second represents the period where American Jews gave the strongest support to the state of Israel and the 'post-Zionist' phase alludes to the time in which criticism of Israel's policies, and namely of the occupation of Palestine became more widespread. However, in Furman's perspective, post-Zionism does not entail an actual rejection of the State of Israel (1997, p. 6). Even though Roth might be placed within the 'post-Zionist' category of Furman's classification, his perspective of the state of Israel is multi-faceted and ambivalent.

Philip Roth notoriously underwent heavy criticism from the Jewish establishment in the early years of his literary career, being accused of perpetuating anti-Semitic stereotypes. While his reputation as a Jewish novelist improved with time, criticisms persisted particularly in relation to Roth's depiction of women and sexuality. Even after his death in May 2018, various Jewish publications disputed his status as the quintessential Jewish American novelist since his work focused so heavily on the male perspective. Thus, for instance, Tamar Fox published an article in *Alma* titled "Philip Roth Hated Jewish Women," and in *Kveller*, Emily Burack suggested ten Jewish American women writers as an alternative reading to Roth. Questions related specifically to Roth's Jewish identity appear less relevant for European readers. His books were particularly popular in France, as highlighted by various enthusiastic obituaries which identify him as a "literary superstar" and tend to highlight the American and universal aspects of his oeuvre. Likewise, his reception in Italy was overall positive. In contrast to the skepticism of some American Jewish publications, Italian Jewish opinions on Roth emphasize his impact on post-war Italian communities, on which he wrought a sort of 'deprovincialization'

(Gillio 2018, n.p.). English-language Israeli media outlets also generally offered a positive view of Roth, highlighting his long career and growing reputation. Interestingly, a *Jerusalem Post* article praises Roth for his emphasis on unbridled sexuality:

> Roth's unapologetic embrace of lust and male sexuality demolished the cringing whininess of Woody Allen and other avatars of American Jewish angst. In that sense, one can anoint Phillip Roth with the olive oil dispensed by the powerful Israeli-type Jew as opposed to the Diaspora Jew. (Abbey 2018, n.p.)

Philip Roth himself held a sometimes-contradictory stance concerning his identity as a Jewish American author:

> At times Roth has been all too happy to acknowledge the importance to his development as a writer of his relationship with his Jewish readership [...]. At other times, however, he has deliberately distanced himself from the idea that his work addressed or responds to the concerns of a particular audience. (Brauner 2007, p. 127)

Nevertheless, his work has explored a variety of issues related to Jewish life, from post-war assimilation in his early work to the legacy of the Holocaust in *The Ghost Writer* and the specter of anti-Semitism in *The Plot Against America*. This perspective also encompasses a representation of Israel. As noted by Karen Grumberg, "Roth's preoccupation with Israel distinguishes him from most other Jewish American authors and reflects his awareness of the tense discourse linking place to authentic Jewish identity" (2009, p. 39).

Breaking boundaries, fragmenting identities

The Jewish state appears early on, in a rather ludicrous perspective, in Roth's controversial breakthrough novel *Portnoy's Complaint*, as the narrator is deprived of his sexual potency whilst dallying with the almost caricatured stereotype of a sabra[1] girl. The subsequent representations of the Jewish American experience of Israel that appear in *The Counterlife* and *Operation Shylock* are less farcical and more complex, yet also point to situations of destabilization rather than comfort or sense of belonging for Roth's protagonists. In these two texts, contacts with the Jewish state blur rather than solidify the characters' sense of selfhood as Jews. This notion of ambiguity is highlighted by the form of the novels, which cloud and

---

1   A *sabra* is an Israeli-born Jew.

disrupt traditional narrative conventions, as well as by their plots. Indeed, as observed by Debra Shostak:

> The texture of each novel is thick with the reflexive play of language, whereby each self produced for narrative display is manifestly artifact of speech and/or writing. In *The Counterlife* Roth signals this effect with repeated references to the verbal as the medium through which impersonation takes place [...] and, more globally, through the novel's structure of chapters that, in replacing each other sequentially, consistently reinvent the 'being' of the central characters [...]. Likewise, in *Operation Shylock*, the whole of the novel functions as one long linguistic performance—of Roth becoming Philip through the process of narrating a sequence of events and experiences, obeying the imperative Philip recognizes in turn, in his double. (2004, p. 131)

This linguistic and narrative context is reflected in the actual border crossings contained in the novels, which both include trips back and forth between Israel and the West bank. Hence Roth tests both literary and geopolitical boundaries.

The West Bank (referring to the west bank of the river Jordan) designates the territories occupied by Israel in 1967 after the Six-Day War and is sometimes called, in nationalist Israeli discourse and in particular in that of settlers, by the biblical name of the area, 'Judea and Samaria.' The Green line (a term Roth does not generally use) is the informal name given to the border. The question of nomenclature comes up repeatedly in Roth's exploration of Jewish identity through the lens of attitudes towards Israel/Palestine and in particular issues related to borders and borderlands. Gloria Anzaldúa famously described a borderland as "a vague and undetermined place created by the unnatural residue of an unnatural boundary. It is a constant state of transition" which lacks the clear demarcation of a border and can thus lead to tension and violence (1987, p. 3). According to Scott E. Michaelsen and David Johnson, "the idea of the 'border' or 'borderlands' has also been expanded to include nearly every psychic or geographic space about which one can thematize problems of boundary or limit" (1997, p. 1f.).

The nature of the borderland culture between Israel and Palestine is hazy, having acquired different meanings and shifting in time. David Newman points to the fluid notion of boundaries between Israel and Palestine:

> The demarcation of territory has been a very fluid process in Israel-Palestine during the twentieth century. From the period of the Ottoman Empire through the British Mandate, the establishment of the state of Israel and the partition of Palestine, the Six-Day War and Israeli territorial expansion, the Camp David Peace Accords with Egypt and territorial contraction, followed by the most recent phases of

> Palestinian autonomy and Israeli territorial withdrawal, the map of the region has
> been constantly changing. (Newman 2001, p. 148)

Moreover, Newman identifies the development of a "geography of fear" (1995, p. 23) that developed after the first Intifada in 1987, leading to more difficult and limited contacts between the parts, since Israelis avoided traveling to certain areas for security reasons, while curfews and limitations were imposed on Palestinians. It is significant to observe that while *The Counterlife* presumably takes place in the late 1970s, it was published in 1987 and that *Operation Shylock* clearly takes place around 1988 and refers to the intifada; hence the 'geography of fear' emerges in the novels. Furthermore, according to Andrew Furman, the first intifada, along with other events such as Jonathan Pollard's conviction of espionage for transmitting military secrets to Israel, played a significant part in damaging American Jewish faith and identification with the Jewish state. In particular:

> [t]he nightly news film of heavily armed Israeli soldiers chasing down and occasionally shooting or beating rock-wielding Palestinian teenagers went a long way shattering the heroic image of the Israeli soldier to which most American Jews had clung until that point. (1997, p. 8)

This specific situation (along with an Israeli soldier who does question his role as a potential pursuer of Palestinian teenagers) appears in a section of *Operation Shylock* which will be discussed later. Consequently, with his Israel fiction, Roth takes part in a broader Jewish American problematization of Israel and its policies.

The act of border crossing and the metaphorical crossings of the borders of conventional fictional structures are intertwined in Roth's Israel novels. This represents part of a broader pattern within the writer's oeuvre. The body of Roth's work involves the creation of complex self-fictions, including recurring alter egos as well as works featuring Roth's own persona with greater or slighter degrees of fictionalization. Elaine Safer points out that:

> the subject matter of [his] later novels is the comic handling of fictional systems themselves. Novels engage in postmodern experimentation with multiple narrators in terms of their comic consciousness of their own fictivity. These novels explore all possible ways of doing narrative, as well as the connection between the told and the teller (exhibiting Roth's playful comic use of details from his own life and even the use of his own name, as in *Deception* and *Operation Shylock*). (1996, p. 157)

The list of 'also by Philip Roth' books currently present in his novels contains 'Zuckerman' and 'Kepesh books' (featuring the entirely fictional Nathan Zuckerman and David Kepesh) as well as 'Roth books,' that is, books centering on Roth himself. The latter category goes from straightforward memoir in *Patrimony*, the account of Roth's father's terminal illness, to the *The Plot Against America*, an alternate history narrating the vicissitudes of the Roth family under an American Nazi regime. This nomenclature clearly blurs the distinction between fiction and autobiographical narrative, the creation of alter egos and the revelation of the self. According to this classification, *The Counterlife* is a Zuckerman book and *Operation Shylock* a Roth book. Hence, in dealing with the state of Israel, Philip Roth explores both writerly and national questions of identity.

Creating Jewish "counterlives" between the United States and the West Bank

Nathan Zuckerman, Roth's most prominent recurring alter ego, is a Newark-born Jewish novelist who has achieved fame as well as receiving intense criticism after the publication of a novel titled *Carnovsky* (obviously an echo of *Portnoy's Complaint*). He appears most prominently in the Zuckerman Bound Trilogy, which develops a Jewish writer's struggles between self-expression and the pressure of origins and family loyalties. The Zuckerman character is also at the center of *The Counterlife*, a novel composed of five sections, each of which alters and shifts the events of the previous one. It is significant to note that the title of the sections (with the possible exception of the last one) all refer to places or spatial shifts: 'Basel,' 'Judea,' 'Aloft,' 'Gloucestershire,' and 'Christendom.' Thus, the formal structure of the novel already alludes to problematic notions of space and identity. The displacement appearing in the titles is reflected in the contrasting narratives: Zuckerman's younger brother Henry dies after coronary surgery in the first part and joins a settlement on the West Bank in the second one; a woman named Maria appears at first as Henry's Swiss mistress and subsequently as Zuckerman's English wife.

While 'Basel' stages a familial and sexual drama amongst assimilated middle-class American Jews, 'Judea' starts with a meditation on the contrast between diasporic and Israeli Jewish identity. The fragmentation of the writerly self is further enhanced by the introduction of yet another alter ego, the Israeli left-wing journalist Shuki Elchanan. Budick points out: "In this book that not only produces counterlives but tends to turn lives and realities inside out, Shuki serves as none other than a kind of Israeli Philip Roth, countering the American Roth, Nathan Zuckerman" (2007, p. 69). Interestingly, in his autobiography *A Tale of Love and Darkness*, the left-wing Israeli novelist Amos Oz on one occasion pictured for himself an

American 'counterlife' as Philip Roth. Oz states that, had his grandparents decided to settle in the United States rather than returning to Europe and eventually emigrating to Palestine, "I would have been born in Brooklyn or Newark, New Jersey, and written clever novels in English about the passions and inhibitions of top-hatted immigrants and the neurotic ordeals of their agonized progeny" (Oz 2003, p. 91). The mention of Newark is a direct allusion to Roth, thus creating an implicit (as well as ironic, considering Oz's tone) form of dialogue between Jewish American and Israeli narrations.

Zuckerman and Shuki's dialogue introduces the topic of the West Bank settlements. Shuki's frustrated comments both trivialize and deride the act of border crossing:

> Pioneers! They work all day in government jobs in Jerusalem and drive home to biblical Judea for dinner at night. Only eating chopped chicken liver at the biblical source, only going to bed on the biblical sites, can a Jew find Judaism. Well, if they want so much to sleep at the biblical source because that is where Abraham tied his shoelaces, then they can sleep there under Arab rule! Please, don't talk to me about what these people are up to, it makes me too crazy. (Roth 2005, p. 79f.)

Shuki's musings serve as a prelude to the reflection on the settlements at the core of 'Judea.' The narrative structure of the chapter follows that of Zuckerman's movement from Tel Aviv, to the Old City of Jerusalem and later to the Hebron settlement to find Henry, thus gradually moving towards increasingly problematic and less legitimate Jewish territories. In the settlement of Agor, more characters serving as mirror images appear: Henry is contrasted not only with his brother but also with Shuki, expressing a patronizing, if not particularly hostile view of Jewish and Arab coexistence in the colonies. His perspective appears to be confirmed by interaction with friendly Arab restaurateurs, yet at the same time it is undermined because Henry brings a gun with him, an act which prompts a metafictional reflection on the part of Zuckerman: "my mind remained on his pistol and on Chekhov's famous dictum that a pistol hanging on the wall in Act One must go off in Act Three. I wondered what act we were in, not to mention which play-domestic tragedy, historical epic, or just straight farce?" (2005, p. 112). Finally, Mordercai Lippman, the settlement leader under whose spell Henry has fallen under and who, according to Shuki, "smells of fascism," serves as a more extreme pendant than Henry both to Shuki and Zuckerman, giving voice to a jingoistic and anti-Arab rhetoric. These various figures increase the element of both ideological and narrative disintegration.

Significantly, the third section of the novel, "Aloft," which is the structural center of the book, is set entirely aboard an El Al plane, suggesting a sense of uprootedness as well as a complete blurring of borders. In a particularly absurd twist, Zuckerman becomes accidentally embroiled in a hijacking attempt. The American-born Mossad agents who brutalize Zuckerman on the plane refer to the ambiguity of place names, and the destructive laceration of the Middle Eastern conflict it reflects: "The West what? If that's the West bank, where is the East bank? Why do you speak in Arab political nomenclature about the West bank?" (2005, p. 178). In the closing of the chapter, Zuckerman performs a grotesque forced aliyah[2] that mirrors Henry's lofty fanaticism: "Consequently, as the steep descent into Israel began, it was I alone, returning to the Promised Land with all my clothing peeled away and shackled to God's bird, the El Al plane" (2005, p. 185). While the outcome of the hijacking incident is never revealed and apparently has never taken place in the remnant of *The Counterlife*, Judea reappears significantly in Zuckerman's English wife's (at this stage mistress), Maria, dream, where she is swimming, "escaping from something" when some boys on a jetty encourage her to climb on a moored boat, shouting "Judea! Judea!", only to be replaced by Maria's first English husband, wearing a green tweed suit. Maria calls the dream "grotesquely obvious." (2005, p. 195). In her interpretation of the dream, green refers to what is quintessentially, almost stereotypically English, associating the color to Gloucestershire, the place that gives the chapter its title. Both Maria and Zuckerman are oblivious to the implication that might refer to the "green line," which would imply that the dream refers not to the contrast between Zuckerman and the English husband as the two men in Maria's life, but rather to the controversies attached to Israel and Palestine, represented by her relationship with Zuckerman.

Meeting the other, meeting oneself in Operation Shylock

Furman points out that, in spite of his skepticism towards standard Zionist discourse and insistence on the fanaticism of the settlers, Roth does not give a voice to Arab figures in *The Counterlife*'s representation of the Israel-Palestine 'geography of fear.' This partly changes in *Operation Shylock*, a novel that pushes to an even further extreme the intermingled dis-

---

2   The term *aliyah* designates a Jewish person's move to Israel.

ruption of traditional narrative structure and personal as well as Jewish national identity. As mentioned before, *Operation Shylock* is a 'Roth' book. Here, Roth interweaves actual autobiographical facts, such as a possibly pharmaceutically induced mental breakdown, with an increasingly surreal narrative concerning an encounter with a double of himself, bearing the same full name and a close physical resemblance, who is the proponent of a movement called 'diasporism,' which aims at bringing back Ashkenazi Israelis to their Eastern European countries of origin. Ulla Haselstein notes that in *Operation Shylock*, Roth "encounters a doppelgänger within himself, the fight for whom serves as a commentary both on the conflict between Israel and the Palestinians and on the political responsibilities and loyalties in his writing" (2011, p. 56). Massimiliano Boni observes that the fragmentation of the self goes beyond that between Philip Roth and his 'impostor' alter ego, since the various characters he encounters embody different facets of Jewish identity (2012, p. 100). Thus, his cousin Apter represents the traumatized Holocaust victim and, by contrast, the novelist Aharon Appelfeld is the intellectual survivor who has channeled his experiences into his art. The doppelgänger, with whom Roth engages into a verbal, as well as ultimately physical struggle (mirroring the biblical story of Jacob wrestling with the angel mentioned in the epigraph of the novel), can be read as an embodiment of internal struggle; finally the character of Smilesburger, who is also a camp survivor and is implied to be a secret agent, is the Jew who has embraced an Israeli identity (Boni 2012, p. 87). The fragmentation of the self reflects the intricacies of the borderlands that serve as the backdrop of *Operation Shylock*.

In the course of the novel, Roth is dragged towards the disruptive border culture after an encounter with a Palestinian former graduate school classmate named George Ziad (possibly based on Edward Said) who, mistaking Roth for his 'diasporist' alter ego, engages into a passionate anti-Zionist tirade, referring to the loss of Jewish culture of values and culture which he associates with the diaspora:

> Yes, they are the authentic ones, the Yehoshuas and the Ozes, and tell me, I ask them, what are Saul Alinsky and David Riesmen and Meyer Shapiro and Leonard Bernstein and Bella Azbug and Paul Goodman and Allen Ginsberg and on and on and on [...]. That's what these 'authentic' Jews will have contributed to civilization—a country lacking every quality that gave the Jews their great distinction! (Roth 1994, p. 125)

Interestingly, while these thoughts are attributed to an Arab character, they are reminiscent of Zuckerman's indifference to Israel and his identification with a specifically American perception of Jewishness in *The Coun-*

terlife, as well as possibly some of the derogatory remarks made for instance by the novelist Avraham B. Yehoshua throughout the years towards
the Jewish culture of the diaspora.[3]

Said, like George Ziad, makes a distinction between Israeli and diasporic
Jewish identity, espousing the ideas of philosophers such as Adorno and describing himself wryly in an interview with Ari Shavit on Haaretz as "the last
Jewish intellectual" (Shavit 2001, p. 445). This symmetry causes a further
identity blur, hinting at the potential similarities between Jewish and Palestinian predicaments in the context of narratives of marginalization, oppression
and exile. Moreover, Ziad himself becomes another possible alter ego since he
"can be seen as one more impersonation for Philip, offering a voice that oppose those of the Israelis. 'Zee' as he is called could, in a Nabokovian twist,
stand for an inverted 'story of Z,' that is, of Zionism" (Shostak 2004, p. 142).

While it is beyond the scope of the present work, it can be noted that the
merging of apparently clashing Jewish and Arab narratives and personal
identities is a theme both of Israeli Jewish and Palestinian/Israeli Arab writing. Thus, for instance, Sayed Kashua's novel *The Second Person* (2011)
stages an Arab character who gradually endorses a Jewish persona; on the
other hand, in the Israeli author Savyon Liebriecht's story, "The Road to
Cedar City," a Palestinian man befriended by an Israeli Jewish woman during a trip in the United States says "you have no idea what it is like to be
homesick for Jerusalem" (Liebrecht 1998, p. 145) and generally voices a
perspective echoing traditional Jewish diasporic discourse of exile. These
elements suggest that Roth's complex reflections on shifting ethnic and national identities may be considered as part of a broader literary context
englobing both Jewish and Palestinian narrations and emphasizing the
common experience of marginalization and loss rather than that of conflict
and mutual hostility.

The mirror images in *Operation Shylock* subsequently multiply as Roth
enters "his second Jewish courtroom in two days" (Roth 2005, p. 140), the

---

3   Just a few days before I gave the paper on which this article is based at the
     ninth MESEA conference in Saarbrücken, Yehoshua attacked Nicole Krauss at
     the International Writers Festival in Jerusalem, dismissing Jewish American
     literature, including the work of Roth. According to *Haaretz*, "He rejected in
     one sweep any non-Israeli Jewish literature, taking particular aim at the giants
     of American Jewish literature of the previous generation, such as Bernard Mal-
     amud, Philip Roth and Saul Bellow. Yehoshua claimed that he was "unim-
     pressed by them since they failed the test by not comprehending the grandeur
     of political Zionism by not opting for it as the sole path for a continued Jewish
     historical existence" (Namdar 2014, n.p.).

first having been Demjanjuk's trial and the second that of a Palestinian teenager in Ramallah. This contrast may allude to two possible jarring views of the Jewish state, as avenging Jewish victims and victimizing Palestinians in turn. At the same time, Roth's representation of the intricacies of the border culture and of the 'geography of fear' veer gradually towards the darkly humorous. Struggling to find his way back to Jerusalem and feeling potentially threatened both by Arabs and Jewish settlers as well as the IDF soldiers he eventually encounters, Roth muses: "And this is what you get from fucking around in the middle of a civil insurrection! [...] This is what you get for your bad jokes!" (Roth 1994, p. 166). He is eventually rescued from his predicament by another key figure in *Operation Shylock*'s exploration of the Middle Eastern conflict, the Israeli lieutenant who is a reader of Roth's novels and who has a role similar to Shuki's in *The Counterlife*, voicing a left-wing, self-critical Israeli position, rendered more dramatic by his status as a soldier.

After the Ramallah episode, the plot of *Operation Shylock* becomes increasingly intricate and surreal, at times borrowing in a parodistic fashion from the conventions of spy novels (especially those using the Middle Eastern conflict as background, such as the British spy fiction writer John LeCarré's *The Little Drummer Girl*) and further enhancing the sense of dissolution of the self. Interestingly, Roth claims to have removed the chapter of the narrative relating the titular "Operation Shylock," supposedly as a result of Smilesburger's advice, something than can be read as a "textual mutilation" that increases the general sense of fragmentation of the novel (Grumberg 2009, p. 54).

Conclusion

The Counterlife and *Operation Shylock* do more than elaborate a reflection on the meaning of Israel for American Jewry from the point of view of a novelist who, early in his career, was accused of expressing self-hate. These novels use the lacerating and shifting boundaries between Israel and Palestine to reflect blurring metaphorical boundaries within fiction, within Jewish identity as well as within selfhood at large. They operate an investigation of the concept of border-crossing, which acquires a meaning beyond that of a physical shift, facing highly controversial dilemmas related to how Jews (both in Israel and at large) might view the Israeli-Arab conflict. It is in this way that, to borrow once again from Koestler's reflection, for Roth, Jewishness becomes indeed "the human predicament carried to its extreme" (Koestler 1965, p. 335).

Works Cited

Abbey, Alan (2018): Famed writer Philip Roth didn't play nice, www.jpost.com/ Diaspora/Famed-writer-Philip-Roth-didnt-play-nice-558221, 21/12/2020.

Anzaldúa, Gloria (1987): Borderlands/La Frontera: The New Mestiza (1st ed. ed.). San Francisco: Spinsters/Aunt Lute.

Boni, Massimiliano A. (2012): "Una Specie di Distillato di Umanità": L'Identità Ebraica in Operazione Shylock di Philip Roth. In: La Rassegna Mensile di Israel 78, no. 3, p. 87–104, www.jstor.org/stable/43497776.

Brauner, David (2007): Philip Roth. Manchester: Manchester University Press.

Budick, Emily Miller. (2007): Roth and Israel. In: Parrish, Timothy (ed.): The Cambridge Companion to Philip Roth. Cambridge: Cambridge University Press, p. 68–81.

Furman, Andrew (1997): Israel Through the Jewish-American Imagination: A survey of Jewish-American Literature on Israel, 1928-1995. Albany: State University of New York Press.

Gillio, Gian M. (2018): Philip Roth visto da Guido Vitale: era la nostra finestra sul mondo, www.articolo21.org/2018/05/philip-roth-visto-da-guido-vitale-era-la-nostra-finestra-sul-mondo/, 21/12/2020.

Grumberg, Karen (2009): Necessary Wounds and the Humiliation of Galut in Roth's The Counterlife and Operation Shylock. In: Philip Roth Studies 5, no. 1, p. 35–59, www.jstor.org/stable/10.5703/philrothstud.5.1.35.

Haselstein, Ulla. (2011): Diasporic Doubles: Philip Roth's Operation Shylock. In: Fluck, Winfried/Pease, Donald E./Rowe, John C. (eds.): Re-framing the Transnational Turn in American studies. Hanover, N.H.: Dartmouth College Press.

Koestler, Arthur (1965): Thieves in the Night: Chronicle of an Experiment. London: Hutchinson.

Liebrecht, Savyon (1998): Apples from the Desert (1st English-language ed. ed.). New York: Feminist Press at the City University of New York.

Michaelsen, Scott/Johnson, David E. (1997): Border theory: The Limits of Cultural Politics. Minneapolis: University of Minnesota Press, www.jstor.org/stable/10.5749/ j.ctttsx6s.

Namdar, Reuven (2014): When Nicole Krauss was bullied in Jerusalem for being a U.S. Jew – Opinion, www.haaretz.com/opinion/.premium-when-nicole-krauss-was-bullied-in-j-lem-1.5250259, 21/12/2020.

Newman, David (1995): Boundaries in Flux: The 'Green Line' Boundary between Israel and the West Bank – Past, Present and Future. In: Boundary and Territory Briefing 1, no. 7.

Newman, David (2001): Boundaries, Borders, and Barriers: Changing Geographic Perspectives on Territorial Lines. In: Albert, Mathias/Jacobson, David/Lapid, Yosef (eds.): Rethinking International Relations Theory: Identities, Borders, Orders (Vol. 18). University of Minnesota Press, p. 137–152, www.jstor.org/stable/10.5749/j.ctttst8f.11.

Oz, Amos (2003): A Tale of Love and Darkness. Orlando: Hartcourt, Inc.

Roth, Philip (1986): Philip Roth talks to the Italian writer Primo Levi about his life and times. In: London Review of Books 8, no. 18, www.lrb.co.uk/the-paper/v08/n18/philip-roth/philip-roth-talks-to-the-italian-writer-primo-levi-about-his-life-and-times, 21/12/2020.

Roth, Philip (1994): Operation Shylock. London: Vintage.

Roth, Philip (2005): The Counterlife. London: Vintage.

Safer, Elaine B. (1996): The Double, Comic Irony, and Postmodernism in Philip Roth's Operation Shylock. In: MELUS 21, no. 4, p. 157–172, www.jstor.org/stable/467647, DOI:10.2307/467647.

Shavit, Ari (2001): "My Right of Return." In: Viswanathan, Gauri (ed.): Power, Politics and Culture: Interviews with Edward W. Said. New York: Vintage Books, p. 443–458.

Shostak, Debra B. (2004): Philip Roth: Countertexts, Counterlives. Columbia, S.C.: University of South Carolina Press.

Photography and Mapping: Geronimo and Indigenous Knowledge in Leslie Marmon Silko's *Almanac of the Dead*

Dorothea Fischer-Hornung

'If they've not read Hiawatha, the photographer has.' [1]

'This portrait is not an Indian.'[2]

For centuries, mapping—and more recently photography—has marked and expressed forms of visualization of human perception and imagination. Both maps and photographs often define borders and identities— entities in the discourse of power. In many of her works, Leslie Marmon Silko establishes how the materialization of the abstract categories of space and time—often mapped in nation-state borders—can both initiate and confirm such discourses. However, these same expressions of material culture can also be a way of deconstructing those very same categories, exploding the borders marked in cartographic representation. The perception of the reality of the photographic image is dissolved through acts of imagination.

The epistemology of the Enlightenment and the West, with its imposition of linear constructions of space in mapping and time in the writing of history, is targeted as a central theme in Silko's *Almanac of the Dead* (1991). The gaze of colonizing forces imposed on the indigenous subject is confronted in the exposure of material culture as one instrument of dominance. Rather than conforming to the mapping and policing of borders—here, the border between Mexico and the United States (U.S.)— Silko's frontispiece, the "Five Hundred Year Map," centers on people and their relationships. It concentrates on connective border relations rather than separating border divisions, challenging the violation of Native lands along nation-state borders, the 'reality' of which is categorically denied by indigenous peoples.

---

1   Paul Fussell, quoted in Dippie 1992, p. 132.
2   Vizenor 1994, p. 44.

Since its inception, photography, like mapping, has been at the center of epistemologies of the 'real.' The viewer's perception of the image, especially in the early days of analog photography, was strictly tied to the idea that portraits of individuals presented the 'reality' of those who were photographed. Initially, there were—especially because of the restrictions presented by long exposure times and complicated development techniques—clearly defined rules of portraiture, including those rules of composition and iconography passed on from the classical fine arts in the West. It was clear to those being photographed that certain forms of decorum were required, which clothes and colors were appropriate and what was to be brought along and worn for a photo session. Further, creative backdrops were common accessories that created the desired atmosphere. In the context of photographic history and at the point in time when the last of the Indian wars were being fought, portraiture of Indians in full tribal regalia became part of the cultural discourse of the Noble Savage threatened by extinction or its binary opposite, the Cruel Savage, whose manifest destiny it was to be extinguished. Those who had threatened the pioneers moving West had been either removed or forced to surrender—the portraits thus illustrating the nobility of a 'dying race.' Much like in the photography of colonialism and anthropology, the subjects being photographed were part of a larger discourse of dominance and violence, whereby what was 'real' was defined by the photographer and the viewer based on the epistemology of the West. It is in this context that Silko inserts her counternarrative of photography of Goyathlay, more commonly known as Geronimo.[3]

Epistemologies of mapping

In the "Five Hundred Year Map" that introduces and defines *Almanac of the Dead*'s imaginary cartography, Tucson, Arizona, is mapped as the center of evil.[4] Only one border is drawn as a strictly horizontal, incision-like parallel mid-way between the North and the South, with Mexico marked

---

3   Silko refers to Goyathlay, a Bedonkohe Apache, as Geronimo throughout *Almanac*. In accordance, I refer to him as Geronimo.

4   In an explanatory boxed text Silko defines the significance of Tucson, the Apache Wars and, implicitly, Geronimo's resistance: "Tucson, Arizona: Home to an assortment of speculators, confidence men, embezzlers, lawyers, judges, police and other criminals, as well as addicts and pushers, since the 1880s and the Apache Wars" (1991, frontispiece).

in large, bold letters just south of the 'border' and Tucson centered due North—the United States is not cited on the map at all. The names of various groupings of characters in the novel are scattered on the map:

> Rather than dividing peoples and land, Silko's map connects disparate peoples over a five-hundred-year period. On the map nineteenth-century Apache 'Geronimo' appears on a list of characters directly before the African American Vietnam War veteran 'Clinton' and directly after white 'John Dillinger,' who was killed after committing a bank robbery in 1934. By linking these disparate people and time periods together on her map and throughout the text, Silko works to disrupt the normative Christian idea, repeated in secular terms in the Enlightenment, that human time and history are linear and disconnected from the earth. (Romero 2002, p. 629)

If after the Enlightenment in the West time was linear and progressive, for Silko and the indigenous peoples of the Americas "time was round—like a tortilla; time had specific moments and locations" (Silko 1996a, p. 136). By centering the map on human relationships and activities, Silko's mapping mimics this rounded, bent sense of time and space. Since two-dimensional mapping necessarily flattens and restricts our conception of the world, Silko undercuts geographies centered on Western coordinates by focusing on individuals and communities rather than locations. Her grouping of individuals bends and thereby transcends time and space. Many characters are linked by the disruptive force—often considered illegal by authorities on both sides of the border—they exert in the Americas. Other groupings are linked in the context of Silko's portrayal of the "Eurotrash oligarchy" (1991, p. 289). Human relations are, therefore, conceptually mapped in Silko's border-crossing, challenging the hemispheric and initiating her deconstruction of Western epistemology.

The acceptance of maps as a "mirror of nature" is, according to J.B. Harley, a defining feature of Enlightenment cartography:

> Most striking is the belief in progress: that, by the application of science ever more precise representations of reality can be produced. The methods of cartography have delivered a 'true, probable, progressive, or highly confirmed knowledge' (Laudan 1977, p. 2). This mimetic bondage has led to a tendency not only to look down on the maps of the past (with a dismissive scientific chauvinism) but also to regard the maps of other non-Western or early cultures (where the rules of mapmaking were different) as inferior to European maps. (Harley 2005, p. 75)

In Silko's postnationalist cartography none of the individuals or communities are separated by the imaginary border between North and South. She emphasizes hemispheric 'free trade' in forms far beyond any stipulations entailed in the North American Free Trade Agreement (NAFTA):

> In *Almanac*, a focus on Native 'free trade' across the US-Mexico border, going back as it does for centuries, is at once a parody of NAFTA-style free trade and a

serious critique of it. The guns, drugs, healers, dealers, and revolutionaries who cross the border with impunity represent a kind of *trans*nationalism that preceded colonization and continued despite colonization; it also presages a truly postcolonial reality. Throughout the text, storylines erase and replace borderlines. (Reed 2009, p. 37, emphasis original)

Silko refuses to separate the legal from the illegal, because the definitions of the terms are based on nationalist and capitalist agendas—trans-Americanity[5] in the context of globalized world systems and the crisscrossed genealogy of the Americas become the fulcrum of relationships:

The people had been free to go traveling north and south for a thousand years, traveling as they please, then suddenly white priests had announced smuggling as a mortal sin because smuggling was stealing from the government. [...] Where were the priest and his Catholic Church when the federal soldiers used Yaqui babies for target practice? Stealing from the 'government'? What 'government' was that? Mexico City? Zeta laughed out loud. Washington D.C.? How could one steal if the government itself was the worst thief?

There was not, and there never had been, a legal government by Europeans anywhere in the Americas. Not by any definition, not even by the Europeans' own definition and laws. Because no legal government could be established on stolen land. (1991, p. 133)

Based on her own experience in traveling in the borderlands between the United States and Mexico, in her essay "The Border Patrol State" she describes how she was stopped, searched, and denied passage despite her legal rights as a U.S. citizen. (Silko 1996c, p. 115–121). She experienced how many citizens on the borders are assigned the status of foreigners in their own country. They are the victims of expansion under Manifest Destiny and territorial agreements established under the Treaty of Guadalupe Hidalgo (1848), which undermined the rights of former citizens of Mexico and left the territorial rights of Native Americans unclarified:

In the Southwest, the United States has assigned Mexican Americans and American Indians a perpetually foreign status, which characterizes their entry into the United States as subjects of conquest and victims of Manifest Destiny. The United States expanded into Mexico's northern territories under the pretext of Manifest Destiny as a way to justify their violent takeover of already-occupied lands. (Archuleta 2005, p. 118) [...] By erasing borders and expanding traditional binaries of Mexican/American or illegal alien/citizen to include indigenous peoples of the western hemisphere, Silko creates a pan-tribal, Western-hemispheric army. Her imagined army contains exploited and subjugated individuals from both sides of the border. (2005, p. 130)

---

5   Cf. Saldívar 2012 for an extensive discussion of the term and its applicability.

Calabazas, a Mexicano Tucson drug runner but also a spiritual guide, describes the absolute rejection of borders by indigenous peoples, with a remarkably constant use of the present and present perfect tense even when speaking of the past. He thus connects the thousands of years of migratory passage in the Americas with free movement over the present-day border:

> We don't believe in boundaries. Borders. Nothing like that. We *are* here thousands of years before the first whites. We *are* here before maps or *quit* claims. We *know* where we belong on this earth. We *have always moved* freely. North-south. East-west. We *pay no attention* to what isn't real. Imaginary lines. Imaginary minutes and hours. Written law. We *don't see* any border. (Silko 1991, p. 216, my emphasis)

This unbroken past and present resistance to imposed divisions and separations provides an example of what Vizenor in his *Manifest Manners* has referred to as 'survivance'—an enabling combination of survival and resistance against the "simulations of dominance" and "the absence of the tribal real" (1994, p. 68f.).

It is in this location, the border that is not one, that Silko locates her novel of the impending dissolution of Western epistemology and culture, as well as the indigenous reacquisition of the land that is the birthright of all native populations. For Silko, this revolution will inevitably begin in the South,[6] gaining momentum through the spirit of the millions of souls who have died since and because of European contact and conquest. And this revolution will be fired by the stories handed down over generations:

> One day a story will arrive in your town. There will always be disagreement over the direction—whether the story came from the southwest or the southeast. The story may arrive with a stranger, a traveler thrown out of his home country months ago. Or the story may be brought by an old friend, perhaps the parrot trader. But after you hear the story, you and the others prepare by the new moon to rise up against the slave masters. (1991, p. 578)

---

6   The Zapatista revolutionaries in the Chiapas play an important part in Silko's conceptualization of a potential indigenous revolution. Walter Mignolo elucidates the redefinition of the word 'democracy' by the Zapatistas in the context of "reciprocity and community social organization for the common good" (2000, p. 743) in confrontation with European liberal politics of the individual, which for Mignolo in the end makes neither approach definitive but a resolution between the two. He refers to the positive results of this process as "diversality" (cf. 2000, p. 742).

Photographic Reality

Indigenous peoples do not recognize, indeed they actively reject, the cartographic incisions represented by borders across Natives lands but imposed by the 'real' nation-state borders between the United States and Mexico. Further, visual representations of indigenous peoples are an additional material form of cultural and personal violation. Silko uncovers the visual violence reflected in the 'historical' photos of Native Americans—epitomized by those taken of Geronimo—but also the simultaneous refraction and rejection of such image violence by the members of the community who are the subject of the photographs. Much like the visual strategies employed in the Five Hundred Year Map, Silko portrays Geronimo as both a photographic and historical trickster figure. With his band of warriors, he was able to escape U.S. government forces for years. What is more, Silko reveals the indigenous resistance to images of Geronimo: Native Americans viewing these images maintain that it was never the 'real' Geronimo on the various photos supposedly taken of the great border-crossing leader before his capitulation. In the tradition of 'spirit photography,'[7] which documents the nineteenth-century fascination with traces of the 'real' on photographic material, Silko sees the spirit of the real Geronimo eternally escaping both his literal capture as well as his capture in images as the eternal Other.[8]

Arguing in a similar vein and with a bow to Walter Benjamin, Susan Sontag emphasizes that because each photograph is just a fragment, "its moral and emotional weight depends on where it is inserted" in time and context (Sontag 1973, p. 105f.). The original photo results from the interaction of the photographer and the individual who is photographed. The very act of taking a photograph is an event by and of itself that invades or interferes with the event as such (1973, p. 11). This relationship becomes what she considers a 'predatory alliance' which became most invasive after the completion of the transcontinental railroad and the 'colonization' of the American West through photography (cf. 1973, p. 64). Tourists descended on the West and were eager for a 'good shot.' In a similar manner, ethnographers and anthropologists hungered after documentation of

---

7   Cf. (Warner 2008, p. 221–235) for an extensive discussion of spirit photography. One could also consider the photos as 'protoholograms,' cf. Bladow 2017, p. 9.

8   Cf. Huizar-Hernández 2017 for a discussion of the difficulty of finding the 'real' Geronimo in the context of his autobiography.

the 'real Indian'; individuals and their culture became relics, 'found objects.' Much like the bourgeois shopper Benjamin explored in *The Arcades Project*, tourists, anthropologists, and professional photographers became consumers and distributors of images, estranged from the subject before their lens. What they captured were only "clouds of fantasy and pellets of information" and "unpremeditated slices of the world" (Benjamin 2002, p. 69). Taking a photograph became identical with the experience of the event and as a result people were turned into "image-junkies" (2002, p. 22). Thus, the camera enables the annihilation of moral boundaries and social inhibitions, freeing the photographer from any responsibility toward the people photographed (2002, p. 41).

Benjamin suggested that in the era before "mechanical reproduction works of art attained an 'aura'—"a strange web of time and space: the unique appearance of a distance, however close at hand" (2011, p. 209)—by their passage through time, incorporating the history of their production, ownership, display, and physical aging:

> One can no longer view them as the productions of individuals; they have become collective images, so powerful that capacity to assimilate them is related to the condition of reducing them in size. In the final effect, the mechanical methods of reproduction are a technology of miniaturization and help man to a degree of mastery over the works without which they no longer are useful. (2011, p. 212)

He felt that "meaning resides in the space between the original and its translation"—meaning results from a work's existence in time and space. Understanding meaning is to interpret or translate the function of a work as it is inserted into a particular space or multiple spaces over different moments of time.[9]

Therefore, the meaning of the photographs both for the subject and the subject's community may be quite different one from the meaning for the photographer or for his or her immediately intended audience.[10] Meaning

---

9   Elizabeth Edwards expands our understanding of the process of translation of the meaning of the photographs into the structure of museums and exhibition, where collections of photographs, which throughout their history have been inserted into various spaces at various times, become structured in a collectivity presented to viewers as a newly interpreted and translated whole. Edwards maintains that photography should be considered as a part of a culture of translation between the culture of the content and the culture of use (2001, p. 194).

10   Malavika Karlekar notes a similar photographic process—the relationship of the colonizer and colonized—within the culture of Imperialism: "Apart from its uses in policing and governance, the photograph soon became indispensable in creating a visual archive on the subject people […]. And, perhaps unsurpris-

is not an absolute, but changes over time and develops an 'aura,' in Benjamin's sense, in its repeated viewing, interpretation, and insertion into ever-changing contexts. In the various interpretations of 'Geronimo' photos, Silko's Native American viewers transpose the meaning intended by those nineteenth-to-early-twentieth-century hunters of images, translating them into their own vision of 'reality.'

Creating the "Indian"

In the collection of photographs of Native Americans taken in the late nineteenth century by photographers such as Edward Curtis,[11] C.S. Fly, and Frank A. Rinehart, the poses often recall classical statuary, with Natives stepping out on a rock or mountain, as the "last of the Mohicans" or reclining on a blanket as an Orientalist fantasy (cf. Dippie 1992, p. 132–142). The photographers had a clear idea of what a Noble Savage should look like: "On viewing a later nineteenth-century photograph of two handsomely attired north-west American Indians, Paul Fussell was prompted to remark, 'If they've not read Hiawatha, the photographer has'" (qtd. in Dippie 1992, p. 132).

The images of Navajos,[12] who were very late in migrating to the plains, are often, for example, photographed as autochthonous in the environment. Photography is used, as James Faris notes, "evidentially (anthropologically) against a Navajo history and their indigenous claims. In a curious perversity, Western 'reality' is imaged, not Navajo" (2003, p. 86f.). He elaborates further, "these photographs are guided by a series of other discourses premised on the hierarchies of civilized/savage, sedentary/nomadic, modern/traditional, anthropological knowledge/local ideology, and West/Other" (2003, p. 88). In this context, he poses a decisive question: "Can there be non-authoritarian photographs?" (1992, p. 256).

---

ingly, it is easy to understand how the emergence of new areas of study such as ethnography, anthropology, archaeology, epigraphy, and so on, ran almost parallel to that of photography" (2013, p. 10).

11   All twenty volumes of narrative text and photogravure images of Edward Sheriff Curtis's *The North American Indian* taken between 1907 and 1930 with the intent to record traditional Indian cultures are available online in Northwestern University's digital collections: http://curtis.library.northwestern.edu/.

12   Cf. Reuters 1993 "Navajos Weigh Return to Old Name: Diné." for a discussion of Navajo self-identification as Diné.

Photography, therefore, becomes a metaphor for, as well as an instrument of, power. It is invested with the ability to appropriate and decontextualize time and space as well as those who exist within it: "The photograph isolates a single incident in history. It can make the invisible visible, the unnoticed noticed. [...] The inevitable detail created by the photographer becomes a symbol for the whole and tempts the viewer to allow the specific to stand for generalities, becoming a symbol for wider truths, at the risk of stereotyping and misrepresentation" (Edwards 1992, p. 7)—in Gerald Vizenor's words an "ideological disanalogy" (2012, p. 102). Various portrayals of Native Americans elicit Vizenor's repetitive rejection of the 'reality' of such images in his unqualified statement: "This portrait is not an Indian" (Vizenor 1994, p. 44). The photograph itself becomes the performance, and, like ritual or theater, it reflects an unlimited world of possibilities (cf. Edwards 2001). Since photographs are performative versions of the 'real,' various forms of 'reality' are possible: "they are realism mediated by the medium and concentrated in images—even if this reality is a radically constructed one" (Steiger 2008, p. 194).

Photographs become "the index fossils of historical reality" (2008, p. 195), the mechanical reproduction of the object: "As a footprint is to a foot, so is a photograph to its referent" (Batchen 1997, p. 212). However, realism is ascribed to photography, "dependent upon the medium's technical character and on the social praxis and discursive context determining it" (Steiger 2008, p. 196). This enables the representation of Native Americans, on the one hand, as 'noble' but, on the other hand, simultaneously as an anachronism with no future (cf. Dippie 1992).

Beyond the stereotypical portrayals of Geronimo and other Native Americans, actual nineteenth century photo forgeries have been documented—C.S. Fly's photos of the meeting between Geronimo, Naiche, their Chiricahua Apache followers, and General Crook, taken at Cañón de los Embudos, Mexico, serve as a pertinent example:

> Fly had developed his series of Embudos peace conference photographs by the end of the first two days of negotiations. They consist of nineteen views of seventeen different scenes, which he numbered 170 to 188. Numbers 187 and 188 are enlarged details of other photographs in the set, and there are two variations [...] of numbers 171 and 176, each with minor composition differences. [...] The series offered for sale contained only one candid view, number 186. It was Fly's first shot, taken within an hour or two of General Crook's arrival. Indeed, he entitled it 'An Instantaneous View of the Council between General Crook and Geronimo.' Immediately after the conclusion of the first meeting, he asked

for and received the cooperation of his subjects in order to attempt a better 'artistic effect.' (van Orden 1989, p. 323)

The spontaneous unposed photo shows a group of rather non-distinguishable group of individuals with Geronimo at the center (Figure 1). The posed image has General Crook clearly positioned in the foreground, second on the right and Geronimo with his troupes gathered neatly around him (Figure 2). Unfortunately for Fly, who had hoped to record Geronimo's final surrender, which he thought would bring him national recognition and wealth, Geronimo changed his mind during the following night and his ultimate surrender was weeks later—with Fly's photo destined to be thrown on the scrap-heap of non-occurrent, counter-factual history (cf. van Orden 1989, p. 324).

Figure 1: Geronimo unarranged image. Courtesy of the Sharlot Hall Museum, Prescott, Arizona.

Figure 2: No 176. Council between General Crook and Geronimo. Courtesy of the Sharlot Hall Museum, Prescott, Arizona.

Photographic Capture of Existence and Resistance

Against the background of this historically loaded context, the importance of photography—the possession or absence of an image—plays a central role in the lives of characters throughout *Almanac of the Dead*. Seese, for example, is looking for her abducted baby. All she has left of him is a photograph she carries in her purse. Desperate to find him, she consults Lecha, a TV psychic who locates people using her paranormal capacities. However, Lecha is not only a 'seer' but is also primarily involved in the translation and restoration of the Almanacs in the novel's title, for which she hires Seese to assist her. All Seese has left of her son, Monte, is his image, his baby photo:

> The kidnappers had stolen the white leather album filled with Monte's baby pictures. They had also removed a framed photograph of Monte from the wall. All Seese had left were snapshots she'd kept in her purse. David had taken all the negatives with him. The police seemed to want proof that she had really had a child in the first place. But the neighbors did not recognize her or remember Monte in the stroller. (Silko 1991, p. 112)

With the disappearance of the baby's photographic images, the material 'proof' of his existence for the police and Seese's neighbors also disappeared. Her own memories continue to fade throughout the novel, making him increasingly unreal even to her since she had no physical experience of his growing older:

> Probably it was exhaustion, but she was having difficulty remembering Monte's face. Her memories of his face as a newborn had blurred together with her memories of Monte on the day he had disappeared. Even the strange dream Seese had had of Monte as much older child had become part of her memory, and she cried because she could no longer remember how Monte looked. (Silko 1991, p. 700)

Silko also critiques the photographic exploitation, instrumentalization, and commercialization of even the most private events. When David, a photographer, finds the body of his lover, Eric, who had committed suicide, he immediately aestheticizes and commercializes the images:

> [N]one of them [the critics] understood how important the Eric series was; none of them realized David's work was about to redefine the terms *portrait* and *still life.* [...] David was worth more dead than he had been worth alive. The Eric series would appreciate in value, and even pictures of David's corpse would bring a good price. [...] Every ounce of value, everything worth anything, was stripped away for sale, regardless; no mercy [...]. Capitalism stayed ahead because it was ruthless. (1991, p. 563ff., emphasis original)[13]

Photography also plays a major role in Silko's later novel *Gardens in the Dunes* (1999). Edward, a nineteenth century East-coast scientist and photographer, settled with his wife in the California desert. In the course of the plot, they travel extensively in Europe. There, he not only studies rare plants but is well-aware of the promise of high economic returns in the illicit sale of citrus and rubber tree cuttings. Due to his epistemological curiosity, his attempts to document his work in photographs, and to possess valuable samples are his (literal) downfall as he stumbles and injures himself while taking photos in the mountains. Later he is arrested after being caught absconding with Corsican *Citrus medica* (citron) cuttings—indigenous plants shackled by capitalist desire for profit (cf. Ryan 2007).

The significance of photography forms a repetitive theme throughout Silko's work and can be traced back to the very beginning of her career as a writer. Silko's *Storyteller* (1981), a multiple-genred, autobiographical volume, was published immediately after her inaugural and to date most widely read fiction, *Ceremony* (1977). Cynthia Carsten notes that Silko re-

---

13   Cf. Fischer-Hornung 2007, p. 109, p. 116–122 for my discussion of abjection entailed in the making of these photographs in more detail.

sists conventional Euro-American models of autobiography which emphasize the autonomous self and individualism and rather emphasizes the community context, "drawing heavily on Laguna Pueblo oral tradition and history, shared family memories and photographs, as well as photographs of the Pueblo landscape" (2006, p. 108).

Photography frames many of the texts in *Storyteller*, which opens with a noteworthy reference to a Hopi basket full of photos that have a special meaning for Silko's family. These photos help to define her place within the community:

> [...] Inside the basket are hundreds of photographs taken since the 1890s around Laguna. My grandpa Hank first had a camera when he returned from Indian School, and years later, my father learned photography in the Army.
>
> Photographs have always had a special significance with the people of my family and the people at Laguna. A photograph is serious business and many people still do not trust just anyone to take their picture.
>
> It wasn't until I began this book that I realized that the photographs in the Hopi basket have a special relationship to the stories as I remember them. The photographs are here because they are part of many of the stories and because many of the stories can be traced to the photographs. (Silko 1981, p. 1)

Significantly, for the purposes of this study, in *Storyteller*, Silko includes not only numerous photographs but also 'A Geronimo Story.' This story is preceded by a photo of an elderly woman who is crocheting (1981, p. 211), the caption of which appears 61 pages later and reads "Grandma A'mook. Photograph: Lee H. Marmon" (1981, p. 272). On the opposite page, it is followed by a photo of "The Laguna Regulars in 1928, 43 years after they rode in the Apache Wars. *Photograph: Unknown*" (1981, p. 273).[14] The story of the involvement in the hunt for Geronimo by the U.S. army and their support by the Laguna Regulars, as passed down by Laguna storytellers like Grandma A'mook, is framed as a trickster tale—the tricksters being both Geronimo and the Laguna Regulars.

> [...] Silko also seems to use photos to verify stories that read as fiction. Immediately following 'A Geronimo / Story," [...] Silko places a photo of the Laguna Regulars, a band of Leguna men who had participated in the Apache Wars. Nothing in the text surrounding 'A Geronimo Story' indicates that this story has been told to Silko by any member of the Laguna Regulars, yet the placement of the

---

14   The captions of the photos are not found immediately associated with the respective images; rather, they are listed at the back of the book. This split between the images and their captions leaves more room for interpretation of what the images might mean in their immediate context.

photo suggests that its subjects testify to the contents of the story, even if it has emerged predominantly from Silko's imagination. The men in the photo, in other words, assert the reliability of a storyteller's imagination. (Domina 2007, p. 49f.)

As Lynn Domina also points out, the story is but one among many Geronimo stories, implied in the indefinite article in the title. Such stories have been told many times before and always end with Geronimo's disappearance or, in this case and in many others, his total absence: "This particular Geronimo story, in other words, concerns a title character whose presence in the story exists exclusively by virtue of his absences" (2007, p. 60). The Laguna Regulars, despite their knowledge that Geronimo is nowhere near them, go along on the hunt for the entertainment value of the trip. When Captain Pratt arrives, Siteye has an injured foot but determines he has to join the hunt anyway: "'Shit,' he said, 'these Lagunas can't track Geronimo without me,'" (Silko 1981, p. 212) and decides he also happens to need to take his nephew to saddle his horses. Although Captain Pratt and the Leguna Regulars knew Geronimo was not there, they would go anyway: "Geronimo isn't down there. So we're going down" (1981, p. 214). The decision is totally illogical, an ironic non sequitur. It is reversals like these that signal tricksterism for the hearer/reader. And, true to the trickster hero who is never caught, the trickster makes of a no a yes and a yes of a no:

> 'Maybe next time I come we'll find Geronimo,' I said.

> 'Umm,' That's all Siteye said. Just sort of grunted like he didn't agree with me but didn't want to talk about it either. (1981, p. 214)[15]

On the way to the Zuni Mountains, the hunt enables the Laguna Regulars—like tourists—to visit places they have never been to before, such as the Acoma land and the lava land of the Navajos. It also enabled them to sing the spring songs and enjoy the stars of the Milky Way while camped out at night. Siteye notes:

> 'Yes,' he said, 'It's a pretty good place. I don't think Geronimo would even travel out there.' But he would never say this to Captain Pratt. When they finally reach their destination, Pie Town, Siteye notes: 'It didn't look like Geronimo had been there. The corrals were full of cows and sheep; no buildings had been burned.' (1981, p. 219)

However, all the soldiers stationed there acted as if Geronimo would appear any minute:

---

15 Cf. Vizenor (1994, p. 77), "The trickster is a language game, a counter causal liberation of the mind [...]."

> Captain told us that they were keeping all the horses in a big corral in the arroyo because they expected Geronimo any time. We laughed while we rode down the sloping path into the wide arroyo. [...]

> 'Looks like all the white people in this area moved up here from Quemondo and Datil. In case Geronimo comes. All crowded together to make their last stand.' Siteye laughed at his own joke. (Silko 1981, p. 219f.)

His reference to the victory of the Lakota, Northern Cheyenne, and Arap-aho over the US Army during 'Custer's Last Stand' at the Battle of Little Bighorn (1876) serves to underline the absurdity of looking for Geronimo when all signs indicate that he is nowhere in the area. The 'touring' Leguna Regulars found it was simply fun to go along for the ride while simultaneously also hunting for meat to dry as supplies. They make the inhabitants of Pie Town and the US army the butt of their jokes and they triumph in their verbal skills: "Anybody can act violently—there is nothing to it; but not every person is able to destroy his enemy with words" (1981, p. 222).[16]

> Before I went to sleep I said to Siteye, 'You've been hunting Geronimo for a long time, haven't you? And he always gets away.'

> 'Yes,' Siteye said, staring up at the stars, 'but I always like to think that it's us who get away.' [...]

> We stopped. Siteye turned around slowly and looked behind us at the way we had come: the canyons, the mountains, the rivers we had passed. We sat there for a long time remembering the way, the beauty of our journey. Then Siteye shook his head gently, 'You know,' he said, 'that was a long way to go for deer hunting.' (1981, p. 222f.)

Mastering the situation with irony in a subtle play on "get away," Native American trickster stories provide an example of survival strategies.[17] The telling of and listening to stories are acts of empowerment; using the Word is a source of remarkable strength (cf. Nakadate 2001, p. 387f.).

In addition to verbal skills, Silko's characters also adapt various Euro-American gadgets and instruments, empowering them over space and time

---

16   The Laguna Regulars also particularly enjoy the name of Major Littlecock, teasing him about the fact that he, instead of them, could sleep with the horses since he has a "desire for horses at night." Captain Pratt refuses to translate the crude joke, leaving the joke to be understood only by insiders, belittling Major Littlecock as an outsider, with as little to show as his name implies (Silko 1981, p. 222).

17   Vizenor would consider this as an example of "postindian simulations of tribal survivance" (cf. 1994, p. 15).

with ancient pre-Columbian forms of spiritual energy to fulfill self-defined purposes, thereby resisting the power of the West's own capital-bound inventiveness. For example, Rose, an old Alaska Indian woman, could instrumentalize the spirits of the ancestors by rubbing weasel fur on a television and through the repeated telling of their stories, causing 'fields of force,' static energy storms strong enough to down airplanes:

> The old woman had gathered great surges of energy out of the atmosphere, by summoning spirit beings through recitations of the stories that were also indictments of the greedy destroyers of the land. With the stories the old woman was able to assemble powerful forces flowing from the spirits of the ancestors. (Silko 1991, p. 156)

Feeding on the same sources of energy, Silko portrays the spirits of the ancestors, enabling Geronimo's image to appear on the various photos of Geronimo, marking Silko's radical dissolution of Western epistemology. She asks her readers to take seriously what Michael Taussig refers to as 'second contact,' mimesis in performance. The performance of the perspective of indigenous peoples, the Other, elicits a disarmingly ferocious shock—the moment when the anthropological gaze is thrown back on the colonizer by the colonized subject, the moment when colonizers see themselves reflected and refracted in the images produced by the Other.[18] Taussig—and Silko as well—demand that we take this moment seriously as the beginning of the dissolution of the categories of self and alterity, enabling a transcendence of the binary separating the colonizer and the colonized, Self and Other. Silko, like Taussig, asks Western readers to move away from the perceptions that dominate and determine the West's ways of seeing and acting:

> To become aware of the West in the eyes and handiwork of its Others, to wonder at the fascination with their fascination, is to abandon border logistics and enter into the 'second contact' area of the borderland where 'us' and 'them' lose their polarity and swim in and out of focus. [...] Stable identity formations autodestruct into silence, gasps of unaccountable pleasure, or cartwheeling confusion gathered in a crescendo of what I call 'mimetic excess' spending itself in a riot of dialectical imagery. (Taussig 1993, p. 246)

If we take Taussig's concept of second contact and Silko's narrative strategies seriously, this disassembles the very possibility of defining the border between Self and Other, between history and narration, between North and South, as anything more than a shadowy possibility. Photos in Silko's

---

18   Cf. Fischer-Hornung 2002 for a more detailed discussion of Taussig's concept of 'second contact' in the context of *Almanac of the Dead.*

novel become performative events inserted into time in specific places and contexts. Silko depicts Geronimo as a trickster hero who, for decades, could keep literally thousands of American soldiers chasing after him and his band of warriors. However, his singularity is broken and refracted like in a hall of mirrors. In the perception of Native observers there must have been three, perhaps four 'Geronimos' in the photographic images that Americans considered 'the' Geronimo. Numerous characters tell the story of Geronimo as it was handed down to them and from their perspective. Yeome, a keeper and writer of the Almanacs, maintains that the real Geronimo was never captured—neither his image nor his spirit:

> I have seen the photographs labeled 'Geronimo.' I have seen the photograph of the so-called surrender at Skeleton Canyon where General Miles sits in the shade of a mesquite tree flanked by his captains as he makes false promises and lied. But the Apache man identified in the photograph is not, of course, the man the U.S. army has been chasing. He is a man who always *accompanied* the one who *performed* certain feats. He is the man who agreed to *play the role* for the protection of the other man. The man in photograph has been promised safe conduct by the man he protected. The man in the photograph was a brilliant and resourceful man. He may not have known that while he would find wealth and fame in the lifelong captivity, he would not again see the mountains during his life. The man who fled had further *work to do*, work that could not be done in captivity. (Silko 1991, p. 129, my emphasis)

This passage signifies[19] on the claim to the 'real' of photography and underlines the trickster nature of those playing the game of hide-and-seek with the U.S. army. In the text quoted above, the active verbs in the phrases (my emphasis in italics) underline the agency in plotting and performing a staged identity to attain a spiritual freedom beyond the eventually captured body after actual physical surrender. The repetitive phrase "the man" underlines his totally unidentifiable and indeterminate physical identity. Silko's dark trickster humor works to energize the imagination and her narrative strategy refuses to see history purely in terms of polarized good and evil, victim and oppressor. Her refusal to read the history of the indigenous populations purely in terms of victimhood, establishes agency—both positive and negative—in the past and thereby enables positive agency in the present and future. According to Silko, human beings, for better or for worse, have always been agents in their own history.[20]

---

19   Cf. Gates 1988 for a related discussion of tricksterism and signifying in African American culture.
20   Silko elaborates on the destructive role of the indigenous sorcerers and the priesthood in the conquest of the South. For example, she writes: "The appearance of Europeans had been no accident; the Gunadeeyahs [the destroyers] had

The interpretation of the historical Geronimo had undergone significant changes throughout his life and also thereafter. He eluded U.S. forces for years but surrendered in 1886. By the end of his life in 1909, after a decade of captivity, he had also become a symbol of heroic resistance—a sainted savage (Geronimo) transformed from a blood-thirsty invader and killer of innocent settlers (Goyathlay) fulfilling Manifest Destiny (cf. Sonnichsen 1986).[21]

The portrait of Geronimo with one knee on the ground and the arm carrying a rifle resting on his knee pointing upward, taken against a photographic canvas background with cacti arranged around him, is the "earliest known photo of Geronimo, taken by photographer A. Frank Randall at San Carlos reservation in 1884. This is the face [and posture] that launched a hundred articles, stories, and novels" (1986, p. 14). Sontag maintains that despite the seemingly 'real' of photography:

> A person is an aggregate of appearances, appearances which can be made to yield, by proper focusing, infinite layers of significance. To view reality as an endless set of situations which mirror each other, to extract analogies from the most dissimilar things, is to anticipate the characteristic form of perception stimulated by photographic images. (Sontag 1973, p. 159f.)

---

called for their white brethren to join them. Sure enough the Spaniards had arrived in Mexico fresh from the Church Inquisition with appetites whetted for disembowelment and blood. No wonder Cortés and Montezuma had hit it off together when they met; both had been members of the same secret clan" (1991, p. 760).

21 To this day Geronimo maintains a special significance in American culture: paratroopers in the Second World War used Geronimo's name as a battle cry, a practice that spread to others taking daring leaps, including workers on oil rigs and children in swimming holes. In 2011, "the US Navy special operations force (the SEALs) reported to President Obama the successful completion of their action against Osama bin Laden's compound in Pakistan with the code 'Geronimo EKIA' (enemy killed in action). Whether 'Geronimo' referred to bin Laden himself, as early reports indicated, or the mission to kill or capture him, as the White House insisted, the military was employing a long-standing practice in appropriating an indigenous name from the Indian Wars to refer to a contemporary military action [...]. The conflation of Geronimo with the terrorist Osama bin Laden was deeply offensive to many Apaches and other indigenous citizens, who protested in various forums, including Facebook ('Osama is not Geronimo'), YouTube ('Geronimo E-KIA, a poem by the 1491s), and a congressional hearing on racist stereotypes of indigenous people (US Senate Committee on Indian Affairs 2011): although this episode involved assassination rather than captivity, it reveals, once again, the continuing significance of the captivity tradition in the American national imaginary" (Strong 2013, p. 69f.).

The cry for 'authenticity' is, however, strong and based on the assumption that the 'authentic event' really exists—one single event to be interpreted in a single manner. As William R. Handley and Nathaniel Lewis elucidate in *True West: Authenticity and the American West,* "Simply put, discourses of authenticity have contributed to the construction of canonicity, ethnicity, cultural nationalism, regional ideology, and gendered identities" (Handley/Lewis 2004, p. 9). It is these constructions of the image of Geronimo and his trickster role in the perception of the Native American viewers that is the basis of multiple deconstructive—often playful and ironic—strategies in Silko's work.

So, who is the 'real' Geronimo? The Apache warrior who outwitted the troops sent by the U.S. government? The negotiator of peace agreements some interpret as surrender? The farmer in captivity in Florida? The performer who rode in Roosevelt's 1905 inauguration parade? The man who was conscious of his currency as celebrity, selling photos, buttons off his jacket, and hand-made bows and arrows at three world exhibitions?[22] Or the man who negotiated the return of his tribe to Arizona after his death?[23] After his surrender and during his captivity, was he, as Mark Sample maintains, often 'playing Indian'—the trickster in passive disguise? In his autobiography he concludes, "I am glad I went to the Fair. I saw many interesting things and learned much of the white people. They are a very kind and peaceful people" (Geronimo/Barrett 1906, p. 35). Further, Geronimo maintains, "When I was at first asked to attend the St. Louis World's Fair I did not wish to go. Later, when I was told that I would receive good attention and protection, and that the President of the United States said that it would be all right, I consented" (1906, p. 28). He leaves out the fact that he had been offered a lucrative contract elsewhere but that the government would not allow him to leave his captivity at Fort Sill unless he agreed to their conditions of one dollar per day for appearing at the exposition.[24] His representation of his version of the story, however,

---

22　The 1898 Trans-Mississippi and International Exposition in Omaha, Nebraska; the 1901 Pan-American Exposition in Buffalo, New York; the 1904 Louisiana Purchase Exposition in St. Louis, Missouri.

23　Cf. Geronimo and Barrett 1906 for his own interpretation, dictated in the manner of numerous slave narratives to a Euro-American interlocutors, and Sample 2011, p. 9 for a discussion of the complexity of Geronimo's various roles and how he manipulated his 'cultural capital.'

24　Cf. Geronimo and Barrett 1906, p. 29.

leaves agency in his hands and rhetorically removes him from the role of captive—trickster magic.

In the stories passed down about Geronimo, there were purported to be three to four different 'Geronimos' on both sides of the Mexican-U.S. border. They went under different names and, like the inability of *gringos* to distinguish unique details in the landscape, European Americans had equal difficulties in distinguishing the various 'Geronimos': "the Yaquis and the Apaches quickly learned to make use of the Europeans' inability to perceive unique details in the landscape" (Silko 1991, p. 225). In the same way, the inability to distinguish individual images of 'Indians' and 'Geronimo'—"a sort of blindness of the world" (1991, p. 224) provided a productive source of resistance. This was further complicated by the use of various names—Goyathlay, his Apache name, and Geronimo, the name Mexicans gave him:

> This was not his name. No wonder there has been so much confusion among white people and their historians. The man encouraged the confusion. He has been called a medicine man, but that title is misleading. He was a man who was able to perform certain feats. (1991, p. 129)

And it was these feats that caused so much consternation among those who tried to capture him and which enabled varied forms of tricksterism on the part of the Apaches: "the tribal people here were all very aware that the whites put great store in names. But once the whites had a name for a thing, they seemed unable ever again to recognize the thing itself" (1991, p. 224).

In the retelling of the story of 'Old Pancakes,' Mahawala, a Yaqui elder, and Calabazas name the various performers of Geronimo in the photo images: Red Clay (the final Geronimo who died in Oklahoma), Sleet (the youngest of the Geronimos), and later, 'Old Pancakes,' an old drunkard and joker, who just claimed to be Geronimo to save the other fake Geronimos from death (cf. Silko 1991, p. 224–232). Yaquis "understood that a person might need a number of names in order to conduct all of his or her earthy business" (1991, p. 227). In a play on the historical practices of photographers in the West, Silko incorporates a historical description of how the photographic images of Geronimo's surrender were staged:

> The photographer who made the photographs had been at Fort Apache for a number of weeks by the time he learned from the camp mule master which of the Apaches was 'Geronimo.' The photographer had perfected his Arizona desert backdrop and had time enough to commission Apache women to create a huge feather war bonnet unlike any headpiece the Apaches had ever seen, let alone worn. Sleet had dressed exactly as the photographer had directed, then stood slightly to one side so that the long, trailing cascade of chicken and turkey feathers could be fully appreciated in the profile view. (1991, p. 226)

Mahawala ends his story by signifying on the death of Geronimo in Florida, far removed from his tribal people and lands: "Of course in the hands of a sorcerer who can say what might happen. Don't take any chances. Look where poor Old Pancakes ended up" (Silko 1991, p. 232). He knew, of course, that Old Pancakes/Geronimo had ended up as a captive and destitute farmer in Florida, never able to return to his tribal lands.

In a further 'joke' on the actual behavior of the historical Geronimo in his tours of the various world exhibitions and wild-west shows, Silko describes how Geronimo 'played' his audience—in Vizenor's words: "This is not an Indian."

> Each of the so-called Geronimos had learned to demand prints of themselves as payment for posing. At meetings in the mountains they had compared photographs. The puzzle had been to account for the Apache warrior whose broad, dark face, penetrating eyes, and powerful barrel-chested body had appeared in every photograph taken of the other Geronimos. The image of this man appeared where the faces of the other Geronimos should have been [...]. The identity of the Apache in the photograph could not be determined, but a number of theories were advanced by both Apaches and Yaquis concerning the phenomenon; the light of the polished crystal, the light of the sun, and the light of the warrior's soul had left their distinctive mark with the Apache face white people identified as Geronimo. (1991, p. 228)

Subsequent to this ironic performance of the 'scientific' methods and argumentation of the Enlightenment and the colonizer—in Taussig's sense, a 'second contact' performance—they conclude, "Of course the real man they called Geronimo, they never did catch. The real Geronimo get away."—old Mahawala—a joke "Calabazas realized that the old ones were serious about this Geronimo story" (1991, p. 224).

But not only Apaches and Yaquis were affected by the magic-like feats of Geronimo, his captors were affected as well. General Miles, who had been accused of capturing the 'wrong Geronimo,' dreams of Geronimo's resistance and liberation.

> In the general's dreams, Geronimo had brushed away shackles and leg irons as if they were cobwebs, and walked away, disappearing as the troops looked on, paralyzed by an invisible force. For more than fifteen years, five thousand U.S. troops, costing $20 million, had stomped through cactus and rock to capture one old Apache man more sorrowful than fierce. (1991, p. 231)

The 'spell' that Goyathlay/Geronimo reaches from the ancestors long before the life of Geronimo into the late twentieth century of the novel in the retelling of the story—its explication and elaboration by those who came after. The Apaches were nervous about the images of the dead Geronimo, whereas the Yaquis simply saw that "The spirit of the ancestor had cast its light, its power, in front of the faces of the three Geronimos" (Silko 1991, p. 323).[25]

Silko weaves the story of Geronimo in and out of her vastly encompassing novel, illustrating the resistance of the Apache warrior to the forces on both sides of the southwestern border. Employing the strategies of oral story-telling, she intertwines various ancestor stories about the assistance the ancestors provided in the past as well as the guidance they would offer in the present and future: "the story they told [and she tells] did not run in a line for the horizon but circled and spiraled instead like a red-tailed hawk" (1991, p. 224).

An example of the force of these stories told in various forms is illustrated and framed by the story of Sterling. He is ostracized by his own tribe at the onset of the novel after revealing the secrets of the 'Great Snake' to a film crew. During his tribal exile, he reads and hears various stories of historical outlaws and rebels, searching for the meaning of outlaws in general but Geronimo in particular. These forces lead him to recognize the condition of exile experienced by many indigenous peoples at the borderlands between Mexico and the United States and eventually enables his return to his tribe by the end of the novel:

> Sterling thought he was probably one of the few Indians interested in famous Indian outlaws. He knew tribal leaders and so-called Indian experts preferred that Indians got left out of that part of American history too, since their only other appearances had been at so-called massacres of white settlers. (1991, p. 40)

He notes that none of the resistance or joy or art of these indigenous people ever make it into the press and that the stories told drastically distort history told through the eyes of the colonizer. About the rise of the capitalist elite in Tucson, Arizona, for example, he notes that the merchants in Tucson never wanted to see the Apache wars end since it enabled them to profit from supplying the troupe. Present-day Tucson provides enough proof of the distorted twists and turns of historical discourse: "the old Tucson mansions along Main Street were the best proof that murders of innocent Apache women and children prospered. In only one generation,

---

25   Silko has her own explanation of such photographic phenomena in her essay "On Photography," the title of which cannot be an accidental reference to Susan Sontag's magisterial volume of the same name: "The more I [Silko] read about the behavior of subatomic particles of light, the more confident I am that photographs are capable of registering subtle electromagnetic changes in both the subject and the photographer" (1996b, p. 180).

government embezzlers, bootleggers, pimps, and murderers had become Tucson's 'fine old families'" (Silko 1991, p. 80).

But more importantly for Silko's overall message and for tying the novel together, he recognizes the arbitrary nature of the categories imposed upon those who are displaced by these profiteers—and that there is a global dimension to this phenomenon. He recognizes the larger context of his individual fate:

> In the short time he had been in Tucson, Sterling had begun to realize that people he had been used to calling 'Mexican' were really remnants of different kinds of Indians. [...] Indians flung across the world forever separated from their tribes and from their ancestral lands—that kind of thing had been happening to human beings since the beginning of time. African tribes had been sold into slavery all over the earth. (1991, p. 88)

But even the discovery of the significance of Geronimo in the history of indigenous resistance becomes ever more complex. Who was to know which convoluted distortion of history would take place in the centers of power— how the story would be told all depended upon who survived and won:

> His knowledge of Mexican history was sketchy, but Sterling did not think they had had anyone like Geronimo since Montezuma. And then it got very confusing because it seemed as if the Mexicans were always having revolutions, and he knew that although the winning side usually executed and jailed the losers for being 'criminals,' both Police Gazette and True Detective magazines disqualified crimes committed during wars and revolutions. (1991, p. 89)

The Apache on the photos is not Geronimo but "He is the man who agreed to play the role for the protection of the other man." (1991, p. 129).

Works Cited

Archuleta, Elizabeth (2005): Securing Our Nation's Roads and Borders or Re-circling the Wagons? Leslie Marmon Silko's Destabilization of 'Borders'. In: Wicazo Sa Review 20, no. 1, p. 113–137, DOI: 10.1353/wic.2005.0001.

Batchen, Geoffrey (1997): Burning with Desire: The Conception of Photography. Cambridge, MA: MIT Press.

Benjamin, Walter (2002): The Arcades Project. Cambridge: Harvard University Press.

Benjamin, Walter (2011): Short History of Photography. Oxford: Oxford University Press.

Bladow, Kyle (2017): Timely Objects and the Revolutionary Formerly Known as Marcos: Rereading *Almanac of the Dead*. In: Studies in American Indian Literatures 29 (2), p. 1–25, https://www.muse.jhu.edu/article/666028, 1/6/2021.

Carsten, Cynthia. (2006): *Storyteller*: Leslie Marmon Silko's Reappropriation of Native American History and Identity. In: Wicazo Sa Review 21, no. 2, p. 105–126, DOI: 10.1353/wic.2006.0012.

Dippie, Brian W. (1992): Representing the Other: The North American Indian. In: Edwards, Elizabeth (ed.): Anthropology and Photography 1860–1920. New Haven, CT: Yale University Press, p. 132–136.

Domina, Lynn. (2007): 'The Way I Heard It': Autobiography, Tricksters, and Leslie Marmon Silko's *Storyteller*. In: Studies in American Indian Literatures 19, no. 3, p. 45–67, DOI: 10.1353/ail.2007.0029.

Edwards, Elizabeth (1992): Introduction. In: Edwards, Elizabeth (ed.): Anthropology and Photography 1860–1920. New Haven, CT: Yale University Press, p. 3–17.

Edwards, Elizabeth (2001): Raw Histories: Photographs, Anthropology and Museums. Oxford: Berg.

Faris, James (2003): Navajo and Photography. In: Pinney, Christopher/Peterson, Nicolas (eds.): Photography's Other Histories. Durham, NC: Duke University Press, p. 85–99.

Faris, James C. (1992): A political Primer on Anthropology / Photography. In: Edwards, Elizabeth (ed.): Anthropology and Photography 1860–1920. New Haven, CT: Yale University Press, p. 253–263.

Fischer-Hornung, Dorothea (2002): Economies of Memory: Trafficking in Blood, Body Parts, and Crossblood Ancestors. In: Amerikastudien/American Studies 47, no. 2, p. 195–222, https://www.jstor.org/stable/41157727, 1/6/2021.

Fischer-Hornung, Dorothea (2007): 'Now we know that gay men are just men after all': Abject Sexualities in Leslie Marmon Silko's *Almanac of the Dead*. In: Kutzbach, Konstanze/Mueller, Monika (eds.): The Abject of Desire: The Aestheticization of the Unaesthetic in Contemporary Literature and Culture. Amsterdam: Brill and Rodopi, p. 107–127.

Fly, C. S. (1886): Council between General George Crook and Apache Leader Geronimo. Sharlot Hall Museum - Library & Archives, https://archives.sharlothallmuseum.org/photos/product-details/1969, 1/6/2021.

Gates, Henry Louis (1988): The Signifying Monkey: A Theory of Afro-American Literary Criticism. New York: Oxford University Press.

Geronimo; Barrett, S. M. (1906): Geronimo's Story of His Life. New York: Duffield, www.ibiblio.org/ebooks/Geronimo/GerStory.htm, 1/6/2021.

Handley, William R.; Lewis, Nathaniel (2004): True West: Authenticity and the American West. Lincoln: University of Nebraska Press.

Harley, J. B. (2005): Deconstructing the Map. In: Thrift, Nigel/Whatmore, Sarah (eds.): Cultural Geography: Critical Concepts in the Social Sciences. London: Routledge, p. 71–93.

Huizar-Hernández, Anita (2017): 'The Real Geronimo Got Away': Eluding Expectations in Geronimo: His Own Story; The Autobiography of a Great Patriot Warrior. In: Studies in American Indian Literatures 29, no. 2, p. 49–70, https://www.muse.jhu.edu/article/666030, 1/6/2021.

Karlekar, Malavika (2013): Visual Histories: Photography in the Popular Imagination. Oxford: Oxford University Press.

Laudan, Larry (1977): Progress and Its Problems: Toward a Theory of Scientific Growth. Berkeley: University of California Press.

Mignolo, Walter (2000): The Many Faces of Cosmo-polis: Border Thinking and Critical Cosmopolitanism. In: Public Culture 12, no. 3, p. 721–748, https://www.muse.jhu.edu/article/26217, 1/6/2021.

Nakadate, Neil (2001): Leslie Marmon Silko. In: Fallon, Erin/Feddersen, Rick/ Kurtzleben, James/Lee, Maurice A./Rochette-Crawley, Susan (eds.): A Reader's Companion to the Short Story in English. Westport, CT: Greenwood Press, p. 388–397.

Reed, T. V. (2009): Toxic Colonialism, Environmental Justice, and Native Resistance in Silko's *Almanac of the Dead*. In: MELUS: Multi-Ethnic Literature of the U.S. 34, no. 2, p. 25–42, DOI: 10.1353/mel.0.0023.

Reuters (1993): Navajos Weigh Return to Old Name: Diné. In: The New York Times, 12/17/1993, at https://www.nytimes.com/1993/12/17/us/navajos-weigh-return-to-old-name-dine.html, 1/6/2021.

Romero, Channette (2002): Envisioning a 'Network of Tribal Coalitions': Leslie Marmon Silko's *Almanac of the Dead*. In: The American Indian Quarterly 26, no. 4, p. 623–640, DOI: 10.1353/aiq.2004.0008.

Ryan, Terre (2007): The Nineteenth-Century Garden: Imperialism, Subsistence, and Subversion in Leslie Marmon Silko's *Gardens in the Dunes*. In: Studies in American Indian Literatures 19, no. 3, p. 115–132, DOI: 10.1353/ail.2007.0025.

Saldívar, José David (2012): Trans-Americanity: Subaltern Modernities, Global Coloniality, and the Cultures of Greater Mexico. Durham, NC: Duke University Press.

Sample, Mark (2011): 'A Very Kind and Peaceful People': Geronimo and the World's Fair. Sample Reality, www.samplereality.com/2011/05/03/a-very-kind-and-peaceful-people-geronimo-and-the-worlds-fair, 1/6/2021.

Silko, Leslie (1999): Gardens in the Dunes. New York: Simon & Schuster.

Silko, Leslie Marmon (1981): Storyteller. New York: Little, Brown & Co.

Silko, Leslie Marmon (1991): Almanac of the Dead. New York: Simon & Schuster.

Silko, Leslie Marmon (1996a): Notes on Alamanc of the Dead. In: Silko, Leslie Marmon (ed.): Yellow Woman and a Beauty of the Spirit. New York: Simon & Schuster, p. 135–145.

Silko, Leslie Marmon (1996b): On Photography. In: Silko, Leslie Marmon (ed.): Yellow Woman and a Beauty of the Spirit. New York: Simon & Schuster, p. 180–186.

Silko, Leslie Marmon (1996c): The Border Patrol State. In: Silko, Leslie Marmon (ed.): Yellow Woman and a Beauty of the Spirit. New York: Simon & Schuster, p. 115–123.

Sonnichsen, C. L. (1986): FROM SAVAGE TO SAINT: A New Image for Geronimo. In: The Journal of Arizona History 27, no. 1 (Commemorating the Centennial of the Surrender of Naiche and Geronimo September 4, 1886), p. 5–34, https://www.jstor.org/stable/41859661, 1/6/2021.

Sontag, Susan (1973): On Photography. New York: Ferrar, Straus and Giroux.

Steiger, Bernd (2008): Photography as the Medium of Reflection. In: Kelsey, Robin/Stimson, Blake (eds.): The Meaning of Photography. New Haven, CT: Yale University Press, p. 194–197.

Strong, Pauline Turner (2013): American Indians and the American Imaginary: Cultural Representation across the Centuries. Boulder, CO: Paradigm.

Taussig, Michael (1993): Mimesis and Alterity: A Particular History of the Senses. New York: Routledge.

van Orden, Jay (1989): C. S. FLY AT CAÑON DE LOS EMBUDOS: American Indians as Enemy in the Field A Photographic First. In: The Journal of Arizona History 30, no. 3, p. 319–346, https://www.jstor.org/stable/41695767, 1/6/2021.

Vizenor, Gerald (2012): Edward Curtis: Photography and Disanalogy. In: Fitz, Karsten (ed.): Visual Representations of Native Americans: Transnational Contexts and Perspectives. Heidelberg: Winter Verlag, p. 101–112.

Vizenor, Gerald Robert (1994): Manifest Manners: Postindian Warriors of Survivance. Hanover, NH: University Press of New England.

Warner, Marina (2008): Phantasmagoria: Spirit Visions, Metaphors, and Media into the Twenty-first Century. Oxford: Oxford University Press.

Neo-cosmopolitan Negotiations: Public and Private Border Crossings in Shirley Geok-lin Lim's *Joss and Gold*

Ludmila Martanovschi

Introduction

This study discusses the neo-cosmopolitan propensities in *Joss and Gold*, Shirley Geok-lin Lim's 2001 novel, which includes sections set in Malaysia, the United States of America, and Singapore. It is a novel which invites readers to engage with cultural issues that transcend borders and to follow characters whose identities are shaped transnationally. The novel has been interpreted as a text that "has reworked some of the most persistent clichés of American multiculturalism and the problems of ethnic as well as cultural hybridity" (Wagner 2005, p. 154) in the context of Asian American women's writing. While acknowledging that the examination of the text as part of multicultural literature in the United States of America is useful, the current analysis goes further. Here *Joss and Gold* illustrates exemplarily the fact that Lim, as an originally Malaysian-Chinese author who now lives in California, speaks not only to American readers but also to a worldwide audience interested in ground-breaking fiction.

In "'A Multilingual Life': The Cosmopolitan and Globalectic Dimensions of Shirley Geok-lin Lim's Writings" (2014), Sneja Gunew uses cosmopolitan theory to address some of the concerns of Lim's novel. Given the focus on multilingualism (cf. 2014, p. 17f.) and the aim of discussing other writings by the same author, especially her acclaimed autobiography, *Among the White Moon Faces* (1996), the critic leaves room for a new, more detailed reading of the novel. Such a reading would examine the neo-cosmopolitan dimensions present in *Joss and Gold* while also evoking further theoretical developments in cosmopolitanism. The following study of *Joss and Gold* proposes exactly this.

Considerations on Neo-cosmopolitanism

Even a concise definition of the term "cosmopolitanism" acknowledges its growing importance to the understanding of contemporary realities and discourses, theorists' efforts to revise it constantly, and the appearance of what has been called "a new cosmopolitanism" (Wisker 2007, p. 179). Moreover, such a definition does not fail to underline the urgency of individual and communal adaptation to a changing world: "as coloniser and colonised, immigrated or indigenous, side by side, people are metamorphosing, developing different, more mixed hybrid identities, reliving histories but also changing their sense of location, identity and language—it is all in flux" (2007, p. 182). In other words, the imperative at the heart of an increasingly globalized world is to engage with its fluidity and constantly shifting identity, never losing sight of the complexities, including the dangers, of this process.

Awareness of such intimations is demonstrated in Berthold Schoene's *The Cosmopolitan Novel* (2010). Throughout his analysis, Schoene considers cosmopolitanism the body of political ideas corresponding to globalization (2010, p. 6) and capitalizes on the need for realism (2010, p. 7) and vigilance, or "careful intellectual scrutiny" (2010, p. 10). After reflecting on the problems of earlier considerations on cosmopolitanism, such as their idealism, Schoene embraces a more critical variant, emphasizing the fact that "the new cosmopolitanism is centered on the development of a strong sense of global community in order to pre-empt war and terrorism, be they motivated by nationalism, religious fundamentalism, or any other arch-ideological conviction or belief" (Schoene 2010, p. 10). This necessary preoccupation proves particularly useful for discussing Lim's novel, which tackles the topic of nationalism in twentieth-century Malaysia.

Relying on John Tomlinson's perspective in *Globalization and Culture* (1999), Schoene further identifies a major tension at the heart of cosmopolitanism, explaining that "cosmopolitan representation's possibly greatest challenge lies in bridging the rift between the world of globalised business, marketing and political decision-making, on the one hand, and its countless sub-worlds of powerless, disenfranchised daily living, on the other" (2010, p. 14). In Gunew's own summary of new cosmopolitanism, she also sees the focus on certain groups' disadvantaged position as central to this version of cosmopolitan theory when she says that "the new cosmopolitanism engages with the perspective of those left out of triumphalist globalization in which the world is constantly referred to as being connected in new ways—the most remote communities are represented as, in effect, virtual neighborhoods" (Gunew 2014, p. 13), further explaining that this "does not compute in terms of access to resources" (2014, p. 13). In her fiction, Lim shows concern for characters whose access to empowering elements such as high social status or financial affluence is limited and focuses on gendered negotiations of the struggle for individual dignity and stability.

A recent collection of essays entitled *New Cosmopolitanisms, Race, and Ethnicity: Cultural Perspectives* (2019) aims at contributing to the debates concerning the neo-cosmopolitan projects of today. When delimiting the scope of the volume in his introductory chapter, Samir Dayal professes that the new cosmopolitanism/s the essays address is/are "more immediately pertinent to local and 'rooted' cultural phenomena and cultural production, at least to the extent that the local is valorized as the obverse of cosmopolitanism and a protection against kinds of cosmopolitanism that threaten the integrity of particular cultures or communities" (Dayal 2019, p. 3). In keeping with the theoretical clarifications and ambitions of this volume, my study also shows that a comprehensive analysis of Lim's novel cannot concentrate on key terms such as gender, race, and ethnicity, without also tackling class, nation, age or sexual orientation. As a matter of fact, the border crossings of my title refer to various instances when the boundaries of such categories are exploded and recontextualized.

The most immediately noticeable neo-cosmopolitan feature of Lim's novel is its composite structure. By moving swiftly between spatial and temporal foci, juxtaposing events that happen in Kuala Lumpur, New York and Singapore at three different main moments in history, while preserving intelligibility for her narrative, Lim illustrates Schoene's definition very clearly:

> Episodic yet cohesive, compositeness forges narrative assemblage out of a seemingly desultory dispersion of plot and characterization. Cosmopolitan representation resorts to the montage techniques of contemporary cinema, effecting rapid shifts in focus and perspective with the aim of cramming as many story lines and clashing imageries as possible into one and the same mise en scène. (Schoene 2010, p. 14)

Indeed, the cinematic logic of the shifts that occur in *Joss and Gold* reflects the contemporary reader's taste for fiction that incorporates the advanced technology of this age, responds to the hunger for time-saving strategies and flatters their ability to synthesize information, even if it reaches them in fractured form. The cohesiveness of the novel has been previously remarked upon, as it has been proven that each section adds to the themes encapsulated in the text. The sense of unity is never lost even as the novel moves from the first part entitled 'Crossing' set in Kuala Lumpur, to the second entitled 'Circling' taking place in New York, and to the third entitled 'Landing' featuring Singapore: "Through the positioning and repositioning of her characters within Malaysian, American, and Singaporean sociopolitical contexts, Lim's *Joss and Gold* captures and redefines the complex nuances of exile and home" (Mayer 2014, p. 163). In my interpretation of the novel, the characters' movement from their home(lands) into exile is discussed in terms of literal border crossings that, on the one hand, have far-reaching public and private consequences and that, on the other hand, are paralleled by non-literal border crossings especially in terms of gender construction and class mobility.

Given the fact that the exilic trajectory is often intrinsically connected to the issue of preserving or losing one's mother tongue and that the use of English and other languages is directly problematized in Lim's novel, the neo-cosmopolitan perspective on English is valuable for the current analysis. Among Schoene's considerations, the observation that, as the world's *lingua franca* today, English "tends to absorb quite literally a whole world of national differences while finding its own original distinctiveness profoundly hybridized by continual re-appropriation" (Schoene 2010, p. 16) dwells on the loss of a prescriptive, standardized English, reminiscent of colonialism, as well as on the shape-shifting nature of English itself, which actually splits into many Englishes. In *Joss and Gold*, the protagonist's primary language is English, but as a speaker who uses it for specialized purposes, Li An is acutely aware of its contamination or else rich hybridization with other local languages such as Chinese or Malay. The very use of phrases coming from these languages in the novel and the effort of finding English equivalents that would not break the fluency of the narrative testifies to Lim's preoccupation with and masterful rendition of the tensions inherent in the Englishes of her characters residing in Malaysia, Singapore and even New York.

Enacting Border Crossings and Negotiating the Consequences

The novel focuses on Li An, a young Malaysian graduate of Chinese descent, who is granted the opportunity to teach English literature at the University of Malaya in Kuala Lumpur. She strives to make sense of and engage intelligently with both the public realm, most notably the political turmoil Malaysia is going through in 1969, and the private realm, the personal turmoil she is facing as a wife who is experiencing attraction to a man other than her husband. The web of characters around her illustrates some of the challenges the Malaysian multicultural society encounters as Malay, Chinese and Indian communities have to negotiate the terms of their emerging national identity. Even if she is married to a scientist from a wealthy Malaysian-Chinese family and her close female friends are also Malaysian-Chinese, and thus immersed in issues pertaining to cultural diversity, she first becomes acquainted with Malay nationalist discourse through several acquaintances. In the first part of the novel, the protagonist spends increasingly more time with an American visitor to Malaysia, Peace Corps volunteer Chester Brookfield. She soon realizes that her attachment to him is questionable in the context of a traditional society which imposes strict rules to protect a woman's reputation, but she claims agency and insists on defining her own life, despite the boundaries imposed on her at that moment. By the end of the novel, whose third part is set in 1981, Li An lives in Singapore raising her daughter, Suyin, in an all-women household, resisting the Madame Butterfly stereotype, i.e. the image of the Asian woman who clings to her child's American father.

The current analysis uses neo-cosmopolitan concepts to follow the protagonist's movement from youth to maturity as she negotiates dimensions of her identity and emerges, at the end of the novel, as an empowered self-sufficient woman whose border crossings constitute as many choices she thrives on. It is Shirley Geok-lin Lim's merit as a Malaysian-born writer and academic working and publishing in the United States of America today, while preserving connections to her native Asia, to have proposed a text at the turn of the twenty-first century that speaks to readers interested in literature whose central themes are cross-cultural communication and feminine empowerment.

In the opening of the novel, in the section entitled 'Crossing,' Li An is depicted as a restless young woman whose temperament, personal tastes, determination and English training seem to make her dreams about getting a grant to study in the United States of America a possible course of action after graduation. She justifies her choice adamantly: "Why not America? Isn't that where everything is happening? It's so boring here. Nothing ever changes. No one is doing anything, no one is writing poetry, no one is painting, no one is singing, no one is going anywhere" (Lim 2001, p. 11). However, the novel takes utmost care in juxtaposing her plan of going away, since nothing happens at home, with an opposite position coming from her husband, diligent Henry Yen. His response to her emphasizes the fact that the vibrancy of that particular moment in Malaysian history should not be missed. He explains that intellectuals have a crucial role in the shaping of the nation's destiny and it is their duty to help to the best of their abilities. Leaving seems a cowardly and self-centered gesture as far as he is concerned. His own plans are focused on studying in Germany and returning to Malaysia to add his humble contribution to local scientific developments. In the following explanatory passage, Henry demonstrates patience and passion at the same time:

> All kinds of things are happening here. This is the time for us to assert ourselves. We are going to be the most important people in the country because we are the people with brains. Malaysia has just become a nation. It's only eleven years since independence, so how can you expect there to be poetry or art yet? It's like science. You have to work hard every day with your experiments, and then someday you will discover that truth which no one else has found. Malaysia is like an experiment. Going to America is a selfish way of acting. (Lim 2001, p. 11)

The young speaker of these words has confidence in his role as scientist and intellectual who needs to make sacrifices and help his country prosper. Even if Henry's argumentation does not convince her entirely, for a while Li An goes along with the idea of accompanying Henry to Europe for a short time, the plan of returning home to contribute to the construction of Malaysia being firmly rooted in his intentions. In the meantime, her infatuation with Chester, who constantly provides inside perspectives on his native culture, strengthens her interest in America and desire to emigrate. But, by the end of the first part of the novel, Chester has departed from Malaysia hastily, leaving Li An behind to give birth to their child, Suyin, whom she does not tell him about. The daughter's birth accelerates the dissolution of her marriage and ruins her plans of moving to Europe or America. Without the financial support and the social status associated with being married to Henry, Li An experiences powerlessness and is forced to identify ways of acceding to a better life, free from the prejudices she faced in Malaysia.

The third section of the novel, 'Landing,' discloses Li An's circumstances almost twelve years later. Her energy and purposefulness seem to have been channeled towards finding a middle ground between her homeland and the remote spaces of relocation she contemplated in 1969 as she chooses Singapore and reinvents herself as the editor of *BioSyn-Sign*, the news bulletin of a successful company. As explained in the novel, while providing financial stability, the protagonist's new position involves certain constraints and a lot of responsibility: "With a powerhouse like BioSynergy—or BioSyn, as it was better known—a weekly bulletin was not simply a newssheet, it was a hot document studied by investors, shareholders, and the Monetary Authority of Singapore for clues to the company's health and future" (Lim 2001, p. 176). It is clear that the female editor's creativeness and freedom of expression are carefully checked. And as the novel implies, all her initiatives have to be sanctioned by the male executives for whom the financial rationale takes precedence over other considerations, thus a rather oppressive context, at least for female professionals.

Singapore seems to be a space characterized by in-between-ness, representing Li An's solution of compromise between not emigrating at all and reaching remote destinations full of promise, as in her youthful dreams. Here she manages to weave new perspectives for her self-fulfillment away from her homeland and the traumatic specter it inspires in the wake of the post-13 May 1969 riots and her personal troubles, yet close enough to maintain contact with Malaysia. Analyzing Singapore as emblematic for the theme of exile in *Joss and Gold*, Chingyen Yang Mayer adds further nuances to decoding this urban space:

> As a woman who has transgressed the gender and racial boundaries, Li An is forced to start anew in a place where nobody knows her past. Singapore is a place where she can nurse and rehabilitate her wounds, a safe haven, but it is also a place of banishment. Lim vividly captures Li An's stinging sense of homelessness and alienation even after Li An had been a resident of Singapore for nine years. (2014, p. 168)

In a scene in the final section of the novel, in which she attends a school reunion that gives the author the chance to present a cross-section of Malaysian society in the 1980s, Li An feels the need to justify her choice of relocating to Singapore when challenged by a multimillionaire former classmate, Alex Yeo: "Lots of Malaysians leave. Australia, Canada, UK. We're all over the world. Some of us can't succeed in Malaysia" (Lim 2001, p. 172). Li An seems to voice the sentiments of many minority intellectuals from Malaysia who realize that their efforts are overlooked and their merits are marginalized in the general craze that emphasizes Malay nationalism in the 1970s. Her diasporic status is only partially a choice, since decisive events in 1969 forced her to seek security and stability elsewhere. As Mayer further explains, after giving birth and being divorced, Li An experienced hostility directly: "Malaysia has become a more inhospitable place for a woman who has committed the unpardonable sin of adultery" (2014, p. 168).

The novel epitomizes the confluence of the private and public histories in connection to one night: May 13th, 1969. This particular choice of a narrative knot is very relevant, since it marks a most tumultuous moment, as explained by one of the first critics of the novel, Sharmani Patricia Gabriel:

> On that day, racial clashes broke out in the capital following Malay insecurity over the massive victory by the mostly Chinese-led opposition in the General Elections. The politically dominant Malay community, already insecure about its weak economic standing, felt threatened by the political inroads made by the economically-superior Chinese. Ethnic tensions culminated in the riots, an orgy of killing that lasted a few days. May 13 1969 proved to be the most significant event in the history of the Malaysian nation for it provoked radical modifications to the political, economic and social life of the nation, underscoring, in blood, the particular implications of race, rights and privileges to the peoples of Malaysia. (Gabriel 2002, p. 89f.)

For the protagonist, the memory of that night brings together feelings of guilt, shame, pain and joy at the same time. On the one hand, this is the night when her child is conceived. The curfew imposed on the citizens of the city creates the circumstances that allow Li An and Chester to share the same closed space, give in to the physical attraction that has pulled them together all along, make love and thus enter a new dimension of their relationship. The joy she takes in seeing her daughter grow cannot be separated from those particular hours engraved in her memory. On the other hand, however, it is also the night when Li An's father-in-law is brutally killed in his own house by a furious mob, the event having dire consequences for the entire family: "In dark Petaling Jaya on the night of May 13, with Chester's arm around her waist and the warm length of his body by her side, feeling his pressure on her hip, she had invested the keen sensation with promise, a tenderness she'd believed real, surely more real than the killings and fires in Kuala Lumpur" (Lim 2001, p. 179).

Given her own personal strife and confusion at the time of her pregnancy, Li An cannot heal in the aftermath of the national trauma overshadowing everything around her. Rather than forge coping strategies with the help of her remaining friends on site, Li An confronts the dilemma of leaving in order to escape a stifling life on her own. While the novel does not reveal much about this particular period in her life, choosing to jump more than ten years forward, the reader does find out, in retrospect, that she was deserted by her husband who refused to raise a child whom he recognized as not his. The infant however gained a non-conventional family as Li An's best friend, Ellen, stepped in to help and share some of the responsibilities as the little girl's godmother, and Henry's stepmother, Mrs. Yeh, agreed to her role as grandmother to the very end of her days. Women's alliance in creating a nurturing environment for the child is one of the feminist overtones of the novel and the alternative Lim provides to the dismal ending of *Madame Butterfly*'s story. In a way Lim uses new cosmopolitanism and feminism to solve a problem of ethnic stereotyping and patriarchal dominance, as critics have been quick to notice about the novel: "it strives to counteract ... the prevailing stereotypes of beautiful Asian women encountering white males" (Wagner 2005, p. 154). Li An is clearly constructed as a complex, dynamic, articulate, independent woman, who "stands as a counter to all the Western Orientalist visions of Asian women that depict them as passive, dependent, occupying highly sexualized locations" (Sankaran 2014, p. 174). While Lim's novel does oppose the constant waiting and final suicide of Puccini's protagonist with Li An's self-sufficiency and rejection of the returning American man, it also aspires to address much more, as even a succinct examination of the text testifies: "*Joss and Gold* was originally intended as a modern revision of the *Madame Butterfly* story, but the story outgrows the themes associated with that classic narrative and thus moves to larger, more contemporary complexities spawned by a globalizing world, shifting social and professional roles, and different values" (Morgan 2009, p. 638). The novel self-consciously reveals its position towards the pattern fixed by Puccini's opera, when it allows Chester, the American anthropologist who returned to the United States to become a professor and marry a young woman with a social background similar to his, to reflect: "This was the West's degradation of Asia, the imago of what had gone wrong in Vietnam. Asia was independent of the West, had been independent for centuries, did not need America to know itself" (Lim 2001, p. 202). The capacity to discuss the complex East-West divide, using a sophisticated theoretical vocabulary and inscribing the text with a self-reflexive dimension, betrays Lim's familiarity with current critical debates, while attracting an academic readership fluent in the contemporary scholarly idiom.

Chester's incursion into Malaysia had been about getting to know the other and, ironically, not even eleven years later does he find himself anywhere closer to this objective, the very 'knowability' of a culture being questioned in the novel. When preparing to return to the region with a research grant that would allow him access to revisiting his past, Chester ruminates:

> Malays, Eurasians, Chinese, Tamils, Pakistanis, Sikhs, Indonesians—there was a parcel of them for a small country. I knew Americans shouldn't have been there, adding to the mess, like we were doing in Vietnam, but it was confusing, figuring out what was interference and what wasn't. (2001, p. 156f.)

While talking about political action initiated by nation-states, he is also referring to individual action often influenced by forces above and beyond one single agent. In this very reflection, he might be expressing his regret in connection to his own choices and his incapacity to make more informed decisions.

When Li An meets him for the first time at the end of the 1960s, his commitment to explore the local culture and immerse himself in experiencing Malaysia seems to be his *raison d'être*:

> He didn't have time for Westerners, because he spent as much time as he could with Malaysians. But he didn't keep to one group. He had Chinese friends, who soon included Henry and herself, and Indian friends like Dorisammy and Gopi, and Malay friends like his roommates, Abdullah and Samad. (Lim 2001, p. 30)

The locals discuss their various political perspectives with Chester, an outsider; thus the novel helps the reader less knowledgeable about Malaysia understand its complex ethnic diversity. Anticipating the race riots of that year, a memorable scene in chapter four has Li An and Henry, the Malaysian Chinese couple, confront Chester, whose ideas about the local construction of nationhood must have been borrowed from his friends, Abdullah and Samad. The latter identify as Malay and must have championed "the fairness of a *Bumiputra* (Sons of the Soil) policy—one to which Henry takes great exception" (Sankaran 2014, p. 181). When Chester shows limited consideration for his hosts and little understanding of ethnic intricacies by blurting out "The Chinese aren't really Malaysian, are they?" (Lim 2001, p. 34), Henry retorts in defense of his community whose living in Malaysia for many generations justify their sense of belonging: "Our traditions are Chinese, but that doesn't make us less Malaysians. What makes Malay a real culture and Chinese not real" (2001, p. 34). His immediate response is followed by Li An's patient contextualization:

> You wouldn't know that recently people here have been having the fiercest arguments about what is a Malaysian. You sound just like the ultra-Malay politicians who want to kick the Chinese out of the country. My mother's family has been in this country for five or six generations, and some of the Malays are really immigrants who have just arrived from Indonesia in the last few years. You can't make any judgments based on who or what is 'original.' (2001, p. 34)

Her speech represents as much an admonition for her American friend, whose reaction she considers thoughtless and disrespectful, as a lesson to any anthropologist who draws rash conclusions with no regard for local histories, attitudes and feelings. She goes on to express her opinion that a more inclusive and fairer Malaysia is possible: "Give us a few more years and we'll be a totally new nation. No more Malay, Chinese, Indian, but all one people" (2001, p. 35).

Despite his hosts' convictions and faith in the viability of a multicultural model, the American Peace Corps volunteer is somewhat justified in being confused and swaying in his views from one side to another. His roommates are ardent supporters of the perspective that Malaysia should belong to the Malay only. Furthermore, they believe the Malay should have privileges. Abdullah, a young journalist, uses pathos in his nationalistic writing while adopting a conciliatory tone in explaining the same principles to his friends. Even following the riots, when he gives Li An a ride home, thus providing friendly help, he insists: "I told you the Chinese cannot push us too far. This is our country. If they ask for trouble, they get it" (Lim 2001, p. 82). She cannot retort on the spot, but her thoughts register the need for cross-cultural negotiations and a fresh perspective steeped into local realities of multi-ethnic coexistence: "His truth was wrong; she was sure it was wrong. You cannot be born and live in a place all your life without that place belonging to you. How could you not grow roots, invisible filaments of attachment that tied you down to a ground, a source of water? If a tree were pushed off the earth it stood on, deprived of its water, it would die" (2001, p. 82).

The same certainty that her identity is intrinsically based on the place in which she was born, even if her allegiances have developed a multiplicity of directions and she is ready to explore cosmopolitan ramifications and transnational connections, is echoed in her diary pages as well: "All this talk about Chinese rights makes me sick too. Malay rights, Chinese rights. No one talks about Malaysian rights. I am Malaysian. I don't exist" (2001, p. 75). In showing that even in her diary, a most intimate form of writing, usually not meant for anyone else's eyes, this educated young woman contends with the political issues of the day, Lim identifies yet another way of demonstrating the interconnectedness between the private and the public realms. Once the riots disprove Li An's vision of a tolerant model for Malaysia, her decision to raise her child in Singapore, and therefore Lim's decision to project this city as a refuge for people with neo-cosmopolitan views, is a stage for their, that is the character's and the author's, search for viability, for acceptance, and for feminist self-affirmation.

Conclusion

In her turn, the character of Li An's daughter exemplifies further border crossings, which translate into unconventional ways of relating to her family and of establishing transnational connections to her father figures. In the final section of the novel eleven-year-old Suyin meets Chester Brookfield, who wants to explore fatherhood at a point in his life when he has had a vasectomy as he and his wife have decided that they will not have children. Chester is introduced as her mother's old friend from

America (Lim 2001, p. 213), but their spending time together convinces the girl that he holds the key to a significant dimension of her mother's past and her own future. The moment he invites Suyin to visit New York opens up the prospect of discovering a remote, yet exciting new cultural space and thus of escaping the confines of her immediate surroundings. Almost concomitantly, Suyin begins to relate to another father figure, Henry Yen, whose stepmother's death as well as legal and financial arrangements prompt him to connect to the girl whom Mrs. Yen always treated as her granddaughter and whom the old lady chose as her heiress. Acting as "executor of Grandma's estate" (2001, p. 254), he travels from Malaysia to Singapore to explain certain business matters to Suyin, while re-establishing a familial bond he had severed minutes after seeing the Amerasian infant for the first time. Challenging not only a traditional understanding of the family, but also that of the father and his role in a child's life, Lim grants not only one, but two male presences in Suyin's life. Demonstrating appetite for cross-cultural connections and emotional attachments, Suyin communicates with them both. Rather than dwell on the shock that such a drastic change in the girl's reality could have produced, the author chooses to celebrate the preadolescent character's capacity to adapt to novelty and to negotiate meaningful relationships with both men.

In contrast to the negative connotations of the labels that children have used for her such as "mixed breed devil," Suyin translates such phrases for her own purposes and re-appropriates them in her own terms. She playfully reads the promise of sustaining connectedness and familial nonconformism in a derogatory appellation that otherwise could have been harmful to her self-image:

> Chap cheng kwei, Chap cheng kwei—mixed breed devil, she had finally learned, was what her classmates had called her from her first day in school. Perhaps that was what it was to be a chap cheng kwei, to have all these strange relatives whose existence she had never known, living in Kuala Lumpur, in Singapore, in America. Here, there, and everywhere. (2001, p. 255)

"Here, there, and everywhere" is an almost poetic way of reflecting on the need for coming to terms with the fluidity of the contemporary cosmopolitan condition, for negotiating public and private relationships and pressures, for enacting border crossings that would ensure individual and communal sustenance, for navigating spatial, temporal and other challenges human beings face. By capturing such key preoccupations of our age, Lim's memorable novel becomes a landmark in contemporary fiction, proving that literary endeavors can still illuminate human experience, thus deserving careful (critical) consideration.

Works Cited

Dayal, Samir. (2019): Introduction: New Cosmopolitanisms: Rethinking Race, Geography, and Belonging. In: Luczak, Ewa B./Pochmara, Anna/Dayal, Samir (eds.): New Cosmopolitanisms, Race, and Ethnicity: Cultural Perspectives. Warsaw: De Gruyter, p. 1–24.

Gabriel, Sharmani Patricia (2002): Identity, Culture and the National Narrative: Shirley Geok-Lin Lim's Joss and Gold. In: Southeast Asian Review of English 44, p. 87–93.

Gunew, Sneja (2014): 'A Multilingual Life': The Cosmopolitan and Globalectic Dimensions of Shirley Geok-lin Lim's Writings. In: Asiatic: IIUM Journal of English Language and Literature 8, no. 1, p. 12–24.

Lim, Shirley Geok-lin (2001): Joss and Gold. New York: The University Press of the City University of New York.

Mayer, Chingyen Yang (2014): Longing and Belonging, Exile and Home in Shirley Geok-lin Lim's Joss and Gold. In: Asiatic: IIUM Journal of English Language and Literature 8, no. 1, p. 162–172.

Morgan, Nina Y. (2009): Lim, Shirley Geok-lin (1944-). In: Huang, Guiyou (ed.): The Greenwood Encyclopedia of Asian American Literature. Westport, Connecticut and London: Greenwood Press, p. 635–640.

Sankaran, Chitra (2014): Writing Back: Ethics and Aesthetics in Joss and Gold. In: Asiatic: IIUM Journal of English Language and Literature 8, no. 1, p. 173–184.

Schoene, Berthold (2010): The Cosmopolitan Novel. Edinburgh: Edinburgh University Press.

Wagner, Tamara Silvia. (2005): Realigning and Reassigning Cultural Values: Occidentalist Stereotyping and Representations of the Multiethnic Family in Asian American Women Writers. In: Huang, Guiyou (ed.): Asian American Literary Studies. Edinburgh: Edinburgh University Press, p. 152–175.

Wisker, Gina (2007): Key Concepts in Postcolonial Literature. Basingstoke, New York: Palgrave Macmillan.

Russian Jewish Emigrant Writers Leaving for the West: David Bezmozgis, Maxim Shrayer, and Vladimir Vertlib[1]

Bettina Hofmann

In his memoir, *Little Failure* (2014), Jewish American writer Gary Shteyngart relates his immigration from Leningrad to New York City in 1979 when he was seven years old. As his plane lands in Vienna, his first stop in the West, the adult narrating-I comments: "Momentarily, we will land in a world unlike any we could have imagined, the one many will tell us is free. But nothing is free" (Shteyngart 2014, p. 82).

Shteyngart is not the only contemporary immigrant writer from a communist country to invoke this trope of the free world. The Chinese American Ha Jin has named his first novel set in the U.S. *A Free Life* (2007), and the Jewish Canadian David Bezmozgis, who emigrated as a child from Latvia, i.e. like Shteyngart from the Soviet Union, has called one of his novels *The Free World* (2011). These authors point out the price immigration exacts from people who, more or less, voluntarily change their countries, as the quoted apodosis "But nothing is free" foreshadows. Even if immigration is followed by material success, the change of language and other cultural modes such as types of labor, friendship patterns, food habits, etc. claims a psychological and social price.

In the literature of immigration, this process is usually described in terms of assimilation or integration with a clear dichotomy of 'before' versus 'after.' Most immigrant narratives put an emphasis on getting adjusted to conditions in the new country, with few references to the life lived before. This paradigm was established by Jewish immigrant writers from Eastern Europe at the turn from the nineteenth to the twentieth century. Mary Antin, Abraham Cahan, and Anzia Yezierska, probably the best-known writers of that group, identified America with freedom from political and economic oppression, from anti-Semitism, and other constraining

---

1   A slightly different version of this article, "Transitland Italien," (2018) appeared in German in Bischoff/Tippner (2018) *Jahrbuch für europäisch-jüdische Literaturstudien.*

traditions such as religion that were characteristic of Europe.[2] These writers appropriated the American, and in particular the Puritan, discourse of exceptionalism and contrasted the (mostly) negatively connoted 'before' in Russia with the positive 'after' in America. Anzia Yezierska's short story "America and I" (1923/1994) may serve as an illustrating example, where already in the second paragraph, America is identified with the Promised Land and set into opposition to Russia: "Choked for ages in the airless oppression of Russia, the Promised Land rose up—wings for my stifled spirit" (Yezierska 1923/1994, p. 1865).[3] Emphatically, the narrator of the story, and one can confidently assume the author as well, draws an analogy to the Puritan experience and thus claims to be part of this greater master narrative: "And I, the last comer, had her share to give, small or great, to the making of America, like those Pilgrims who came on the *Mayflower*," the narrator concludes (1923/1994, p. 1872). When conditions in America do not live up to their promise, the narrator rather finds fault with her own shortcomings than blame others: "But the great difference between the first Pilgrims and me was that they expected to make America, create their own world of liberty. I wanted to find it ready made" (1923/1994, p. 1871). Psychologically, this self-criticism lets her preserve her ideals even when they are disappointed.

After the Russian Revolution, with the consolidation of the Soviet system and the introduction of restrictive immigrant quotas in the U.S. in the 1920s, Jewish immigration from Eastern Europe to North America came to a halt. A new wave started in the 1970s when about 250,000 Jews— Gary Shteyngart's family belongs to this cohort—were allowed to leave the Soviet Union. When the Soviet authorities again stopped handing out visas, the *refusenik* movement was born. In 1987 exit visas were issued once more so that, accelerated by the disintegration of the Soviet Union, a new exodus took place in the late 1980s/early 1990s, which Bezmozgis's and Shrayer's families joined. Destinations for those emigrants were, next to Israel and the United States, also Canada, Australia, and Germany.[4] Like their predecessors at the turn to the twentieth century, this cohort quickly produced quite a number of writers who soon published in their

---

2   Cf. Fine (1988); Girgus (1984); Wald (2003); Wirth-Nesher (2006) for a discussion of this first cohort of Russian Jewish immigrant writers.
3   Cf. Billeter Sauter (2011) for an analysis of the female immigrant experience in Anzia Yezierska.
4   Cf. Ben-Refael (2006); Gold (1997); Orleck (1999) for the history of emigration from the Soviet Union and immigration to the U.S.

newly adopted languages. Wladimir Kaminer and Vladimir Vertlib would be examples for writers who settled in Germany and Austria and chose German,[5] while Ellen Litman, Anya Ulinich, and Lara Vapnyar are now popular figures on the literary scene in the U.S. These authors have taken up many patterns the foregoing immigrant group established while also revising and introducing other features.[6]

The writers of the early twentieth century focused on the hopes, expectations and also disappointments in the new world and compared conditions between 'before' and 'after.' Of course, the expectations of the new world are different at the beginning of the twenty-first century. It is interesting to see what the authors of the contemporary scene focus on. Some direct their attention not so much to the process of integration upon arrival but rather on the journey itself when crossing different borders, i.e. on the space and time of transition. They tell of the time of indeterminacy, the state of limbo in-between, when the old world has been left while the new order is not yet in sight. Three texts that prominently deal with this inconspicuous and innocuous time between departure and arrival are David Bezmozgis's novel *The Free World* (2011), Maxim Shrayer's memoir *Waiting for America* (2007), and Vladimir Vertlib's autobiographically informed novel *Zwischenstationen* (1999), i.e. 'way-stations' or literally 'in-between stations.' With their settings in Austria and Italy, the texts reflect the historical stopovers the majority of emigrants had to make. Like thousands of actual emigrants, among them the authors mentioned, the protagonists of all three books first pass through Vienna, which, as the capital of Austria, was considered neutral space between the West and the East during the Cold War. Many of those who did not immediately leave for Israel went on to Italy as a second layover before their destinations and destinies were decided and they eventually proceeded to their final points of arrival.

Maxim Shrayer's, *Waiting for America: A Story of Emigration* (2007) is a memoir offering a nostalgic look back on the youth of the protagonist. His family joins the first wave of what proved to become a major exodus from the Soviet Union in 1987. Due to the long process required to obtain all necessary documents, they stop over in Ladispoli, a seaside resort north of Rome, where most of the text is set. As in the other narratives under

---

5   Cf. Gilman (2011) for a comparison between Kaminer and Vertlib. Gilman judges the latter to be the "'official' multicultural Jewish writer in Austria" (2011, p. 272).

6   Cf. Hofmann (2008) for further discussion of Jewish American writers in the new millennium.

discussion, little is said about the life the family leaves behind in Moscow. The book starts with the plane flight and from then on tells a tale of progress of the twenty-year-old autodiegetic narrator who develops from a poor *refusenik* into a successful American professional, with wife and children in Chestnut Hill, a posh suburb of Boston.

Having left the Soviet Union, the family needs to decide where to go. The narrative depicts a typical dilemma reflected in the other texts as well, namely the difficult and crucial choice of destination, in particular between Israel and other countries. While the father has strong Zionist ties, it is the mother's desire to immigrate to the U.S. that finally prevails. It is striking that Shrayer depicts the process of becoming part of western society, be it Italy or another country, in erotic terms. A representative example for the emigrant experience is to be found when the narrator relates the liaison of the fellow emigrant Aptekman with an Italian pharmacist:

> In retrospect I can see why Mrs. Perelman and our whole refugee enclave were so taken with the affair of Aptekman and the bombshell from the *farmacia*. [...] Stealing glances over their shoulders or shamelessly staring at the Italian woman as she kissed and transformed Aptekman, other Soviet refugees imagined themselves in her arms. They, too, were ready to be caressed and seduced by Italy as they waited at her plenteous shores. (Shrayer 2007, p. 104)

The West is a paradise of erotic and sexual plenty. It is personified as an attractive woman that needs to be courted and conquered. Italy is a first object of desire, but its attractions pale against the allurement of the U.S. On one of his first days in Rome, the protagonist flirts with Nordic beauties from the U.S. on the Spanish Steps. "My English at the time was grammatically accurate and vastly unidiomatic" (2007, p. 63), the narrator explains his failure to arouse further interest in the girls. By using his lack of language competence to explain his lack of luck with the women, the opposite is simultaneously implied: Once he is able to express himself in English, he will also succeed in love. Thus, English is both a means and object of desire.

The protagonist gets one step closer to conquering a woman and thereby the West when in Ladispoli he takes up with an Italian girlfriend, Raffaella, who shares with him his dream of America. Raffaella owns a broken sedan made in 1965. This car becomes not only a site for their sexual adventures, but it is equally important for their daydreaming of America.[7]

---

7   Cf. Dettelbach (1976) for an analysis of the different meanings of the car in American culture.

The old car is their secret, intimate place where they "tell each other about the American lives we had never had" (Shrayer 2007, p. 120). It is important to note that America is first of all a place of the imagination, constructed by help of movies, books, and hearsay before it is actually encountered by experience.

Among the authors who shape the narrator's idea of America in particular is the writer Vladimir Nabokov, himself a Russian émigré to the U.S.: "Reading Nabokov in Ladispoli was my culture shock. I was reading Nabokov and waiting for America" (2007, p. 185). Again, this introduction to America is described in sexual terms: "Reading Nabokov's Russian stories in Italy, less than a month after leaving the Soviet Union, was not unlike losing one's virginity. It was both riveting and emptying" (2007, p. 182).

The book and the period of waiting before finally being allowed to enter the country ends with an episode when the author, together with his mother, takes a day trip to Capri. They themselves are poor refugees who cannot afford any treats, but they observe a content American couple, almost a caricature of clichéd American tourists. The man has a "great belly," and both man and wife eat "gargantuan" sandwiches and drink coke: "They were so blissfully comfortable in their own skin, so untouched by fears and inhibitions, so unworried about their future. They were so incredibly American" (2007, p. 224). At this point, he makes a vow:

> Mama, let's make a promise, a compact. Let's come back here one day. [...] Maybe I'll fall in love and get married. And the four of us will sit in this café and look at Sorrento across the bay, and order club sandwiches, many club sandwiches, and of course champagne. And we'll talk about our new life in America and remember our old life in Russia. (2007, p. 225)

Here it is the sheer quantity of food and sensual pleasure that equals the promise of America.[8] Most interesting, however, is that he calls this resolution "a compact," a term that evokes the Mayflower Compact and thus makes him part of American society by linking him to one of the first immigrant groups. The narrative ends when mother and son walk down the hill, hungry but optimistic: "No words could describe our paradisal poverty" (2007, p. 225). In retrospect the time of transition in Italy becomes romanticized. Shrayer presents a classical rags-to-riches story, from hard-

---

8   Cf. Diner (2001) for more information about the abundance of food in the new world as a classic trope for all kinds of immigrants.

ships overcome to due success clad in a traditional heteronormative love story of sexual desire.

Vladimir Vertlib's life story *Zwischenstationen,* also a partly autobiographic text,[9] shows many similarities to Shrayer's in terms of time and setting. Yet it is different in organization and mood, less celebratory and less self-confident. In contrast to Shrayer's life story, which was embedded in a whole community of extended family and other Russian émigrés, Vertlib concentrates on the itinerant life of the nuclear family, i.e. father-mother-son, of the first-person narrator. The family's movement is random and chaotic, not goal-oriented or linearly progressive at all. Their route is mindboggling: Russia—Israel—Austria—Italy—Austria—Holland—Israel —Italy—Austria—USA—Austria. There is no direction, no purpose, eventually no salvation, either. In this random movement, Vienna becomes the anchor, "der Fixpunkt," to which the family involuntarily return again and again (Strasser 2006, p. 110). When they find themselves stuck in Italy for the second time, father and mother put it onto their ten-year-old son to decide where they should go next:

> I started to cry. I did not want to return to Israel, and I had no good memories of Austria either when thinking of all the cheerless apartments and the many people who had called me 'Tschusch' and 'foreigner.' I sobbed loudly. 'I do not want to go anywhere' was the only thing I managed to put forward. 'This means you would like to stay in Ostia,' my father deduced. Again I shook my head. 'This is not logical,' mom concluded. 'If you do not want to go anywhere, then you want to stay. You are a big boy and you are able to understand logical connections.' (Vertlib 1999, p. 159; my translation)

This is the dilemma posed by an *aporia* that cannot be solved and which is unfairly put upon the son's shoulder. Of course, it is the parents themselves who have maneuvered the family into this situation. They phrase the decision of choosing a new country as a mathematical equation, i.e. in terms of logic. Yet such choice is not primarily a rational but rather a profoundly emotional decision that involves affiliation, loyalty, and trust. The parents, however, are totally alienated and lack emotional attachment to any country. Instead, they show profound skepticism toward whatever place they find themselves in. They are critical toward every regime, ideology, and religion. This makes them remain in transit and in limbo almost permanently. This feature makes Christa Gürtler regard the novel as be-

---

9   Cf. Heero (2008) for a detailed discussion of which features may be considered autobiographical and which are rather fictional.

longing in the tradition of German *Exilliteratur*, the literature of exile, in whose history Vertlib strives to inscribe himself (Gürtler 2001, p. 113).

When they are in Ostia, Italy, ca. 40 km south of Ladispoli, also in the greater Rome area, for the second time, the family approach a philanthropic Russian organization meant to help emigrants. There they meet an unsympathetic, one might be tempted to call her anti-Semitic, Russian expatriate woman who advises them to return to Israel since it is a country they may call their own. Throughout the interview, she eats sweets from a box on her desk without offering any to the family. At the end, when the parents have received no help from her, the boy reaches into the box and crams a few chocolates into his mouth at once. This seemingly bizarre action does not simply express his greed. Rather, he wants to partake of the luxury and sweetness too that he is barred from enjoying. Taking away what others are enjoying in front of him seems to be the only possibility to get his share of the richness of the West.

The parents then argue about the option offered by the Russian woman, to go to Argentina while the boy immerses himself, as always, into his books about partisans fighting the Germans. The climax occurs a few pages later when he helps another Russian woman who illegally sells pierogi at her stall. When she steps away leaving him to handle the business himself for a few minutes, he is robbed of all the day's earnings. Upset about yet another failure, he takes his suitcase with his old Russian books and throws it into the sea. By this he drowns the ideals of his childhood and discards the notion of becoming a hero. This scene is a turning point in his growing up. In hindsight, he also leaves the Russian language behind, for the next 'way-station' is Austria again where he will eventually make German his own.

Before he returns to Austria for good, the family try to make it in the U.S. Members of the ultra-orthodox community help them to get hold of tourist visas with the prospect of getting permanent permits to stay in the U.S. But they expect the family to practice the religious traditions and send their son to a *yeshiva*. When the family do not comply, they do not receive further help, which eventually leads to their deportation. It is an ironic twist that in their extreme individualism the Vertlibs seem to be more American than the Americans themselves. The day before his deportation, the protagonist visits the Boston Public Library one last time, a place both of learnedness and democratic spirit. The librarians good-naturedly laugh at him because they have discovered that he used the security number of an old lady when borrowing books. But he perceives the women's innocent laughter as a cruel joke on him. The detection of his forged identity card is followed by his exclusion from American society.

This scene can also be read as an intertextual comment on Mary Antin's autobiography *The Promised Land* (1912/1997), in which she celebrates the progress of her life in America. The Boston Public Library is also crucial for her Americanization: "Did I not say it was my palace? Mine, because I was a citizen; mine, though I was born an alien; mine, though I lived on Dover Street. My palace—*mine!*" (1912/1997, p. 266, emphasis original). Vertlib cannot share in her enthusiasm. He has been denied all these privileges and is expelled, not only from this site of English books but is finally excluded from the American dream altogether.

The outlook on history and its implications for the future is very different in Bezmozgis's novel. In contrast to Vertlib's memoir, the concept of family is more extended in Bezmozgis. The Krasnanskys, like their predecessors from the turn of the preceding century, who came in three-generational families, consist of grandmother Emma, grandfather Samuil and their two sons Karl and Alec. Alec is married to Polina and Karl to Rosa. Karl and Rosa have two sons, Yury and Zhenya, seven and five years old. Already the names are telling: Samuil is a Biblical name and identifiably Jewish. His sons' names, in contrast, are not markedly Jewish. Instead, the couple's name "Karl and Rosa" strongly evoke the German Socialists Karl Liebknecht and Rosa Luxemburg, thus underlining a socialist legacy for the next generation while the names of the third generation appear simply Russian.

The story time of the novel covers five months. It is interesting to note that the names of the months, namely from July to November, are given a prominent position, while the year in which the action takes place is not mentioned in the text proper. Only on the inside cover of the book is '1978' mentioned as the setting. In contrast, the respective month of the action is always printed conspicuously on a separate sheet before the chapters. This piece of information is not simply a realistic device establishing a plausible setting in time. It is actually an inter-textual marker pointing to the classical narrative of migration to America, namely William Bradford's *Of Plymouth Plantation* (1651/2003), where he tells about his voyage to the new world in 1620. His and the other Pilgrims' journey also started in July and ended in November. Another parallel is the fact that it was not smooth sailing for the Pilgrims, who first boarded the *Speedwell* in Holland. When their first ship sprang a leak and proved unfit for crossing the Atlantic, they then had to make do with the *Mayflower,* and after a layover in England they could finally leave for America in September.

By chronicling the history of the Pilgrims' voyage, their difficulties and hardships, Bradford recounts the history of a very small group whose experience, however, he invests with universal meaning. After landing, Bradford complains about the "desolate, hideous wilderness" the Pilgrims found themselves in (1651/2003, p. 78) and writes: "Neither could they, as it were, go up to the top of Pisgah to view from this wilderness a more goodly country to feed their hopes" (1651/2003, p. 78). The reference to Pisgah, the mountain from which Moses saw the Promised Land, shows Bradford's strategy that became typical of Puritan writing. By way of parallelism and typology, as Miller (1939/1982) and Parrington (1930) have demonstrated, the Pilgrims are identified as the new chosen people. The blueprint for their experience is to be found in *Genesis*. Both this book of the Bible and Bradford employ the historical genre that shows the workings of God in human events. By taking the story of Exodus as a blueprint for their own experiences, the Puritans created a utopian vision of the new world.

It needs to be stressed that Bezmozgis takes his detour via the Puritans to make this link to the Biblical story of Exodus. He could have made this connection directly, by only using the motto from *Genesis* 12:1 that precedes the page before 'July.' After all, the Krasnanskys are Jews and as such are easily connected with the Biblical concept of the chosen people. Like Yezierska before him, Bezmozgis, by evoking the Pilgrims, adopts American ideology and lays claim to American history. Simultaneously, Bezmozgis also aligns himself with the legacy of the preceding Jewish American writers who had taken up the Puritan discourse to demonstrate their Americanness.

By taking up this discourse, Bezmozgis also claims to be part of a larger historical legacy, both of Jewish American literature in particular and American literary heritage in general.[10] This positioning in a literary historical context, however, is not the only function of establishing the parallel to the Pilgrims. Indeed, the purpose of the established parallel is striking. For Bradford, as for the ancient Israelites, the main purpose of going to a new land was not simply to look for material prosperity, even though that was a welcome effect because it might be a manifest sign of God's grace. Leaving for the new world entailed rather a spiritual journey toward

---

10   In his latest novel, *The Betrayers* (2014), Bezmozgis rewrites Anton Chekhov's "The Lady with the Dog" (1899) and thus connects himself to yet another strand of world literature, namely Russian.

salvation. Setting out for another country meant they were finally free to do as would please God. Thus, his writing formulates a utopian vision for a moral life that is to remind the reader to uphold these ideals.

In his novel, Bezmozgis pursues this parallel he has carefully set up. First of all, the Krasnanskys must be read not as random creations of individual characters or else as real persons in fictional guise but as types. Second, the events depicted are not random either but of general historical importance. Of course, the two outstanding events of historical upheaval in the twentieth century that affected both particular Jewish and world history are the Russian Revolution and the Holocaust during the Second World War. The novel demonstrates how the characters have been affected by these events and have responded to them.

In this context, also the setting is of importance. It is in Rome where these characters can freely contemplate both their past and their future. Only in this time of transit and transition, a time almost outside of history, can they look back to the past without having to fear censorship by the state. And it is here where their thoughts are not blinded by hindsight yet, either. Rome, however, is not only a neutral non-space between leaving and arriving. It is also symbolic for the decline of Western history. Samuil, who like the other characters shows some compulsion by constantly comparing the West with the East, considers the city from the vantage point of a communist party member: "Their history: imperialist aggression, dogmatic theocracy, totalitarian monarchy, and fascism" (Bezmozgis 2011, p. 21). The decay, however, is not just ideological. In a decisive scene in Ostia Antica, Alec falls prey to Russian criminals who, ironically, deal with orthodox icons in a dilapidated antique synagogue. This is the state of Europe: a demolished site of old religions that are bartered and a place which leaves everyone wounded and worse off.

Samuil, the patriarch and one of the focalizers in the novel, dwells most on the past. He has joined the family despite himself—since his youth he has held on to the communist ideals that he feels he is betraying by leaving the Soviet Union. In flashbacks he remembers the abject poverty of his ancestors. The next generation exchanged religious piety for modern European culture that promised cosmopolitan flair: Samuil and his older brother Reuven read Thomas Mann and learned Esperanto. When those bourgeois notions disappointed, two dynamic ideologies offered themselves, namely Zionism, which was taken up by a cousin, and communism, the path Samuil pursued, following his older brother Reuven's example.

The communist experiment has failed, and now, due to Samuil, the family is stuck for indeterminate time in transit in Italy. Since regulations demand the health of immigrants, Samuil's frail state prevents the family from entering a country other than Israel, where they do not wish to go. Only by his death at the end of the novel are they free to move to Canada. Here the parallelism to the Bible becomes obvious: Samuil, like Moses, is not allowed to enter the Promised Land but must die on the way. His last moments show him on the outskirts of Rome where he is stranded due to a strike by Italian railroad workers, whose walkout has left the passengers to fend for themselves. Blind to the failures of the communist system even unto his death, Samuil sincerely compares the absence of strikes in the USSR favorably with the Italian workers for he is convinced that the Russian workers have nothing that they would strike for. The walk back to the city, however, proves too strenuous. In an eerie desert-like atmosphere, Samuil dies alone by the side of the tracks that seem to be leading nowhere. He has been loyal to the idea of communism to the end, but as it eventually turns out, his clinging to the old ideals have ultimately been prompted by family loyalty. Reuven, the brother who had introduced Samuil to communism, had been killed by a German bomb in 1942. Keeping up Reuven's ideals of a communist utopia has been Samuil's act of loyalty to him.

In contrast to the disciplined, strenuous, and plain life of Samuil, his son Alec exhibits an experimental, anarchic quality that has led him to pursue an extramarital affair in Rome. He is, by pursuing a hedonistic and carefree lifestyle, the Roger Williams of the twentieth century:

> Whereas the only thing Alec detested more than being ordered around was having to order someone else around. Basically, he was of the opinion that the world would be a far more interesting and hospitable place if everyone—genius and idiot alike—was allowed to bumble along as he pleased. 'More freedom to bumble' neatly described his motive for leaving the Soviet Union. (Bezmozgis 2011, p. 93)

Thus Alec 'bumbles' into an affair, his idea of sexual freedom, about which his father wants to tell him off when he sets out on the fatal train trip to his son.

It is clear that the family is not going to stay in Italy for good. But due to their isolation in the Soviet Union, they have only vague ideas about what other countries are like. One character calls the first who try their luck in a new place "minesweepers" (2011, p. 29). This military metaphor stresses the dangers and hardships involved in the task. Additionally, as a homophone, 'minesweeper' can be also read as 'mind-sweeper.' This would point to the need to reset one's mind, to turn it into a blank slate and begin anew in the country.

At first, the Krasnanskys hope to follow a cousin to Chicago. Thus, they intend to follow what sociologists call 'chain migration,' namely to follow in the footsteps of others who have paved the way. The cousin, however, decides to sponsor another family instead, so that the future is again left open. "Now we have nowhere to go" (Bezmozgis 2011, p. 48), Emma, the grandmother, says upon hearing the news. Emma, whose name also resonates with the Hebrew word for mother, is the matriarch of the family who always finds solace in the company of her relatives. Therefore, the rejection by the cousin in the U.S. devastates her. Alec immediately contradicts her: "On the contrary, now we can go anywhere" (2011, p. 48). His counter is reminiscent of the apocryphal dialogue of German Jewish exiles during the Third Reich. When one complained of having to emigrate to South America, a place so far away, the other quipped, "far from where?" While Emma's reaction exemplifies the nurturing mother who defines herself through the family, Alec's response is traditionally male by primarily asserting his identity in freedom from others.

Emma then tries to cheer herself with the thought, "[W]e had it much worse during the evacuation" (2011, p. 26). By this she points to the historical continuity of having to pack up and leave. The evacuation she is talking of is, of course, the one during World War II when they fled from German-occupied Latvia to Uzbekistan. It is interesting to note that the worst feature about the war was that the family was torn apart, not other deprivations such as hunger or persecution.

Families torn apart were also a feature of Soviet life. In one of the flashbacks Samuil remembers how his Zionist cousin was deported to Siberia never to return. Samuil could possibly have saved him from the NKVD, but loyalty to the party did not let him consider this. The cousin comments matter-of-factly shortly before being deported: "Samuil and Reuven bet on one horse. I bet on another. My horse lost" (2011, p. 173). Seen this way, history simply consists of luck but has no meaning, no direction and hence no salvation. In this sense, luck has simply turned again, this time against Samuil.

However, the family members now do not opt in favor of Zionism, which would entail going to Israel. Another emigrant, Israel Lyova, who describes himself as a "serial dissident" (2011, p. 275), considers the Zionist state as a failed option. He had immigrated to Israel, where his wife and son still live. Yet the state of Israel rekindled the trauma of war in the character Israel. As he relates, Israel Lyova, while still a Soviet citizen, was a soldier who participated in the invasion of Czechoslovakia in 1968. As an Israeli he now would have to be an occupier once more. He expresses the trauma of being an aggressor and waging war by the tropes of rape and murder:

> To return to Israel is, for me, pathological, and to return to Kishinev[11] also pathological. Which is worse? How to answer such a question? Which is worse: rape or murder? To a normal person, neither is acceptable. So that's all. *Zehu,* as they say in Hebrew. . . So far I've been a citizen of two utopias. Now I have modest expectations. Basically, I want the country with the fewest parades. (Bezmozgis 2011, p. 277)

In a way, this disillusionment with utopian visions lets the Krasnanskys eventually opt for Canada since it is "[S]afer, cleaner, and in climate not all that different from Latvia" (2011, p. 69). It is gradual improvement, not a totally new vision that makes them choose this country. And, of course, in contrast to the U.S., it also has fewer parades. Before they leave for Canada, Samuil is buried. No one can say Kaddish, the traditional Jewish prayer for the dead. This means that traditional religion is already dead. Instead, everyone present knows the *Internationale*. Like a prayer, the communist anthem expresses the hope for a better world. Probably this is the last time it will be sung. The vision of achieving a better world by way of communism is dead and buried now. But the parallels to Bradford suggest that there is still hope in history. The quest for a utopian vision may not have been totally buried yet. However, it remains open in what ways the Krasnanskys, particularly Yury and Zhenya as the new generation, will continue the quest for a better society in Canada.

The Russian Jewish writers discussed here have followed in the footsteps of their literary predecessors of the turn to the twentieth century when writing about crossing borders for good. They also adopt the analogy of the Jewish immigrant experience to the Puritan project of the seventeenth century that was established by Anzia Yezierska and is now extended by David Bezmozgis. It is interesting to note, however, that the Promised Land for him is not the United States, but Canada. The search for a new home ultimately means the quest for a just society. Even in Shrayer this allusion to the Puritans can be found. However, no idealistic project is visible in this personal rags-to-riches story. Here the West is foremost a place of sensual, especially sexual pleasure. And while the United States is the epitome of such luxury in Shrayer, America is a place

---

11   Kishinev, nowadays Moldova, is notorious for its pogrom of 1903 (cf. Zipperstein 2018).

of utter disillusionment in Vertlib. Unlike Yezierska, who found fault with herself when America did not live up to its ideals, Vertlib does not blame himself for America's shortcomings. There is an ironic twist in his tale that it is in Austria, the country of un-repenting Nazis, and not in the U.S. where he will eventually become a citizen and a writer.

In contrast to the Jewish writers of immigration before them, these authors are less interested in what lies behind or before them after they crossed the border. Instead, they all focus on the 'way-station' Italy, which already shows some features of their final destinations but is also a place that they can leave behind without regret. By concentrating on the voyage, instead of point of arrival or departure, the still indeterminate state of transit is stressed. It is a state of limbo where old values are shed and new ones have not been adopted yet. Thus, this is a time of intense introspection where the imagination reigns. Here expectations and also misgivings are formed about the life they are about to enter. This way, Italy surprisingly becomes a site for formulating utopian visions.[12]

---

12   This is of course quite a new perspective when one considers the use of place for American writers such as Nathaniel Hawthorne or Henry James.

Works Cited

Antin, Mary (1997): The Promised Land. New York: Penguin (Original work published 1912).

Ben-Refael, Eliezer (2006): Building a Diaspora: Russian Jews in Israel, Germany, and USA. Leiden: Brill.

Bezmozgis, David (2011): The Free World. London: Viking.

Bezmozgis, David (2014): The Betrayers. London: Viking.

Billeter Sauter, Irene (2011): New York City: 'Gilt Cage' or 'Promised Land'?: Representations of Urban Space in Edith Wharton and Anzia Yezierska. Frankfurt: Peter Lang.

Bradford, William (1651/2003): Of Plymouth Plantation. In: Baym, Nina (ed.): The Norton Anthology of American Literature (6th ed.). New York: Norton, p. 75–94 (Original work published 1651).

Dettelbach, Cynthia Golomb (1976): In the Driver's Seat: The Automobile in American Literature and Popular Culture. Westport, CT: Greenwood Press.

Diner, Hasia R. (2001): Hungering for America: Italian, Irish, and Jewish Foodways in the Age of Migration. Cambridge: Harvard University Press.

Fine, David Martin (1988): The Beginning: American-Jewish Fiction, 1880-1930. In: Fried, Lewis/Brown, Gene/Chametzky, Jules/Harap, Louis (eds.): Handbook of American-Jewish Literature: An Analytical Guide to Topics, Themes, and Sources. New York: Greenwood Press, p. 15–34.

Gilman, Sander (2011): Gibt es neue Ostjuden in der deutsch-jüdischen Gegenwartsliteratur. In: Lorenz, Dagmar/Spörk, Ingrid (eds.): Konzept Osteuropa: Der "Osten" als Konstrukt der Fremd- und Eigenbestimmung in deutschsprachigen Texten des 19. und 20. Jahrhunderts. Würzburg: Königshausen & Neumann, p. 259–278.

Girgus, Sam B. (1984): The New Covenant: Jewish Writers and the American Idea. Chapel Hill: University of North Carolina Press.

Gold, Stephen J. (1997): Jews, Soviet. In: Levinson, David/Ember, Melvin (eds.): American Immigrant Cultures: Builders of a Nation. New York: Simon & Schuster Macmillan, p. 529–535.

Gürtler, Christa (2001): Zwischen Kulturen und Sprachen: Zur zeitgenössischen deutschsprachigen Literatur von Zsuszanna Gahse bis Vladimir Vertlib. In: Schwob, Anton/Krumm, Hans-Jürgen/Schacherreiter, Christian/Schmid-Bortenschlager, Sigrid/Schrodt, Richard (eds.): Vol. 4: 'Und gehen auch Grenzen noch durch jedes Wort': Grenzgänge und Globalisierung in der Germanistik; Beiträge der Tagung der Österreichischen Gesellschaft für Germanistik in Ljubljana 2000. Wien: Praesens Verlag, p. 107–115.

Heero, Aigi (2008): Vladimir Vertlibs Zwischenstationen—ein autobiografischer Roman? In: Tarvas, Mari (ed.): Tradition und Geschichte im literarischen und sprachwissenschaftlichen Kontext. Frankfurt: Peter Lang, p. 23–35.

Hofmann, Bettina (2008): 'A Blessing, not an Affliction': Jüdisch-amerikanische Schriftsteller eröffnen neue Perspektiven auf Osteuropa. In: Domsch, Sebastian (ed.): Amerikanisches Erzählen nach 2000: Eine Bestandsaufnahme. Darmstadt: text und kritik, p. 210–232.

Hofmann, Bettina (2018): Transitland Italien: Jüdische Auswanderer aus der ehemaligen Sowjetunion erzählen von der Durchgangsstation Italien auf dem Weg nach Kanada, Österreich und in die USA. In: Bischoff, Doerte/Tippner, Anja (eds.): Mobile Identitäten: Figurationen in der zeitgenössischen europäisch-jüdischen Literatur. Jahrbuch für europäisch-jüdische Literaturstudien. Berlin: De Gruyter, p. 142–155.

Jin, Ha (2007): A Free Life. New York: Pantheon Books.

Miller, Perry (1982): The New England Mind. Cambridge: Harvard University Press (Original work published 1939).

Orleck, Annelise (1999): The Soviet Jewish Americans. Westport, CT: Greenwood Press.

Parrington, Vernon Louis (1930): The Colonial Mind. Vol. 1. Main Currents in American Thought. New York: Harcourt, Brace.

Shrayer, Maxim (2007): Waiting for America: A story of Emigration. Syracuse: Syracuse University Press.

Shteyngart, Gary (2014): Little Failure. New York: Random.

Strasser, Alfred (2006): Einmal Leningrad - Wien - New York und zurück: Stationen einer Odyssee in Vladimir Vertlibs Roman Zwischenstationen. In: Germanica: Voix étrangères en langue allemande 38, p. 103–113, DOI:10.4000/germanica.378.

Vertlib, Vladimir (1999): Zwischenstationen. München: dtv.

Wald, Priscilla (2003): Of Crucibles and Grandfathers: The East European Immigrants. In: Wirth-Nesher, Hana/Kramer, Michael p. (eds.): The Cambridge Companion to Jewish American Literature. Cambridge: Cambridge University Press, p. 50–69.

Wirth-Nesher, Hana (2006): Call it English: The Languages of Jewish American Literature. Princeton: Princeton University Press.

Yezierska, Anzia (1923/1994): American and I. In: Lauter, Paul (ed.): Vol. 2: The Heath anthology of American literature (2nd ed.). Lexington, Mass.: Heath, p. 1865–1872 (Original work published 1923).

Zipperstein, Steven J. (2018): Pogrom: Kishinev and the Tilt of History. New York: Liveright Publishing Corporation.

Crossing the Boundaries of Class, Gender, Race, and Genre

Constructions and Transgressions of Class, Gender, Race, and Genre in Hari Kunzru's *The Impressionist*: A Narrative About Former and Current Globalizations

Elke Sturm-Trigonakis

Introduction

The construction of boundaries (spatial, anthropological, social, or gender-based) is one of the fundamental practices of what constitutes culture; they separate and unify while concurrently creating liminal zones which are in principle open to both sides. Furthermore, boundaries, thresholds, and transitions ask for the location and definition of the Self, indicating identity, or, at least, parts of identity (Görner 2001, p. 11). This paper considers Michel Foucault's emphasis on the complementarity of the construction and transgression of boundaries which automatically refer to and trigger each other (cf. Benthien/Krüger-Fürhoff 1999, p. 7); it then analyzes the boundaries of social class, gender, and ethnicity in Hari Kunzru's novel *The Impressionist* (2002). Chris Jenks defines transgressions as a "conduct which breaks rules or exceeds boundaries" (2003, p. 3), and indeed, Kunzru's protagonist has to go through a plethora of metamorphoses in order to reach an identity of his own. Son of a British officer in India and an Indian woman, Pran Nath has grown up in a rich Kashmiri family in Agra in the second decade of the twentieth century, but is thrown out when his father (in reality his stepfather) discovers his English blood. He lands in a brothel and is sold as *hijra*[1] to the Nawab of Fatehpur near Lahore, where he has to live as Rukhsana satisfying—among others—the sexual desires of the British resident Major Privett-Clampe. The Major calls him Clive and makes him recite English poetry in an English schoolboy's uniform. After this experience he receives further English education at a missionary's house in Mumbai and as Robert/Bobby, he successfully makes his first steps as an Englishman. Taking the passport and the passenger ticket of a murdered young man, he travels to England as Jonathan Bridgeman and studies Anthropology at Oxford. At the end of the novel,

---

1   The term *hijra* designates an alternative sex and gender role in India.

we find him in West Africa after a British expedition to the Fotse tribe, travelling with a Bedouin caravan.

According to Anne McClintock, class, race, and gender are the three "formative categories of imperial modernity [...] come into being in historical relation to each other and emerge only in dynamic, shifting, and intimate interdependence" (1995, p. 61). While 'postcolonial discourse,' however, greatly favored any kind of 'writing back' and 'subaltern speaking,' there is now a shift: during the nineteenth and the first half of the 20th centuries, a focus on transgressions prevailed. Meanwhile, the foregrounding of liminality and the creation of Third Spaces has gained importance in postmodern times (Hohnsträter 1999, p. 244). This transition has led to an innovative approach to colonial matters beyond the former dichotomy of colonizer vs. colonized, center vs. periphery, or wealthy north vs. poor south often seen in contemporary literary texts about experiences of imperialism (cf. Sturm-Trigonakis 2013, 2014, p. 190–194; McClintock 1995, p. 13). Our age of global entanglement has likely created a new sensibility for "accelerated phases of globalizations," as Ottmar Ette describes them in *TransArea* (2012). He locates the first phase in the sixteenth century and its European global expansion; the second phase around 1800 with the last 'discoveries,' (e.g. Australia); the third phase from 1850 to 1920 as the era of the worldwide extension of European imperialism; and finally, the last phase from 1945 until now (Ette 2012, p. 8–26). I aim to argue that a plethora of contemporary literary representations of these four globalizations constitute their subjects in a way that allows for classifying them as New World Literature (New *Weltliteratur*), thus exceeding former reductions of essentialist monocultural and/or nationalist discourse. At the content level, these current texts avoid polarizations regarding cultural, ethnic, or social environments, instead giving preference to in-between and hybrid characters, spaces, and time layers (cf. Koselleck 2003). At the expression level, this hybridity also dominates through multilingualism in the widest sense and, as can be shown through Kunzru's novel, through a transformation and adaption of established literary genres; in our case, the picaresque novel (Sturm-Trigonakis 2013, p. 65f.). This paper begins with an analysis of the configurations of class, gender, and race in *The Impressionist*, before discussing textual negotiations of actual and former phenomena of globalization in order to position the text into a wider map of 'post-postcolonial' literature and especially New World Literature.

Class

Though it has almost become commonplace, it may be important to remember that the origin of boundaries lies in a conceptualization of space which can often be identified with social entities. This means that spatial metaphors mark inclusion in or exclusion from a particular social structure (cf. Anselm 1995, p. 197f.). In Kunzru's text, the protagonist Pran moves from one place to another several times, including journeys from India to Europe and to Africa. Each movement corresponds to a crossing of social boundaries, with either an exclusion from or an inclusion within particular social structures. At the outset, he experiences exclusions against his will. Later on, however, he cautiously approaches the other side of the social boundary, grasping the opportunity to a seemingly final inclusion into English society, only to consciously decide at the end to stay out of any social group and to live as a traveler in an unbound existence.

The first traumatic exclusion happens when "Pran Nath Razdan: the beautiful, the son and heir" (Kunzru 2002, p. 42) is thrown out from the protection of his family's house, suddenly finding himself out on the street outside of the "familiar door with its iron studs and hinges, its scuffed blue paint" (2002, p. 41). He is lost amid a malicious crowd and without money, in a state of utter loneliness. The beggar at the corner in front of his family mansion sends him to his 'own people,' the Agra Post and Telegraph Club, where "the horrid blackie-whites gather together to swap their own stories of disgustingness, the disgustingness of natives, the foul Indianness of native ways and the firm manner in which they, the husbands, put down their employees, and they, the wives, chastise their servants, if they have them" (2002, p. 47). Pran asks a young man for some food, and this man's self-hatred results in his lashing out at Pran, who must flee from his violent blows (2002, p. 49). In this scene, the text reveals the interdependence of social class and race with its principle 'the darker the lower,' a phrase which may still be deeply relevant in social class-heavy societies such as the U.S. or Brazil.

Pran's social descent reaches its lowest point when he is sexually assaulted by the pedophile Major Privett-Clampe at the palace of the Nawab of Fatehpur (2002, p. 97ff.). After that terrible experience, he is made to sweep floors, scrub pans, and massage hijra feet, and "everything about his life is now inverted. [...] Pran Nath Razdan is falling away. In his place, silent and compliant, emerges Rukhsana" (2002, p. 101). As McClintock notes, the social categories here are once again dynamically interwoven. In this case, social class and gender are inseparable; Pran has lost his former arrogance and aggressiveness and instead takes the role of a 'compliant' girl who is placed at the bottom of the social ladder, a social class even lower than a boy without family and protection like Pran. That Pran himself has internalized this social and gender categorization but is not willing to toe the line becomes obvious in Mumbai at Reverend Macfarlane's house, when he—now going by the name of Chandra or Robert alias Pretty Bobby—sweeps the floor, thinking, "this is not his job. It is the sweeper-woman's job" (Kunzru 2002, p. 191). Consequently, as soon as he is ready, "he straightens up, lighting a cigarette. He holds it elegantly, instantly transformed from servant to cocktail-party guest. To complete the picture he leans on the wall beside him, crossing one leg over the other. A fashion plate. A man of leisure." (2002, p. 191). This first scene of Bobby's life in Mumbai anticipates his social advancement and his growing willingness to adopt different identities, accompanied by his first serious steps into Englishness. 'Robert' for the reverend, 'Chandra' for the reverend's wife Elspeth (cf. 2002, p. 193), and "Pretty Bobby, crown prince of the most notorious of all red light districts, the sewer of India: Falkland Road" (2002, p. 201) establishes himself in Mumbai as a connected man "brokering deals and procuring hard-to-find services for those with a discreet manner and an open wallet" (2002, p. 236). Although he remains on the outside of exclusive places such as the 'Royal Bombay Yacht Club,' he is able to find clients there nonetheless (2002, p. 237). During the day, he is an eager student of Macfarlane's anthropological studies, where he improves his English. Twice a week, he accompanies Mrs. Macfarlane to Mrs. Pereira's 'Theosophical Society,' where he not only comes into touch with a mingled society of Indians and Europeans, but also experiences his sexual attractiveness to both sexes, enjoying and using his power over others (2002, p. 239–242).

Thus, his years in Mumbai provide him with knowledge about different social groups within the imperial society of the colony; mingling with these groups, he not only learns their particular functioning, that is, their behavior, values, and norms, but he also begins to use his knowledge in the form of blackmailing (2002, p. 241) and cheating (2002, p. 242) in order to improve his own social position. Meanwhile, he trains his ability to perform different roles according to the societal environments he is moving in.

In Oxford, the protagonist, now as student Jonathan Bridgeman, cultivates "several groups [...], in a large but highly compartmentalized range of acquaintance" (2002, p. 344). He reaches the social summit when he is invited by Prof. Chapel to participate in an anthropological expedition to

Fotseland in West Africa, and has a love affair with the professor's daughter, Star (Kunzru 2002, p. 396ff.). She rejects his marriage proposal, however, because of his conventional Englishness, preferring the Afro-American jazz pianist Sweets to him (2002, p. 413ff.). His most terrible personal and emotional downfall happens alongside his greatest social triumph and his potential arrival in the upper-middle class of Oxford University teachers. The irony of his fate lies in Star's preference of an Afro-American person, which reveals all his efforts for perfect Englishness to have been useless and demonstrates the insignificance of categories such as class or race with regard to deeper human relationships. As a result, Jonathan is no longer motivated to insert himself into any social group and agrees when his expedition comrades in Africa blame him for his lack of "team spirit" and for not being a "joiner" (2002, p. 469). Thus, logically, the protagonist's social upward and downward movement in the narrative proves that in the end, he is no longer defined by a name, but is referred to just through the personal pronoun "he" and is surrounded only by sand, the camels, and unnamed drovers (2002, p. 481). Again, however, this last station in his life—at least for the reader—is sketched through a highly orientalized, nearly kitsch image supposing nothing else than a new act of performance by the protagonist. Therefore, it underlines the performativity of the text itself and the ironic distance of the narrator from his own text, which is a typical device of picaresque narration.

Social class boundaries, as they are presented in *The Impressionist*, are almost infrangible in Indian and English society as well as in mixed-race social groups. Their foundations are grounded in parameters, such as family and origin, manners and behavior, clothes, education, and financial status. Furthermore, they are closely interdependent with other determining categories such as race or gender. Though the protagonist attempts to integrate himself with different groups at different points of the novel, the text underlines that the protagonist is rejected by society for not having roots in it, which signifies a harsh criticism towards the intolerance and closeness of all social entities. Here the text most succinctly articulates the contemporary perception of this phase of globalization during British imperialism around 1900.

Gender

McClintock states that "all nations depend on powerful constructions of gender" and that "no nation in the world gives women and men the same access to rights and resources of the nation-state" (McClintock 1995, p. 353). Furthermore, "women are typically constructed as the symbolic bearers of the nation, [...] but are denied any direct relation to national agency," while men play a metonymic role representing the nation as a whole (1995, p. 354f.). One of her main points of departure is the notion "that gender is not synonymous with women" (1995, p. 7) and this is precisely what *The Impressionist* is about, since it subverts and satirizes traditional definitions of sex as well as the function of gender roles for the national project.

One of the key scenes is Pran's first contact with the eunuch Kwahjasara, chief hijra in the palace of Fatehpur, who introduces Pran to his new existence as Rukhsana:

> 'Remember you know nothing. You *are* nothing. Now, Rukhsana, how many sexes are there?'
>
> 'Two?'
>
> 'Fool! There are thousands! Millions!' (Kunzru 2002, p. 81)

"One simple cut," the *hijra* promises, and "the door to an infinity of bodies, a wonderful infinity of sexes" (2002, p. 81) will open, a promise which terrifies the boy. During the following weeks in the palace, it becomes obvious that Pran/Rukhsana is chosen to serve as the object of Major Privett-Clampe's pedophilia. After taking photographs of the Major 'in action,' the British resident is planned to be blackmailed to get his support to overthrow the Nawab. This intrigue has been planned by the Nawab's brother, along with one of the Major's subordinates, under the pretense that the Nawab's impotence will endanger the continuity on the throne of Fatehpur. The plan fails, but after sexually violating Pran/Rukhsana, the Major detects "some English" (2002, p. 108) and "some white blood" (2002, p. 109) in the boy, puts him in an English school uniform, makes him recite English poetry (2002, p. 109–112), and names him Clive (2002, p. 131). In this way, the protagonist changes and re-changes the gender role ascribed to him in different ethnic and social spaces, thus demonstrating the arbitrariness of these categories.

Kunzru's narrative strategy strives against asymmetrical gender conceptions of colonizer and colonized and, furthermore, of orientalist fantasies and white men's dreams of dark women (cf. Young 1995, p. 150f., p. 178). In the text, Reverend Macfarlane seduces a girl in Assam (Kunzru 2002, p. 227–232), but at the beginning of the novel it is the young Indian girl who seduces the British officer. Prof. Chapel's daughter, Star, leaves Jonathan for an Afro-American musician in Paris, and at the end marries the Nawab of Fatehpur (Kunzru 2002, p. 480). All these patterns signify the undermining of stereotypes of fixed power and gender positions. The women are not always victims, nor does sexual attraction only flow from the white male colonizer to the colonized colored female, nor are the eunuchs mere victims. Therefore, I agree with Robert J.C. Young's perception of colonialism as a "machine of war, of bureaucracy and administration [...] but also a machine of fantasy, and of desires" (1995, p. 98). Kunzru's text demonstrates, nevertheless, that this machinery has worked itself into both directions, influencing and changing the gender discourse in both societies. As Stephen H. Gregg emphasizes, this was perceived and fought by considerable propaganda efforts to protect the representatives of the empire from any kind of corruption by bad influences, especially on their sexual behavior; for instance, through effeminacy or miscegenation (cf. 2005, p. 21ff., p. 12f.). Kunzru presents a parody of the official discourse: the English Major is sexually attracted to little schoolboys, whereas the Nawab, who pretends to be impotent because of a curse, changes into a tiger of insatiable sexual appetite, sparing not even Lady Wyndham, the British resident's wife (Kunzru 2002, p. 174). Narrated in a hypertrophic and burlesque style, the text returns agency, as far as gender and sex are concerned, to all members of the colonial project, independent of race or social class. With its blurring of any established configuration of what gender discourse was supposed to be within the Empire, the novel attacks the boundaries of British and Indian imperial knowledge about perceptions of sexuality and gender during this era.

Race

"You are what you feel. Or if not, you should feel like what you are. But if you are something you don't know yourself to be, what are the signs? What is the feeling of not being what you think you are?" (2002, p. 52). These are Pran's desolate deliberations after he has been thrown out of his home and then out of the Anglo-Indian Post and Telegraph Club in Agra. This scene is key to setting the entire story in motion, for Kunzru's novel fundamentally negotiates matters of identity, unfolding the adventures and survival strategies of a young man who does not fit in any ethnic group. This is because firstly, his phenotype allows him to be widely grouped in with the Indian as well as the English population; and secondly, because the people around him are used to seeing what they expect or what they want to see, as the text demonstrates. Sketching the wide gamut of reactions towards the protagonist, the text detects and criticizes constructions of race and ethnicity, which are constitutive for societies as a mechanism of exclusion.

The basis for exclusion is the definition of the Own. Kunzru's text presents this through the discourse on the pureness of blood. Young Pran Nath with his copper-tone hair, his nearly green eyes, and the "milky hue" of his skin is the pride of the entire family, "So pale! Such a perfect Kashmiri!! [...] Proof [...] of the family's superior blood" as Pandits in Kashmir, one of the highest and most reputed castes of India (2002, p. 20). Regarding his social status, Pran's stepfather, a lawyer obsessed with "the promotion of hygiene, tradition, cultural purity, cow protection, and correct religious observance" (2002, p. 23) and with a "horror of touching a casteless beefeater,"—that is, English people (2002, p. 33)—represents the Indian version of racial discrimination while also embracing social discrimination against other Indian citizens (2002, p. 34f.). Ironically, he dies from the Spanish flu, which "obliterates all distinctions, hybridizing the whole world into one awful undifferentiated mass" (2002, p. 35). Thus, his character subverts the pretended Western monopoly of hygiene norms, parodying "the Victorian obsession with cotton and cleanliness" (McClintock 1995, p. 211) which found its peak at the beginning of the decline of British imperialism. In an atmosphere of "impending crisis and social calamity," soap promised to "preserve, through fetish ritual, the uncertain boundaries of class, gender, and race identity in a social order perceived threatened by the fetid effluvia of the slums, the belching smoke of industry, social agitation, economic upheaval, imperial competition and anticolonial resistance," (1995, p. 211). The protagonist, during his first experimental steps into the English side of colonial society, is also concerned with the "question of smell," defining "rancid butter" and "a hint of raw beef" as the "underlying whiff of Empire" (Kunzru 2002, p. 249f.). Naturally, this is implied to smell worse than Indian spices, and thus the text once again underlines the narrator's ironic approach to the concept of English superiority.

The English counterparts to this Indian lawyer of pureness are Reverend Macfarlane and the anthropologist Prof. Chapel, both of whom pretend to explain differences of race through so-called scientific methods, reflecting the scientific discourse of that era (cf. Almond 2002, p. 276, p. 279). The consequences of this belief in the superiority of the white descendants of the Aryan peoples lead to anti-Semitism in England—as happens to Gertler (Kunzru 2002, p. 315, p. 328)—and various degrees of discrimination of British colonial subjects. The novel also questions the assumption of anthropology as "the very highest mark of civilization" making "all the earth [...] available" and giving "everything and everyone [...] a place" (Kunzru 2002, p. 375). This pseudo-intellectual argument serves as an excuse to hide the true intention of colonialism; that is, economic expansion and the subsequent exploitation of the colonized (cf. 2002, p. 448f., p. 467f.). In the text, however, the colonized are able to strike back: though at first sight Prof. Chapel seems to degrade the (colonized) Africans to mere objects of observation, the text reverses the supposed established balance of power away from the English toward the Africans, on the level of expression as well as content. The burlesque description of the Fotses' "Gofo," an economic speculation system which seriously endangers the professor's life (2002, p. 371ff.) is reminiscent of contemporary exchange transactions. The fact that the Fotses know about the transmission of diseases through contact with water (2002, p. 373), and their diligently planned murder of the white intruders (2002, p. 344–375) signal the conscious exercise of agency on the part of the Africans, revealing their societal structures as highly complex and differentiated. Under these circumstances, the professor being awarded a "Medal for Progress in the Study of Backward Peoples" (2002, p. 373) highlights again the narrative use of irony. The professor's inability to step beyond his own culturally determined point of observation, serves as an ironic contrast to the protagonist who is able to perceive the English as well as other perspectives (cf. 2002, p. 468).

Part of this critical examination of the British superiority narrative consists of references to fetishization and exoticization of alterity; for example, in the Empire Exhibition at Wembley (cf. 2002, p. 379–382), or through Prof. Chapel's daughter Star's use of Fotse bangles (2002, p. 358, p. 363) and her decoration of a flat in Mayfair *à la Africaine* (2002, p. 379). Mrs. Macfarlane's rather romantic 'going native' would be another example of the narrative's ironic style. She insists on calling Robert/Bobby by the Indian name Chandra and urges him to join Ghandi's nationalist party, arguing that he should be proud of his nation and proud of who he is (2002, p. 199, p. 256). Despite her good intentions and her rejection of her husband's declared belief in white superiority (2002, p. 219), she is only able to perceive one aspect of Indian reality—that is, an exclusively spiritualistic and esoteric view. She approaches Raja Rao's claim to India as an idea rather than a concrete country and a reality (cf. Almond 2002, p. 284). As soon as Chandra shatters her romantic idea of him and India, she throws him out of her house. As an irony of fate, however, she is arrested by Indian policemen under suspicions of supporting the anti-colonial movement (Kunzru 2002, p. 271).

Generally, all the English characters in the novel use their higher educa-tion to claim to be intellectual border crossers as well as tolerant and sup-portive of non-English cultures and ethnicities. They tend to behave, how-ever, in an explicitly arrogant and discriminatory manner exploiting other people: if not directly for economic purposes, then at least implicitly for their own promotion and to compensate for their personal problems. Con-sequently, wherever they travel, they never go beyond the narrow bounda-ries of their class, their gender, and their Englishness.

Thus, it is the protagonist with the plethora of names and identities and his eagerness for social ascent who performs many kinds of real transgres-sions, at first driven by the struggle to survive, then later by his desperate aspiration to truly belong somewhere. From the moment that he becomes aware of his mixed-race origins and the low social status of the "horrid blackie-whites" (2002, p. 46, p. 43–49), he endeavors to become part of the English community because the way to the Kashmiri upper class of the Pandits which he initially felt he belonged to (cf. 2002, p. 52) has by now become closed off to him. After a phase of confusion and uncertainty which culminates in his desperate outcry, "So what am I?"—not *who* am I, importantly—(2002, p. 257), he starts leaving this India-centered atopia. He begins with small steps, first by imitating English manners in the red light district in Mumbai as Pretty Bobby with the use of a wrist-watch (2002, p. 201), then by playfully exploring conversation with English people, "free to reinvent himself, slipping into a new gora identity like one of Shahid Khan's jackets" (2002, p. 249). Through comparison with a re-al-life contemporary figure, the Pakistani billionaire businessman Shahid Khan, the text contextualizes itself in the modern day, while the adjective *gora* has its origin in the Hindi word for 'white' or 'fair' (cf. Lexico Dictionaries Powered by Oxford 2020) and transports the Indian perspec-tive into the English text.

The text strategy offers remarkable insight into English society from a point of view of alterity. In London, the protagonist views "the originals of copies he has grown up with, all the absurdities of British India restored to sense by their natural environment" (Kunzru 2002, p. 299) and he—now as Jonathan Bridgeman—systematically learns Englishness like the vocabulary of a foreign language (cf. 2002, p. 301ff., esp. p. 302, p. 315, p. 335). He manages to survive the Chopham Hall school, which is "a ma-chine for producing belonging, and accordingly everything is done in groups" (2002, p. 314), and then studies at Oxford, another "machine for the formation of character" (Kunzru 2002, p. 346). Jonathan incorporates himself into Oxfordian student society by mimicry, attempting to be "the average undergraduate," emphasizing "everything that is honest, true and English" (2002, p. 345), and goes as far as uttering a speech in defense of whiteness (2002, p. 347) that earns him an invitation from the fascists (2002, p. 348). With all his efforts, he manages to become a perfect Englishman, but dramatic irony causes the moment of his supposedly highest triumph, when he begs Star to marry him, to turn into his deepest fall when she rejects him because he is "exactly like everybody else" and "the most conventional person" she knows (2002, p. 415). She prefers the Afro-American Sweets to him since he has a soul—contrary to Jonathan, so she argues (2002, p. 415).

With its emphasis on national and ethnic identities as the results of education, the text reverses the idea of colonialism as "a conquest of knowledge" (Cohn 1996, p. 16). Having reached expertise in Englishness, the protagonist finally achieves full agency over his identity in Africa, on neutral terrain. As soon as the expedition steps on African soil, Jonathan shows solidarity with their African servants' group instead of acting as their "master" (Kunzru 2002, p. 433), a behavior which demonstrates his questioning the Englishness he has learned. After nights filled with panic because he loses "his personal landmarks," becoming "radically uncertain about where or who or why he is" (2002, p. 443), he is saved from dying alone from disease by the Fotse, whose "old man" diagnoses "that he has been possessed by a European spirit" (2002, p. 475) that he can draw out by applying brands all over his body (2002, p. 477), "leaving only a nightmare, a monstrous disorder" (2002, p. 477).

Kunzru's text offers a plea against hypertrophic adaptability: the British resident on an elephant's back hunting tigers is as ridiculous as the Nawab's brother with his decadent British entourage in the palace of Fatehpur. Therefore, both Indian and British upper classes function as decisive players in the colonial game, in a situation which is mutually beneficial to them. The British Empire cannot be maintained without Indian upper-class collaboration, and the Indian aristocracy gains financial and political power over their subjects through the support of the British. The foundation of this colonial system of power consists of fixed identities and a well-defined place in society for each participant. Thus, the protagonist with his changing roles and solidarities signifies a challenge and even a threat for both sides. Hybridity was discussed in British as well as in Indian society (Young 2008, p. 6–15), and from 1880 on, when the position of the British Empire in India became more and more precarious, there was a real paranoia concerning miscegenation (*métissage*) in the public debate (cf. McClintock 1995, p. 46f.). Until the late 18th century, cultural not racial difference dominated the discourse of differentiation between Europeans and Non-Europeans (cf. Gregg 2005, p. 5, p. 16), there grew an increasing obsession with fixed identities as the Empire seemed to stumble into instability (Young 2008, p. 4, p. 95). Pran Nath as a trespasser of boundaries in every sense of the word undermines the essentialist ideas of colonial discourse and reveals the fragility and the hypocrisy of the colonial project, on both sides. No protagonist archetype could better serve this purpose than the classical picaresque hero.

Genre

Aguirre et al. characterize the trickster in Native American myth as a liminal figure (2000, p. 69), defining marginality as a "closed binary system the two constituents of which (center, margin) deny, oppose or, at most, interact with each other" whereas liminality is described as "an open, plural system the constituents of which include a known area A and, at least, a poorly understood area B, plus a recognition of a threshold separating but also relating A and B, the threshold itself having a variable breadth" including "texts, genres or representations centered around the notion of the threshold, or whose fundamental theme is the idea of a crossover, a transgression or an entry into the Other" (2000, p. 8f.). Kunzru's protagonist is a perfect trickster with a high awareness of his own liminal state, a picaresque figure (*pícaro*) from his childhood on, with different masters, vertical and horizontal movements through society and space without really belonging anywhere (cf. Kunzru 2002, p. 242, p. 344), a suspicious origin, double-bind-dilemma, several metamorphoses etc. (cf. Guillén 1969; esp. Bauer 1994, p. 10–13). A plethora of scenes in the novel allude to classical picaresque texts: the first advisor is a blind beggar as in *Lazarillo de Tormes* (one of the seminal works of picaresque fiction), and the burlesque chaos during the tiger hunt reminds us of the grotesque narrative in Quevedo's *Buscón* (cf. Spitzer 1927/1969). There is an awakening of the *pícaro*, when "Pretty Bobby knows what he wants to be" (Kunzru 2002, p. 254). The protagonist, "a ghost, haunting thresholds, pools of electric light [...] at the limit of perception" (2002, p. 237), could be themed as invisible as in Ralph Ellison's *Invisible Man,* while his usurping of Jonathan Bridgeman's identity evokes Thomas Mann's famous hero Felix Krull from *Confessions of Felix Krull.* All his activities are driven by a deep-rooted self-interest, which in critical situations always leads him to opportunistic behavior. Although he pays with radical loneliness for his dishonesty and cowardice (cf. Kunzru 2002, p. 329f., p. 385), he is unable to overcome his egotism. Furthermore, like most of the *pícaros*, he has a talent for mimicry, adapting himself to nearly every societal environment he comes across: "he is such a chameleon," as Elspeth Macfarlane notes (2002, p. 205). His quick and agile intelligence helps him in this, making him a "too avid," almost "aggressive" pupil of Reverend Macfarlane (2002, p. 238). He is able to seize opportunities whenever they appear, especially when pertaining to his ultimate goal of remaining financially independent. He commits a series of crimes such as blackmailing a homosexual person (2002, p. 241) or spying for the ostensible spiritual medium Mrs. Pereira (2002, p. 241f.); here, however, he acts without financial urgency, driven by an inner compulsion to delinquency similar to that of Moll Flanders, Daniel Defoe's best thief of London.

In short, the text is part of an intertextual picaresque network. It criticizes and satirizes the society around the protagonist, sketching realistic scenarios of English and Indian spaces at the height of British imperialism. By introducing a mixed-blood hero, however, the text not only reinterprets the traditional suspicious origin of characters such as Lazarillo or Buscón, but also integrates itself in a recent innovative wave of picaresque literature which increasingly involves migrant or multicultural protagonists in order to illustrate liminal societal circumstances.[2] Thus, the text not only performs the typical societal transgressions of any *pícaro*, but also demonstrates ethnic hybridity and liminality, satirizing postcolonial fetishism of any hybrid as positive by creating an untrustworthy trickster. This trickster cannot be considered as a mere victim of unjust and discriminating social circumstances but is often enough also the perpetrator of crime and injustice, making use of his in-between status for his own purposes.

---

2   Cf. Xavier Velasco, *Diablo Guardián* (2003); Jan Faktor, *Georgs Sorgen um die Vergangenheit oder Im Reich des Heiligen Hodensack-Bimbams von Prag* (2010); Michael Köhlmeier, *Die Abenteuer des Joel* Spazierer; or Junot Díaz, *The Brief Wondrous Life of Oscar Wao* (2007). For criticism cf. Bruno Blanchman, "Existenzielle und ästhetische Dezentrierung. Wandlungen des pikaresken Paradigmas im französischen Gegenwartsroman"; Christoph Ehland, Robert Fajen (eds.), *Das Paradigma des Pikaresken. The Paradigm of the Picaresque.* Heidelberg: Winter, 2007. 289–300.

Conclusion: The Impressionist as New World Literature

With its emphasis on explicit and implicit multilingualism throughout the text and its negotiation of matters of globalization, Kunzru's novel allows for classifying it as New World Literature, or *New Weltliteratur* (cf. Sturm-Trigonakis 2013), for it tells a story located in a former phase of globalization from the perspective and through the narrative means of our current one. In contrast to postcolonial "sanctioned binarism" (McClintock 1995, p. 15) and "Fanon's Manicheism" (1995, p. 361), the text demonstrates many forms of colonialism and criticizes the universality of colonialist patterns of behavior. However, it also questions concepts of postcolonialism (cf. McClintock 1995, p. 13; Simanowski 1998, p. 36ff.), as the protagonist's ultimate decision of whether or not to remain in Africa does not signify the creation of a cozy third space. Instead, taking refuge in the endless expanse of the desert is tantamount to roving through an atopia, a space as nameless as the hero who has liberated himself from all essentialist identity characteristics or inscription in any recognizable time or space. In this way, both globalization phases illuminate each other, giving our globalized contemporaneity a historical context and relativizing 'typical' categorizations of our time regarding power hierarchies, gender, colonialism, and ethnicity. The text could be read as a plea against assimilation to 'essentialist' national identity markers, since Englishness is contested as well as Indianness or Kashmiriness, thus revealing the constructedness of these 'imagined communities.' The work, however, also demonstrates the concrete consequences of these imaginary boundaries in real life and emphasizes that hybridity—the magic and celebrated in-between concept of our globalization—is not necessarily the ideal answer to boundaries. Thus, it criticizes the contemporary—perhaps naïve—trust in liberal societal concepts such as hybridity, multiculturalism, diversity management, or the cultural melting pot, which might stem from the erroneous judgment of generations of historians who had supported the building of supposed national cultures and mentalities (cf. Weiler 2006, p. 346f.). Furthermore, the text shows that the mechanisms of colonialism are universal and trans-temporal: in former phases of globalization as well in our contemporary one, globalization functions as a cognitive pattern, be it under the disguise of economic, military, or cultural superiority, or be it for support of development or of political independence. In his classical history *England in the Nineteenth Century* (Thomson 1978), David Thomson argues that "despite the extravagances of much that was said and written in these years about 'the white man's burden,' British imperialism even in this, its most dynamic and aggressive phase, was never racialist. Other contemporary imperialisms were racialist" (1978, p. 210f.). Today, such a statement may be met with incredulity at the least. Kunzru's novel speaks against such one-sided judgments and makes the point clear that the transgression of boundaries of any kind has always been a dangerous endeavor and that those transgressors have had a difficult fate.

At the end of the novel, the hero-trickster with the plethora of names and identities remains excluded from any society and ethnicity, finding his peace of mind (or not) only in radical outsiderness, as a foreigner on a foreign continent, in a narrative concluding with an open ending: "For now, the journey is everything. He has no thoughts of arriving anywhere. Today he will sleep under the enormous bowl of the sky. Tomorrow he will travel on." (Kunzru 2002, p. 481).

Works Cited

Aguirre, Manuel et al. (2000): Margins and Thresholds: An Enquiry into the Concept of Liminality in Text Studies. Madrid: Gateway Press.

Almond, Ian (2002): Lessons from Kipling and Rao: How to Re-Appropriate Another Culture. Orbis Litterarum 57, p. 257–287.

Anselm, Sigrun (1995): Grenzen trennen, Grenzen verbinden. In: Faber, Richard/ Naumann, Barbara (eds.): Literatur der Grenze - Theorie der Grenze. Würzburg: Königshausen & Neumann, p. 197–210.

Bauer, Matthias (1994): Der Schelmenroman. Stuttgart: Metzler.

Benthien, Claudia/Krüger-Fürhoff, Irmela Marei (1999): Vorwort. In: Benthien, Claudia/Krüger-Fürhoff, Irmela M. (eds.): Über Grenzen: Limitation und Transgression in Literatur und Ästhetik. Stuttgart: Metzler, p. 7–16.

Cohn, Bernard S. (1996): Colonialism and its Forms of Knowledge: The British in India. Princeton: Princeton University Press.

Ette, Ottmar (2012): TransArea: Eine literarische Globalisierungsgeschichte. Berlin: De Gruyter.

Gregg, Stephen H. (2005): Introduction. In: Gregg, Stephen H. (ed.): Empire & Identity: An Eighteenth-Century Sourcebook. Basingstoke, New York: Palgrave Macmillan, p. 1–25.

Guillén, Claudio (1969): Zur Frage der Begriffsbestimmung des Pikaresken. In: Heidenreich, Helmut (ed.): Pikarische Welt: Schriften zum Europäischen Schelmenroman. Darmstadt: Wissenschaftliche Buchgesellschaft, p. 375–396.

Görner, Rüdiger (2001): Grenzen, Schwellen, Übergänge: Zur Poetik des Transitorischen. Göttingen: Vandenhoeck & Ruprecht.

Hohnsträter, Dirk (1999): Im Zwischenraum. Ein Lob des Grenzgängers. In: Benthien, Claudia/Krüger-Fürhoff, Irmela M. (eds.): Über Grenzen: Limitation und Transgression in Literatur und Ästhetik. Stuttgart: Metzler, p. 232–244.

Jenks, Chris (2003): Transgression. London: Routledge.

Koselleck, Reinhart (2003): Zeitschichten: Studien zur Historik (1st ed.). Frankfurt am Main: Suhrkamp.

Kunzru, Hari (2002): The Impressionist. London: Hamish Hamilton.

Lexico Dictionaries Powered by Oxford (2020): Gora, www.lexico.com/definition/ gora, 30/12/2020.

McClintock, Anne (1995): Imperial Leather: Race, Gender and Sexuality in the Colonial Contest. New York: Routledge.

Simanowski, Roberto (1998): Einleitung: Zum Problem kultureller Grenzziehung. In: Turk, Horst/Schultze, Brigitte/Simanowski, Roberto (eds.): Kulturelle Grenzziehungen im Spiegel der Literaturen. Nationalismus, Regionalismus, Fundamentalismus. Göttingen: Wallstein, p. 8–62.

Spitzer, Leo (1969): Zur Kunst Quevedos in seinem "Buscón". In: Heidenreich, Helmut (ed.): Pikarische Welt: Schriften zum Europäischen Schelmenroman. Darmstadt: Wissenschaftliche Buchgesellschaft, p. 40–60 (Original work published 1927).

Sturm-Trigonakis, Elke (2013): Comparative Cultural Studies and the New Weltliteratur. West Lafayette: Purdue University Press.

Sturm-Trigonakis, Elke (2014): Contemporary German-Based Hybrid Texts as a New World Literature. In: Beebee, Thomas O. (ed.): German Literature as World Literature. New York: Bloomsbury, p. 177–195.

Thomson, David (1978): England in the Nineteenth Century. London: Penguin Books (Original work published 1950).

Weiler, Bernd (2006): Das Unbehagen in der Multikultur oder Über die Bedeutung von Grenzen im Zeitalter der 'Neuen Völkerwanderung'. In: Burtscher-Bechter, Beate/Haider, Peter W./Mertz-Baumgartner, Birgit/Rollinger, Robert (eds.): Grenzen und Entgrenzungen: Historische und kulturwissenschaftliche Überlegungen am Beispiel des Mittelmeerraums. Würzburg: Königshausen & Neumann, p. 333–350.

Young, Robert (1995): Colonial Desire: Hybridity in Theory, Culture and Race. London, New York: Routledge.

Young, Robert J. C. (2008): The Idea of English Ethnicity. Oxford: Blackwell Publishing.

"Border-Perforating Catastrophes": The Failure of Border Security in *The City & The City* and *The Bridge*

Nadine M. Knight[1]

Both China Miéville's novel *The City & The City* (2009), and the American television show *The Bridge* (Reid/Stein/Stiehm 2013-2014) begin with crimes that explicitly call attention to a nationalized border: a dead body torn in half precisely on the border between the United States and Mexico in *The Bridge;* a dead body that has illegally 'breached' the divide between two cities in a fantastical region suggestive of Eastern Europe in *The City & The City*. Both works engage and subvert detective plots, most notably in each plot's emphasis on jurisdictional wrangling and the need for visual evidence in solving their crimes. I argue that *The City & The City* and *The Bridge* use detective plots to show how nationalized borders invite crime, and that militarized intervention is easily subject to "border-perforating catastrophes," (Miéville 2010, p. 66). The cities of our present and our future, these works suggest, are cities that must relinquish the sanctity and security of their borders.

Gloria Anzaldúa, in her landmark work *Borderlands/La Frontera,* writes of the border as a place that is inherently criminalized: "Borders are set up to define the places that are safe and unsafe, to distinguish *us* from *them* […] A borderland is a vague and undetermined place created by the emotional residue of an unnatural boundary. It is in a constant state of transition," (2012, p. 25, emphasis original). In an article about border security in the emerging twenty-first century, Peter Andreas notes that "[g]lobalization […] has also created more border policing work for the state" (2003, p. 84). The result emphasizes visual displays of power to represent national security: "Border control agencies grow and expand partly because of the symbolic power they gain from their role as border maintainers […] Thus, the policing face of the state is becoming more prominently displayed" (2003, p. 111). Similarly, in *Walled States,* Wendy

---

[1]   I would like to acknowledge the invaluable comments of the anonymous readers, as well as feedback from the audience at the 2014 MESEA conference, Caroline Kita, and Catherine Keyser as I worked on this project.

Brown argues that the emphasis on physical barricades invoke "the visual scenography of a state of emergency" that is often politically expedient (2010, p. 77). When nations generate a militarized spectacle of border security, they create a psychological boundary between citizens and noncitizens that also relies upon a fantasy of heightened and obvious visibility. Once physical borders are raised, we believe that we can determine belongingness according to racial or ethnic attribute that render one—visibly and unerringly—either a citizen or a foreigner.[2]

Both *The City & The City* and *The Bridge*, in their very titles, suggest a tension of separation that yearns to be erased, either through the physical structure of a bridge or through the balanced redundancy of the two cities. Both texts are set in locations where the border came to the inhabitants. The fictional linked cities of Besźel and Ul Qoma emerged from an inexplicable and hazily detailed event known as Cleavage, while the 1848 Treaty of Guadalupe Hidalgo dispossessed and relocated Mexicans who had not moved, but around whom a new national border was erected.[3] The detectives at the center of each text are challenged to interrogate their unconscious manifestations of what Walter Mignolo calls "border thinking," including the effects upon "those who did not move, but around whom the world moved" (2000, p. 72). If visual demarcation is at the heart of border security and verifiable citizenship, then both citizens and agents of the law must train their visual acuity.[4] Both works demonstrate the exhausting mental gymnastics required of citizens in a border zone, brought into sharp relief by the detective plots that govern each text.

As Ronald R. Thomas reminds us, "at the center of virtually every detective story is a body upon which the literary detective focuses his gaze and employs his unique interpretive powers" (1999, p. 2). Detectives must

---

2   This tension is exemplified by Arizona Senate Bill 1070 (the "Support Our Law Enforcement and Safe Neighborhoods Act"), which passed in 2010 and was immediately subject to protest at the state and national level. Protesters contended that its policies would encourage racial profiling and the equation of nonwhites with noncitizens. Cf. Cohen/Mears 2012; Archibold 2010; Cisneros 2012.

3   José David Saldívar, for example, reminds us just how young this border is, and that it essentially changed people's status "overnight" (1997, p. 18). Kasey Butcher highlights the complex cultural ties in noting that "eight in ten El Pasoans are of Mexican descent while seven of ten speak Spanish and many others are bilingual or Spanglish speakers" (2015, p. 404).

4   Cf. Rzepka (2005, p. 3, p. 41) on the mapping of crimes on national/racial stereotypes.

be carefully attuned to see and sense any small detail that may help solve the crime, and good detective work reveals how easily crime and evidence can erase national boundaries. The border, particularly in Miéville's novel, actively thwarts the detective's vision: the inhabitants have all been trained to "unsee" (Miéville 2010, p. 65) the Other in order to maintain a "frantic liminality" (2010, p. 61) between neighboring nations. As the two works model the political and epistemological importance of border maintenance, they also become increasingly burdened by the border. National and sensory sovereignty are impossible to uphold in each work, and the detectives become disillusioned, corrupted, and destroyed. Taken together, both works ask us to demand a new transnationalism that will advance social justice and restore our freedom of vision.

Of "topolgangers" and thought crimes: The City & The City

The City & The City is, as Kirsten Tranter describes, a "noir police procedural set in a world close to our own, where reality is tweaked" (2012, p. 418). City borders are of the utmost importance in the novel's exploration of fantastical feats of what Miéville's narrator, Inspector Tyador Borlú, calls "urban semiosis" (2010, p. 279). In this novel, two cities, named Beszel and Ul Qoma, are entirely separate nations—but they occupy the same physical space. Nevertheless, the cities maintain two separate architectures, ethic identities and languages, governments, police, and emergency services. These cities are not neighboring; they are imbricated. This is particularly true in border-overlapping 'crosshatched' areas, such as public parks, that force citizens to remain ever-vigilant lest they wander into a foreign patch of grass merely by noticing it.

Niall Martin discusses real world counterparts to Miéville's cities ("Belfast, Berlin, Jerusalem, Johannesburg") as constitutive of "urban modernity" (2013, p. 713), which necessitates a protective dulling of the senses: "whether in formalized zoning policies or the unwritten rules governing eye contact in certain locations [...] filtering and not-seeing and avoiding are essential skills in navigating any urban environment" (2013, p. 713f.).[5] It is important, then, to examine this skill in terms of unseeing

---

5   Other critics variously cite "old East and West Berlin" (Jones 2013, n.p.), "wartime Sarajevo or Cold War Berlin" (Hamilton 2009, n.p.), or, most broadly, simply "post-Soviet" (Moorcock 2009, n.p.) as parallels for this text. Michael Moorcock's review of the novel also comments on the forced urban

citizens and the surveillance state that produces them. Denise Hamilton's review of the novel emphasizes this connection: "The double-speak and disappearances are common to any modern police state. The 'unseeing' is exactly how individuals and nations block out unpleasant realities, whether it's the homeless man on the corner or the latest genocide" (2009, n.p.). Miéville's novel wrestles 'unseeing' from the realm of the figurative and makes it forcibly literal. Rather than a fortified, contiguous zone designated by longitude and latitude or along a geological formation, the border between Besźel and Ul Qoma is invasive, omnipresent, and most strikingly, constituted almost entirely through acts of selective vision.

Existence in each city is thus at once utterly scopophilic and scopophobic. The daily life of the citizens of each city is a monumental and strictly regimented task of only acknowledging one's own city: you may see the newspaper stand of your own city, for instance, but not the "foreign" café right next to it. Seeing and sensing—selectively and correctly—is the law and an act of nationalism. Miéville's characters must constantly police their senses and even more disruptively, they must "dutifully" deny their senses (Miéville 2010, p. 132). They unsee, unhear, and even unsmell the other city. This conceit illustrates Wendy Brown's argument that "nation-state walling responds in part to psychic fantasies [...] by generating visual effects and a national imaginary" leading to "psychic containment" (Brown 2010, p. 109). In Miéville's novel, there is a constant paranoia and surveillance to make sure that everyone is seeing their city while unseeing, unsmelling, unhearing the other, because even reflex actions, such as the "somatic breach" of jumping at an unexpected car noise, is a punishable offense (2010, p. 52). Border hyperconsciousness forces a rigid performance of citizen-identity at the expense of physical and mental liberty.

While Besźel and Ul Qoma have an official border-crossing location, a building known as Copula Hall, most of the border is invisible. The training of one's situational national perception is thus quite rigorous: before getting their visas tourists must take a lengthy course in the "key signifiers of architecture, clothing, alphabet and manner, outlaw colours and gestures, obligatory details" of each city, including "supposed distinctions in national physiognomies" (Miéville 2010, p. 76). Even Inspector Borlú, a lifelong citizen of Besźel and one raised in this strict nationalist tradition,

---

blindness as "a metaphor for modern life in which our habits of 'unseeing' allow us to ignore that which does not directly affect our familiar lives" (2009, n.p.).

must undergo a refresher course before he can travel to Ul Qoma to assist in the murder investigation. As Borlú reports:

> They sat me in what they called an Ul Qoma simulator [...] on which they projected images and videos of Besźel with the Besź buildings highlighted and their Ul Qoman neighbours minimised with lighting and focus. Over long seconds, again and again, they would reverse the visual stress, so that for the same vista Besźel would recede and Ul Qoma shine [...] I was unseeing Besźel. [...] I was seeing Ul Qoma. (Miéville 2010, p. 133f.)

This strict governance of vision pays truth, it seems, to Foucault's claim that "visibility is a trap" (1995, p. 200). The beginning of Foucault's famous "Panopticism" chapter begins with the regulations for quarantining a town during plague. Foucault concludes that "it is a segmented, immobile, frozen space. Each individual is fixed in his place [...] Inspection functions ceaselessly. The gaze is alert everywhere" (1995, p. 195). The border between Besźel and Ul Qoma, particularly in "crosshatched" public spaces, can render citizens similarly immobile, for they must remain fixed in their place, in their own cityspace. To do otherwise is to risk punishment, detainment, and disappearance.

Miéville's invisible border presents a fascinating twist on what Ronald Thomas points out is a standard convention of the detective genre: the detective's apparent "uncanny act of second sight" which allows him to notice what all others have missed in a crime scene (1999, p. 3). Daniel Hourigan pinpoints the inevitable crisis this creates: "how does Borlú do his detective work if he must persistently undetect the world around him to varying degrees? How can this agent of the law be the enforcer that his position demands of him?" (2013, p. 158). While Hourigan moves his argument to a study of the legal complexities, we must also consider more closely Borlú's impeded vision as a critique of border security as indicative of national security. The novel's very first sentence highlights the detective's problem: "I could not see the street or much of the estate," Inspector Borlú tells us (Miéville 2010, p. 3). This is a crime scene that—as far as anyone knows at first—is indisputably in his city, in his purview, and yet Borlú's very first introduction to the crime scene is a confession of failure. This is further emphasized when he finally examines the victim, a murdered student: "She looked unseeingly at me," he says of the corpse, and then tells us that "I looked away [...] it felt prurient to watch" while the crime scene tech handled the body (2010, p. 7). In this specific instance it is Borlú's duty to watch, and he is incapable. In *The City & The City*, Borlú's 'second sight' could access the city of Ul Qoma; but it is also that which he is banned from ever seeing, thus depriving the detective of his foundational skill. Such are the dangers, the novel suggests, of creating a populace forced to turn a blind eye as part of their citizenship.

In addition to the failures of vision which obstruct the investigation in the opening scene, Miéville shows how border regulations make cases almost impossible to solve. In an intricate twist, the victim was killed in Ul Qoma but her body dumped in Besźel, creating a jurisdictional tangle that neither Borlú nor his Ul Qoman counterpart, Senior Detective Dhatt, knows how to legally resolve. Borlú wishes that Breach would take over the case: Breach, whose representatives are known as 'avatars,' is the mysterious and terrifying organization that investigates and resolves any illegal breaching of the border, usually by disappearing the transgressors. Breach metes out border justice in this world. However, the killer has very carefully not broken the border laws. That is to say, he went through the Copula border crossing with his victim, so his crime is not one of breach. This effectively handcuffs Borlú and Dhatt, emblematic of what Brown contends is the "functional inefficacy" of modern border security (2010, p. 35).

To protect the original killer, an assassin kills Borlú's main witness. Bringing the assassin to justice, however, flirts with the farcical, a noirish chase scene rendered almost slapstick because of the arcane rules of seeing and unseeing that govern these border cities. Borlú chases the assassin—but neither he nor his target are allowed to "see" each other:

> I kept my eyes not on him but looking at some spot or other in Ul Qoma that put him in my field of vision. I tracked him without focusing, just legally […] This was not, could not be, a chase. It was only two accelerations. We ran, he in his city, me close behind him, full of rage, in mine. (Miéville 2010, p. 236f.)

So here a detective is prevented from full and direct pursuit, forced to pretend that he just happens to be traveling with synchronized speed and direction as the perpetrator. As Niall Martin points out, "he is charged, literally, with policing what may and may not be seen. As both an inspector and a policeman, Borlú becomes increasingly aware of a rupture present within the law that he himself embodies" (2013, p. 714). The border is now an accessory to crime, rather than a protective barrier.

We see a similar paralysis of law enforcement at the end of the novel, when the first killer, a rogue scholar named Bowden, attempts his escape. In order to do so, Bowden refuses to respect the laws of visibility and performativity that uphold the border between the two cities. This illustrates what Kent Ono describes as the "figural border" (2012, p. 28) represented in the migrant body: "The body itself is a reliable text, is discursive…revealing aspects of identity that can be regulated as on this or that side of a given border" (2012, p. 30). But Bowden shows what happens when a body refuses to be discursive, refuses to make citizenship visible; he proves that the border is unmistakably delusional and unsustainable. Bowden "walked with equipoise, possibly in either city. Schrodinger's pedestrian," Borlú tells us (Miéville 2010, p. 295). In a passage drawn out to ludicrous extremes, Borlú calls Dhatt (his counterpart in Ul Qoma) and Corwi (his partner in Besźel) and asks them to stroll their cities and carefully not-watch the murderer until he gives some indication of where he is so they can legally see him and arrest him; but "Bowden had not yet transgressed for their attention: they could not touch him" as long as he "did not drift but strode with pathological neutrality away from the cities' centres" (2010, p. 296). Bowden navigates the cities as an "expert" who can "mediate those million unnoticed mannerisms that marked out civic specificity" (2010, p. 297). Here we see how easily one can game this system of mental border patrolling, by refusing to play along with expected mannerisms, appearance, or even direction of gaze. How can we know, the novel asks, where someone truly belongs or what their citizenship is? Despite the performative theater of border patrols, we cannot actually read belonging on a body; we have to hope that strangers make us comfortable and openly declare their citizenship. Rather than swift justice we have theater, and a police officer's own laws render him ineffectual. This is the ultimate failure of national security.

Tellingly, Borlú can only bring both Bowden and the assassin to justice by breaking the law. While situated in Ul Qoma, Borlú commits breach by shooting the assassin who is in Besźel. Of all the violent acts accumulating in the text, this is the only one which results in immediate punishment. Under Breach jurisdiction, Borlú is rendered unconscious, incarcerated and berated: "[the assassin] never breached. […] He never breached. You did" (2010, p. 244). Borlú realizes, with no small amount of fear, that "[t]hey could disappear me without difficulty" (2010, p. 244). The final irony of Borlú's situation is that being taken by Breach is what gives him the official capacity to disregard Bowden's careful refusal of nationality. Borlú can only effectively police crime when he is stripped of his national identity and his original sworn duties to Besźel's Extreme Crime Squad. And yet, Bowden is still only brought to justice through a falsehood: Bowden technically never breached, but the Breach avatars declare that "if we say he breached, he breached" (2010, p. 309). Even Breach, the authority of last resort in this novel, must forgo any adherence to strict law and consistency. Pragmatism and falsehood corrupt proper procedure.

Borlú's apprehension of both murderers carries devastating collateral damage. Being put into Breach not only removes Borlú from his previous affiliation with the Crime Squad, but, most wrenchingly, it results in a complete self-abnegation. He can't go home again: "if you breach, even if it's not your fault, for more than the shortest time… you can't come back from that [...] You'll never unsee again" (Miéville 2010, p. 310). Borlú has been "press-gang[ed]" into the ranks of Breach, as has every avatar before him (2010, p. 311). Borlú is not allowed to say his farewells to his lovers or his partners from either city: he hovers near them but they, per the rules of the border, cannot acknowledge him. He does not even retain his name and rank: "Inspector Tyador Borlú is gone," he reports in the novel's last paragraph. "I sign off Tye, avatar of the Breach," (2010, p. 312). The sense of utter loss is visible even in the new truncation of his name, as Matt Denault points out (2010).[6]

Miéville's novel literalizes the dehumanization of border security and its attendant surveillance state. Protecting the border becomes a theatrical gesture at best, a devastating dissolution of self at worst. In Miéville's work the detective hero is criminalized and, effectively, permanently incarcerated by Breach. The space he now occupies is liminal and corrupt, created solely to oppress the citizenry: Breach admits that the border is an empty and meaningless object, but, the avatar tells him, "That's why unseeing and unsensing are so vital. No one can admit it doesn't work. So if you don't admit it, it does" (Miéville 2010, p. 310). As part of Breach, Borlú is now sworn to enforce an unhealthy system, one that actively works to ensnare its citizenry in unnatural mental and physical boundaries.

"White arms, brown legs": Racialized divisions of The Bridge

The difficulties of 'crosshatched' urban spaces and the jurisdictional uncertainty of correctly crossing and (un)seeing in *The City & The City* make the border-crossing apparatus in *The Bridge* seem startlingly straightforward. The border here is in plain sight, and the difficulties explored in this show are less about the intricacies of how the border has been constructed and how the citizens have been trained, but rather on exposing the racial, linguistic, and classist borders that span and strain El Paso, TX and Ciudad Juárez, Mexico to the point of exhaustion. As in *The City & The City*, here, too, the border exacerbates crime. In addition to the wildly escalating

---

6   Denault observes that "Borlú has been reduced; he has lost his name, his personhood, become subsumed as an enforcer of the system" (2010, n.p.).

works of a serial killer that tie up detectives from both countries in repetitive jurisdictional wrangling, the border is easily and repeatedly perforated by narcotrafficking, sex slavery, femicide, and gun running.

With its debut in 2013, *The Bridge* tapped into American anxieties that escalated with the 2016 election of Donald Trump. Undocumented immigrants, the 'coyotes' who transport them, an American refusal to speak Spanish, and the DREAM Act are all referenced in the pilot episode.[7] Television reviewers repeatedly mention the timeliness of the setting; these concerns, the show suggests, are exclusively the problem of the US-Mexico border and color-line. Emily Nussbaum, in her *New Yorker* review of the series, points out that the show—a remake of a Scandinavian series, *Bron/Broen*, set on the border between Sweden and Denmark—was originally supposed to be set on the Canadian border for a similar climate and geography: "Hard to imagine Detroit and Windsor, Ontario, the producers' original idea, working nearly so well," (2013, n.p.). Alessandra Stanley's *New York Times* review hits upon this as well, noting that "Ciudad Juárez and El Paso, on the other hand, are rich in cultural divides and social discord [...] El Paso is, if nothing else, a crucible for the current debate over immigration reform," (2013, n.p.). In the American public consciousness, the northern border is not nearly so fraught as the southern one, nor, most significantly, so easily racialized.

José David Saldívar begins his work, *Border Matters,* by noting the "intensive militarization of the U.S.-Mexican border" since the 1980s and the growth of the war on drugs (1997, *Préface* p. ix). The militarization of the border, with huge technological and manpower demands for surveillance and control, has become a fixed part of the transnational economy.[8] While

---

7   The Development, Relief, and Education for Alien Minors Act is meant to help undocumented immigrant youth work toward U.S. citizenship through higher education or military service. See the National Immigration Law Center (2011) for a summary and timeline of proposals.

8   See also Peter Andreas, who also cites post- 9/11 security fears for the "intensification of border controls" and the increase of surveillance (2003, p. 79). Kent Ono discusses how the transition from the war on drugs to the war on terror accelerated the militarization of the border (2012, p. 25). Tony Payan argues that the "war on immigration" is sandwiched between the war on drugs and the war on terror in a deepening of militarization (2006, p. xiii). Moreover, Payan points out the excess levels of surveillance that have now created a "panopticon border": "The increase in the number of Border Patrol agents, the watchful human eyes, is also quite evident. All of these are at the disposal of the state to create the panopticon border of the twenty-first century, where everyone is under surveillance at all times" (2006, p. 114).

Saldívar, Peter Andreas, and Tony Payan are concerned with contemporary militarization (and criminalization) of the border, Richard Slotkin provides a reminder that the U.S.-Mexico border has long been fraught and associated with security concerns and criminality, and that "racially alien and criminal Mexicans" replaced Native Americans as the go-to villain in the early decades of film (Slotkin 1998, p. 251). In *The Bridge*, the establishing shots of Juárez invariably focus on poverty, loss, or forced prostitution, while El Paso's establishing shots are far more likely to be of the clean and modern police department or suburbia. Birgit Spengler further observes that the show gives a "brownish hue" to the Mexican scenes, and these "visual differences are reinforced through the increasingly frequent use of mariachi music that introduces sections of the plot set in Mexico" (2016, p. 120). The visual/auditory border between Mexico and the United States is rigidly clear on screen as it is not in real life.

The Bridge (2013-2014) opens with bodily trauma. A female body has been laid across the border, and a wealthy rancher is dying of a heart attack while his ambulance is delayed by the crime scene's shutdown of the border crossing. The border zone is thus immediately situated as a place where humans fail and fall apart in a literalization of the border's long history of violence, bisection, and displacement. As in *The City & The City*, the opening scene depicts a cascade of failures. First, there is a power outage at the border crossing, with lights snapping off and video screens going to static; the border guards are, physically and technologically, blinded while the body is dumped on the midpoint of the Bridge of the Americas between El Paso and Ciudad Juárez. When American Detective Sonya Cross (Diane Kruger) arrives on the scene, she is wearing earphones; she arrives with one of her senses obstructed. She then exposes the failures of the border guards, as they cannot provide her with the make and model of the killer's car. "It's your job to know," she tells the guard with irritation. "Our job is border security and interdiction, not dead bodies," he replies, as if somehow the work of border security has never actually led to, or in fact propagated, dead bodies (Reid/Stein/Stiehm 2013e).[9]

---

9   All quotations taken from personal transcription and subtitles. As Andreas points out, "making the border more difficult to cross has also made it a more lethal border for unauthorized entrants, with hundreds of people dying every year" (2003, p. 88). Payan claims that as many as 500 people have died in the attempt every year between 1998-2004 (2006, p. 119). See also Brown on the increased difficulty of crossing (2010, p. 38) and for the estimate of "at least

The Bridge's opening scene is about sensory and surveillance failure, and the standard detective trope of jurisdictional wrangling is not about ego here, as it often is in other detective shows. Rather, it is about race, citizenship, and a scale of importance of victimization where a dead white woman and a dying white man take precedence. Mexican Detective Marco Ruiz (Demián Bichir) arrives on scene and his first question to Cross is to ask for the victim's identification. "She's American," Cross tells him with certainty. The victim's nationality, tellingly, comes before her personal identification. Cross then names the victim but repeats, "She's American. The car came from El Paso. It's ours" (Reid/Stein/Stiehm 2013e). The issue of nationality arises again when Cross and Ruiz clash over letting an ambulance pass through. Cross, ever rigid in her understanding of the law and interpersonal relations, is uncaring of the medical crisis within the ambulance. Ruiz, more sensitive and sympathetic, waves the ambulance through. Their argument is framed not by opinions of crime scene integrity, but with their interpretation of national desires and interests:

> Cross: There are hospitals in Mexico.
>
> Ruiz: They're American, they wanted an American hospital.
>
> Cross: Why does that matter?
>
> Ruiz: It does.
>
> Cross: You had no right. This is a U.S. case.

Ruiz, overwhelmed by the asymmetrical crime statistics between the two cities, is initially quite willing to let Cross take the murder case. His full involvement is initially only at his captain's behest that Ruiz shadow Cross and "keep the Americans out of our business" (Reid/Stein/Stiehm 2013b). As with the border guards in the pilot episode who pretend that murder is not part of their business, here, from the other side, the Mexican police captain also wants to deny that there is a mutual interest and responsibility for solving and preventing transnational crime.

The true nature of the crime behind the murdered woman left on the border between the two countries further highlights the entanglement of race and class with nationalist assumptions. When the crime scene techs move the woman's body, it splits in half at the waist. As the body is examined at the morgue, Cross learns that there are actually two victims here: the top and bottom halves of the woman don't match. Race and nationality

---

five thousand migrant deaths" along this border from the late 1990s to 2010 (2010, p. 91).

are inextricably linked: "White arms, brown legs," Cross observes at the ME's prompting (Reid/Stein/Stiehm 2013e). Cross reads the victims as an American body on the American side of the border, and a Mexican body on the Mexican side. The darker skin of the bottom victim's legs signal her as non-American—there is no question, in the American mind, that brownness is unequivocally Mexican—so Cross calls Ruiz to identify this second victim. As Josue Cisneros points out, such fixed divisions of a race-nationality axis have only become more codified with anti-immigration ventures in the past decade, such as Arizona's SB1070, which, he argues, works "to codify the Mexican-Latina/o-brown-illegal-immigrant body and to situate citizenship in the performative affect of these bodies" in which to be white is to be American (2012, p. 137). Birgit Spengler argues that this scene "critiques the violent and racist distinc-tion" between the nationalities and "that their separation constitutes an open and potentially devastating wound for both 'sides'" (2016, p. 111). The detective tasked with solving this crime relies solely on her vision— and her racialized assumptions—of the 'proper' sides of the border for each victim in a way that undermines solidarity among the victims.

The murderer chose the victims precisely because of their racialized representation. In a voice message left for the detectives to hear, the killer makes it seem as if his work is about racial justice: "There are five mur-ders a year in El Paso. In Juárez, thousands. Why? Why is one dead white woman more important than so many dead just across the bridge? How long can El Paso look away?" (Reid/Stein/Stiehm 2013e). For the detec-tives and the audience, these murders call attention to the hypocrisy of na-tional blindness: that we willfully avert our gazes from the mass disap-pearance and murder of the women—here specifically, the surge of femi-cide beginning in the 1990s in Juárez.[10] We 'unsee' the endangered demo-graphic on the other side of the border. As Kathleen Staudt observes, "the crimes are nearly invisible" (Staudt 2012, p. 87).[11]

---

10 Cf. Seitz (2013) for a sympathetic appreciation of this scene.
11 Staudt estimates that at least 100 women were femicide murders from 1993 in-to the following decade, while hundreds more were likely victims of domestic violence (2012, p. 83); moreover, as *The Bridge* makes clear, the local and state governments "continue to marginalize and/or deny the problems," with newspapers calling reports of the murders "exaggerations and fantasies" in edi-torials (qtd. in Staudt 2012, p. 87). Melissa W. Wright, in her study of antifem-icide protest movements in Ciudad Juárez, empathizes the importance of visi-bility in quoting one activist who said, "[Officials] did not want to see the poli-tics behind the violence. That's what we made them see" (2011, p. 712),

As with Inspector Borlú of *The City & The City*, Detective Cross cannot see everything she needs to in order to complete her job. Cross has difficulty maintaining eye contact with people, must be reminded to feign empathy when talking to victims, and thinks that it is a "waste of time" for a wife to call her husband "just to hear his voice" (Reid/Stein/Stiehm 2013b). In short, she cannot accurately 'see' how to properly interact with subjects. On the other hand, Cross's poor interpersonal acuity make her better at the impersonal scrutiny needed for laborious detective work. She has many of the traits of what Sheng-mei Ma calls the "Aspergirl detective": "the Aspergirl, by definition, lacks empathic capacity, and yet she is the affectless affective girl-woman, human-computer [...] who intuitively solves the crimes" (2014, p. 53f.).[12] Likewise, Cross's character finds collecting evidence and interpreting imagery much easier than social niceties. Cross's dogged attention allows her to exhaustively watch hours of video evidence in order to rescue a woman trapped by the mystery killer in the desert to die, effecting a nick-of-time rescue (Reid/Stein/Stiehm 2013d). However, while Cross's actions save this life, they bring her no closer to solving the mystery killer's identity, and the killer subsequently successfully murders an eyewitness while she is under Cross's protection. Criminal behavior outpaces Cross's visual and detective powers.

Much like *The City & The City* turned to near-farce to delegitimize its national borders, here, too, the show delegitimizes its proclaimed border politics through the farce of wildly improbable plot twists. The killer is eventually revealed as David Tate (Eric Lange), a former F.B.I. agent who faked his own death and took a new identity. Tate is not making a political statement. Rather, Tate blames Ruiz, his wife's lover in Juárez, for the death of his wife and child in a car accident on the Bridge of the Americas. With this revelation, any outrage or edification sought about the actual plight of the women of Juárez becomes marginalized in favor of escalating sensationalism. Tate sleeps with Ruiz's wife, kidnaps her, kills Ruiz's son in an elaborate drowning, and straps on a bomb vest for a one-on-one showdown with Ruiz where he threatens to blow up the border bridge unless Ruiz executes a hostage. As Jen Chaney states in her *Vulture* recap, "it's clear that Tate is serving no purpose other than satisfying his own self-involved need for revenge" (2013, n.p.); for Spengler, "the borderland corpses appear as pawns" for individualized conflict (2016, p. 125). The

---

12   Cf. McCabe (2015) for more on this neurodiverse trend in detectives in Scandinavian shows and their global remakes.

first season climaxes in a personal vendetta, not border justice. The border is of merely incidental significance at best.

By turning to this bombastic, excessively personal finale, the first season of *The Bridge* refuses to substantively or profoundly engage the real and increasingly urgent issues of transnational inequality and immigration.[13] Indeed, by the season finale the bridge between the two nations is merely atmospheric; Tate would be no less insane if his wife had been driving across the Brooklyn Bridge. Simultaneously fetishized and ignored, the U.S.-Mexico border becomes an increasingly belabored point of reference and an easy scapegoat. Where *The City & The City*'s murders exposed the lies propping up the border, in *The Bridge* the killer's fake message—that no one cares about dead Mexican women on either side of the border—becomes the depressing truth.

Conclusion

As with Borlú, Ruiz brings the killer to justice, but only at great personal expense. Ruiz is diminished, now a lonely, drunk shell of the affable, capable detective we met in the pilot. In the final scene of Season One, Ruiz enters a deal with cartel boss Fausto Galvan (Ramón Franco) to pursue extralegal vengeance against Tate. Much as Borlú becomes Tye, extralegal avatar of justice, we are left with the sense that Ruiz, too, has moved beyond the law. Moreover, Tate and Breach demonstrate that the contemporary surveillance state engendered by border security not only escalates abuses of power but in fact produces well-trained and efficient abusers: both Tate and Breach misuse their state-supplied resources to serve personal interests.

The condemnation of border policies is quite clear in each work; the redemptive solutions less so. *The Bridge* is the more pessimistic of the two works. The end of the first season demonstrates that any perceived progress in solving the problems of the criminalized border is, in fact, circular. After Tate has been captured, Ruiz's captain tells him, meaningfully, "Too bad Tate is in American custody [...] Over here, we'd make him pay," (Reid/Stein/Stiehm 2013a). And Cross tells her lieutenant: "I want

---

13   The second season continues this trajectory, focusing on a fairly conventional exploration of personal vengeance, police corruption, money laundering, and cartel violence.

to work the dead girls of Juárez […] What if an American is involved in this? It's our responsibility to do something." He replies: "Responsibility, maybe. Jurisdiction, no" (Reid/Stein/Stiehm 2013f). We are back where we started, with rigid notions of national jurisdiction and national distrust, unwillingness to transcend these borders, and no one empowered to take any definitive action in protecting endangered women.

The City & The City, in contrast, gestures toward potential disruption to the system and the message that change must come from outsiders who infiltrate (or breach) and subvert the dominant paradigm. In the final paragraph, Borlú/Tye claims that he is "sign[ing] off" (Miéville 2010, p. 312). This implies that he is sending the novel as a broadcast: his testimonial of exactly how Breach works and just how desperate and weak it has become. With this disclosure—which is to say, with the breaking of invisibility—Breach will collapse. We have now seen the joints of the Panopticon, as it were, and that is the first step to learning how to dismantle it. Borlú/Tye's final declaration, "I live in both the city and the city," is a significant step toward dismantling the border (2010, p. 312). Matt Denault reads optimism in these lines, concluding that "Borlú's transformation into an avatar is also a movement of becoming" (2010). It is, perhaps, even a move to the post-citizen: a new demonstration that citizenship is merely a temporary and changeable declaration rather than a fixed, singular, and nationally enforced categorization.

The Bridge and *The City & The City* ask us to reconsider the permanence and effectiveness of enforcing a national border, and if doing so merely condemns citizens to a permanent state of surveillance and warfare. Josue Cisneros highlights the collision of "border vigilantism and racial profiling with performances of citizenship, creating an affective economy in which to perform love for one's country is to fear/police/hate the other" (2012, p. 147). This is a recipe for war and other humanitarian disasters. We hear this echoed in *The Bridge*'s Episode Seven, "Destino" (Reid/Stein/Stiehm 2013c), when the suspect Jack Childress says to Cross, "El Paso del Norte has been falsely split […] There is a war happening here, at the border." The impression of a state of war on the U.S.-Mexico border certainly resonates today. Donald Trump announced his candidacy for presidency in 2015 by declaring that Mexico was "bringing their worst people" to the U.S. and vowing that he would build a "great, great wall on our southern border and […] make Mexico pay for that wall" (Neate 2015, n.p.). Trump's xenophobic platform (which included an attempted ban on immigrants from several majority-Muslim countries) has been a lightning rod for protest even as it energizes his base: an ACLU petition to "Say No

To Trump's Border Wall" had almost 60,000 signatures as of June 2019 (ACLU 2016), while a GoFundMe in support of the wall (since Mexico is not, in fact, paying for the wall) exceeded $20 million in donations at the end of 2018 (Brice-Saddler 2019, n.p.). It is clear that the wall, for the Trump administration, was a rhetorical necessity rather than a true security need: journalists Julie Hirschfeld Davis and Peter Baker contend that, "[h]aving spent more than four years [...] whipping his core supporters into a frenzy over the idea of building a border wall, Mr. Trump finds himself in a political box of his own making" (2019, n.p.).

National borders and the policing thereof continue to be contested and militarized, often with tragic consequences.[14] Slotkin, in *Gunfighter Nation,* writes that "'Mexico' is the mirror in which we appear to ourselves in a glass, darkly" (1998, p. 427). The metaphor of the mirror forces us to acknowledge our visual and psychological conditioning with regard to the border and the Other. In the U.S., vision has now become so intricately tied to notions of national security that the phrase "If You See Something, Say Something®" is registered trademark of the Department of Homeland Security, which has an entire webpage about how American citizens need to train our vision to protect the country (Department of Homeland Security 2014). What a frightening thought: that our vision is now a duty of citizenship but also, as *The City & The City* and *The Bridge* remind us, simultaneously so restricted and catastrophically flawed. True safety, both works make clear to us, will be managed only when we turn our vision away from a strict definition of the border and instead focus our efforts on denationalized cooperation and protecting the vulnerable.

N.B.: This essay was completed before the election of President Biden, who promised reforms in border policy during his campaign. As of August 2021, construction of the border wall has been paused.

---

14   According to a report for *NBC News*, as of June 9, 2019, 24 detainees have died in ICE (Immigration and Customs Enforcement) custody since Trump has taken office—a number which "does not include migrants, including five children, who have died in the custody of other federal agencies" (Rappleye/Seville 2019, n.p).

Works Cited

ACLU (2016): Say NO to Trump's Border Wall, action.aclu.org/petition/say-no-trumps-border-wall, 1/2/2021.

Andreas, Peter (2003): Redrawing the Line: Borders and Security in the Twenty-First Century. In: International Security 28, no. 2, p. 78–111, www.jstor.org/stable/4137469, 2/1/2021.

Anzaldúa, Gloria (2012): Borderlands/La frontera: The New Mestiza (4th ed.). San Francisco: Aunt Lute Books.

Archibold, Randal C. (2010): Arizona Enacts Stringent Law on Immigration. In: The New York Times of 23/04/2010, www.nytimes.com/2010/04/24/us/politics/24immig.html, 2/1/2021.

Brice-Saddler, Michael (2019): A group raised over $20 million to 'build the wall.' Now its supporters want answers. In: The Washington Post of 11/05/2019, www.washingtonpost.com/nation/2019/05/11/group-raised-more-than-million-build-wall-now-some-supporters-want-answers/, 2/1/2021.

Brown, Wendy (2010): Walled States, Waning Sovereignty. New York, Cambridge, Mass.: Zone Books.

Butcher, Kasey (2015): Constructing girlhood, narrating violence: Desert Blood, If I Die in Juárez, and "Women of Juárez". In: Latino Studies 13, no. 3, p. 402–420, DOI:10.1057/lst.2015.33.

Chaney, Jen (2013). The Bridge Recap: This Is Not a Game. In: Vulture of 12/09/2013, www.vulture.com/2013/09/bridge-recap-season-1-old-friends.html, 2/1/2021.

Cisneros, Josue David (2012): Looking 'Illegal': Affect, Rhetoric, and Performativity in Arizona's Senate Bill 1070. In: DeChaine, D. R. (ed.): Border Rhetorics: Citizenship and Identity on the US-Mexico Border. Tuscaloosa: University of Alabama Press, p. 133–150.

Cohen, Tom/Mears, Bill (2012): Supreme Court mostly rejects Arizona immigration law; gov says 'heart' remains. In: CNN Politics of 25/06/2012, edition.cnn.com/2012/06/25/politics/scotus-arizona-law/index.html, 2/1/2021.

Denault, Matt (2010): Review: The City & The City, by China Miéville, linguafantastika.com/2010/07/china-mieville-the-city-the-city/, 30/7/2014.

Department of Homeland Security (2014): If You See Something, Say Something®, www.dhs.gov/see-something-say-something, 2/1/2021.

Foucault, Michel (1995): Discipline and Punish: The Birth of the Prison. New York, NY: Vintage Books.

Hamilton, Denise (2009): The City & City, by China Miéville. In: The Los Angeles Times of 25/05/2009, www.latimes.com/books/la-et-book25-2009may25-story.html, 2/1/2021.

Hirschfeld Davis, Julie/Baker, Peter (2019): How the Border Wall Is Boxing Trump. In: The New York Times of 05/01/2019, www.nytimes.com/2019/01/05/us/politics/donald-trump-border-wall.html, 1/2/2021.

Hourigan, Daniel (2013): Breach! The Law's Jouissance in Miéville's The City & The City. In: Law, Culture & the Humanities 9, no. 1, p. 156–168, DOI:10.1177/1743872111404849, 2/1/2021.

Jones, Chris (2013): Dystopian tale of divided cities at Lifeline. In: Chicago Tribune of 26/02/2013, www.chicagotribune.com/ct-ent-0227-city-review-20130226-column.html, 2/1/2021.

Ma, Sheng-mei (2014): My Aspergirl: Stieg Larsson's Millennium Trilogy and Visualizations. In: The Journal of American Culture 37, no. 1, p. 52–63, DOI:10.1111/jacc.12106, 2/1/2021.

Martin, Niall (2013): Unacknowledged cities: Modernity and acknowledgement in China Miéville's The City & The City and Marc Isaacs' All White in Barking. In: European Journal of Cultural Studies 16, no. 6, p. 710–724, DOI:10.1177/1367549413497692, 2/1/2021.

McCabe, Janet (2015): Disconnected Heroines, Icy Intelligence: Reframing Feminism(s) and Feminist Identities at the Borders Involving the Isolated Female TV Detective in Scandinavian-Noir. In: Mulvey, Laura/Rogers, Anna B. (eds.): Feminisms: Diversity, Difference and Multiplicity in Contemporary Film Cultures. Amsterdam: Amsterdam University Press, p. 29–43, www.jstor.org/stable/j.ctt16d6996.7, 2/1/2021.

Miéville, China (2010): The City & The City. New York: Del Rey.

Mignolo, Walter (2000): Local Histories/Global Designs: Coloniality, Subaltern Knowledges, and Border Thinking. Princeton, N.J.: Princeton University Press.

Moorcock, Michael (2009): Review: The City and the City by China Miéville. In: The Guardian of 30/05/2009, www.theguardian.com/books/2009/may/30/china-mieville-fiction, 2/1/2021.

National Immigration Law Center (2011): DREAM Act: Summary - National Immigration Law Center, www.nilc.org/issues/immigration-reform-and-executive%20actions/dreamact/dreamsummary/, 2/1/2021.

Neate, Rupert (2015): Donald Trump announces US presidential run with eccentric speech. In: The Guardian of 16/06/2015, www.theguardian.com/us-news/2015/jun/16/donald-trump-announces-run-president, 2/1/2021.

Nussbaum, Emily (2013): Clue. In: The New Yorker of 05/08/2013, www.newyorker.com/magazine/2013/08/12/clue-8, 2/1/2021.

Ono, Kent A. (2012): Borders That Travel: Matters of the Figural Border. In: DeChaine, D. R. (ed.): Border Rhetorics: Citizenship and Identity on the US-Mexico Border. Tuscaloosa: University of Alabama Press, p. 19–32.

Payan, Tony (2006): The Three U.S.-Mexico Border Wars: Drugs, Immigration, and Homeland Security. Westport, CT, London: Praeger Security International.

Rappleye, Hannah/Seville, Lisa R. (2019): 24 immigrants have died in ICE custody during the Trump administration, www.nbcnews.com/politics/immigration/24-immigrants-have-died-ice%20custody-during-trump-administration-n1015291, 2/1/2021.

Reid, E./Stein, B./Stiehm, M. (2013a): All About Eva. The Bridge, Season 1, Episode 12 [Television broadcast]. FX Network.

Reid, E./Stein, B./Stiehm, M. (2013b): Calaca. The Bridge, Season 1, Episode 2 [Television broadcast]. FX Network.

Reid, E./Stein, B./Stiehm, M. (2013c): Destino. The Bridge, Season 1, Episode 7 [Television broadcast]. FX Network.

Reid, E./Stein, B./Stiehm, M. (2013d): Maria of the Desert. The Bridge, Season 1, Episode 4 [Television broadcast]. FX Network.

Reid, E./Stein, B./Stiehm, M. (2013e): Pilot. The Bridge, Season 1, Episode 1 [Television broadcast]. FX Network.

Reid, E./Stein, B./Stiehm, M. (2013f): The Crazy Place. The Bridge, Season 1, Episode 13 [Television broadcast]. FX Network.

Reid, E./Stein, B./Stiehm, M. (2013-2014): The Bridge [Television broadcast]. FX Network.

Rzepka, Charles J. (2005): Detective Fiction. Cambridge: Polity.

Saldívar, José David (1997): Border Matters: Remapping American Cultural Studies. Berkeley, CA: University of California Press.

Seitz, Matt Zoller (2013): Seitz on The Bridge: More Than Just a Tex-Mex Murder Mystery. In: Vulture of 10/07/2013, www.vulture.com/2013/07/tv-review-the-bridge.html, 2/1/2021.

Slotkin, Richard (1998): Gunfighter Nation: The Myth of the Frontier in Twentieth-Century America. Norman, OK: University of Oklahoma Press.

Spengler, Birgit (2016): The Body-That-Is-Not-One: Exception and Belonging on the US-Mexican Border in The Bridge. In: Arizona Quarterly 72, no. 4, p. 105–136, DOI:10.1353/arq.2016.0022, 2/1/2021.

Stanley, Alessandra (2013): Evil Knows No Borders: 'The Bridge' Adapts a Scandinavian TV Crime Series. In: The New York Times of 09/07/2013, www.nytimes.com/2013/07/10/arts/television/the-bridge-adapts-a-scandinavian-tv-crime-series.html, 2/1/2021.

Staudt, Kathleen (2012): Violence Against Women at the Border: Binational Problems and Multilayered Solutions. In: Lusk, Mark/Staudt, Kathleen/Moya, Eva (eds.): Social Justice in the U.S.-Mexico Border Region. Dordrecht: Springer Netherlands, p. 79–91.

Thomas, Ronald R. (1999): Detective Fiction and the Rise of Forensic Science. Cambridge: Cambridge University Press.

Tranter, Kirsten/Miéville, China (2012): An Interview with China Miéville. Contemporary Literature 53, no. 3, p. 417–436, DOI:10.1353/cli.2012.0022, 2/1/2021.

Wright, Melissa W. (2011): Necropolitics, Narcopolitics, and Femicide: Gendered Violence on the Mexico-U.S. Border. Signs: Journal of Women in Culture and Society 36, no. 3, p. 707–731, DOI:10.1086/657496, 2/1/2021.

Dissecting the Colorblind American Dream in Adichie's *Americanah* and Selasi's *Ghana Must Go*

Pirjo Ahokas

Border studies, as an interdisciplinary research area, no longer only concentrates on international political borders. It also investigates issues of identity as well as different kinds of social, cultural, and symbolic borders which perpetuate hierarchical binaries such as 'inside' and 'outside,' 'us' and 'them.' In the United States, a hierarchical racial divide between black and white Americans has historically been used to justify racial segregation and inequality. In contrast, the term 'colorblind' was originally used to refer to equal rights. In this sense, it was still echoed in the goals of the Civil Rights Movement and in Martin Luther King's "I have a Dream"-speech (cf. Brown et al. 2003, p. 2; Pinder 2015, p. 1). The new meaning of colorblindness, which is linked to neoliberalism, neoconservatism, and the new right, has evolved in the post-civil rights era in reaction to race-based affirmative action policies.[1] Claiming that racial equality has already been reached in the United States, today's proponents of colorblind thinking emphasize equal opportunity for all. They pretend not to 'see' racial differences[2] and deny that an unequal racial border continues to separate white and black or other racialized groups of people.

In contrast, critics of colorblindness argue that 'race' and racism have not disappeared from American society. Admitting that overt or 'traditional' racism persists in the present era, they regard colorblindness as a "new," subtle form of covert racism (Burke 2019, p. 10f.), which maintains systemic white privilege. Despite the gains achieved since the Civil Rights Movement, a truly colorblind United States still appears to be an unrealized dream.

Chimamanda Ngozi Adichie and Tayie Selasi are transnational authors of African descent. Adichie's *Americanah* and Selasi's debut novel, *Gha-*

---

1   Cf. Omi/Winant (2015, p. 217–221); Pinder (2015, p. 4, p. 37–41) for the genealogy of colorblind thinking and politics
2   Pinder calls this "new" mode of racism "racism without 'seeing' race" (2015, p. 2, p. 17).

na *Must Go,* were published in 2013, when the United States was regarded as a putatively colorblind society. The novels are primarily set in the late twentieth and early twenty-first century United States. The black African protagonists in both novels unwittingly confront America's racial and racializing boundaries after becoming captivated by the promises of the American Dream.

The notion of the American Dream is associated with the uniqueness of the American experience. Signifying the possibility of attaining wealth, upward social mobility, and happiness, it has always attracted immigrants. However, when expounded by the dominant white culture, the American Dream has historically excluded racialized groups of people. It was reinvigorated "as a popular form of political optimism" in the 1980s, when neoliberal economic practices and thinking were first advocated in the United States (Berlant 1997, p. 3f.). Susan Koshy connects this updated version of the American Dream with the narrative of American colorblind equality. She explains that certain people in a multicultural America, who belong to ethnic minority groups, are capable of morphing from race to ethnicity. This allows them to be incorporated into the American Dream and thereby achieve "whiteness" (2001, p. 183, p. 190). However, Koshy concludes that this "is less possible for blacks" (Koshy 2001, p. 159, p. 190). When the protagonists of *Americanah* and *Ghana Must Go* start their new lives in the United States, they assume that the American Dream offers its promises to everybody who seeks success. Yet I argue that they are chasing what I call the Colorblind American Dream. This can only be achieved through a denial of racial hierarchy and difference.

The discourse of the American Dream plays a crucial role in the new identity formations of Adichie's and Selasi's protagonists, and necessitates their various border-crossing endeavors. Recent theorizations of the border underline that the transformation of identity can be an experience engendered by the act of crossing (Nyman 2017, p. 74). The protagonists' constructions of new identity are suggestive of Avtar Brah's concepts of 'diaspora space' (1996) and diasporic identity, which are linked to various kinds of borders and border crossings. Diasporic identity is created in diaspora space (Brah 1996, p. 242), and the processes of diasporic identity formation involve both the migrants' original homelands and their new locations (1996, p. 196f.). Thus, diasporic identity is described as multilocal. In other words, it is simultaneously local and global (1996, p. 196). In *Americanah* and *Ghana Must Go,* the protagonists' intersectional diasporic identity formation is related to race, gender, and class, as well as the pursuit of the American Dream. The aim of this article is to examine the nature and the function of the borders crossed by the protagonists in their attempts to reach their respective American Dreams. It will also investigate how their border crossings affect and transform their ongoing processes of diasporic identity formation. The narrative strategies used in the novels are evocative of what can be called a diasporic aesthetics. Combining reverse temporality with abrupt shifts in time and place, the nonlinear and fragmentary novels frequently cross the border from the present to the past; from the diasporic location to the protagonists' homeland and back again.

In Pursuit of the American Dream

In an article from 2011, Ramón Saldívar proposed that "a radical turn to a postrace era in American literature" has taken place since the turn of the twenty-first century (2011, p. 574). The concept of postraciality is associated with the election of Barack Obama as the first black president of the United States. Like colorblindness, postraciality maintains that the problem of race no longer exists in the United States. For Saldívar, the postrace era in literature means that "a new racial imaginary is required to account for the persistence of race as a key element" of contemporary America, and authors need new forms to represent it (Saldívar 2011, p. 575). According to him, this new era is signaled by work of a new generation of American ethnic minority authors.[3] Adichie (b. 1977) and Selasi (b. 1979) are roughly of the same age as the writers Saldívar refers to. In *Americanah* and *Ghana Must Go*, Adichie and Selasi depict American society from a different vantage point than the authors discussed by Saldívar. However, they do focus on race and employ intriguing aesthetic devices to represent it.

Significantly, both novels begin *in medias res*: Adichie's protagonist, Ifemelu, is preparing a return trip to Nigeria, her home country, after thirteen years in the States, while Selasi's main character, the Ghanaian Kweku Sai, has already been living back in Africa for many years. The importance of the opening scene in each novel is underlined by them being repeated and developed in subsequent scenes so that it becomes a structuring principle in the novels. The border-crossing protagonists are fictional representatives of what is commonly known as "a new African diaspora."

---

3   Cf. Saldívar (2011, p. 596), note 1 for the names of some of the authors.

Recent immigrants from post-colonial Africa tend to be well-educated.[4] Flashbacks reveal that both protagonists initially crossed the border into the United States on student visas. In our globalized world, different forms of mass media cross cultural borders. Thus, it is no surprise that many African immigrants in recent decades have arrived in "the United States with the hope that the American dream will be theirs" (Li 2018, p. 5). Similarly, Kweku is obsessed with the American success myth, while Ifemelu's American Dream is embodied in *The Cosby Show* (1984-1992), which she watched in Nigeria.

The *Cosby Show* centered on the African American Huxtable family, with its all black cast. The show has been viewed as depicting the epitome of the American Dream, but it can more accurately be connected with the Colorblind American Dream since its popularity "seems to have been dependent on its refusal to include racism in its representations" (Budd/Steinman 1992, p. 6). Mike Budd and Clay Steinman also point out that "the level of consumption and occupation represented on the show would easily put the Huxtable family income in the nation's top 1 percent" (1992, p. 6). Ifemelu is aware of the socioeconomic boundaries which separate her from her more privileged classmates in Nigeria (Ford 2018, p. 47), but she seems to have taken the show's representation of the upper-middle class life of the African American Huxtable family as a reflection of the normal social status of black Americans.

The central scene in *Americanah* takes place in an African hair braiding salon in a rundown, non-white neighborhood, where a heatwave triggers Ifemelu's memory of her arrival in New York during a similar period of excessively hot weather. This recollection starts abruptly in the middle of the ninth chapter as if to intimate that Ifemelu has repressed a painful part of her American life. The reminiscence marks the difference between her fantasy and American reality. In Nigeria, she imagined that "the mundane things in America were covered in a high-shine gloss" (Adichie 2013, p. 106), but her first impressions of New York reveal that she was wrong. Ifemelu's notion that there is a clear boundary between her American Dream and what she sees in front of her is reinforced when she looks out of the window from her Aunt Uju's apartment in the Flatlands district of Brooklyn. She surveys an area that stands in sharp contrast to the prosper-

---

4   Chude-Sokei claims that the new immigrants from postcolonial Africa "tend to be better educated than most native-born Americans of any color" (2014, p. 61).

ous neighborhood of Brooklyn Heights where the Huxtables live in their spacious brownstone in *The Cosby Show*: "The street below was poorly lit, bordered not by leafy trees but by closely parked cars, nothing like the pretty street on *The Cosby Show*" (Adichie 2013, p. 106). These binary observations give rise to Ifemelu's diasporic identity transformation.

The catalyst for Ifemelu's and her Aunt Uju's crossing the border to the United States was the military rule in Nigeria. Ifemelu's aunt was forced to flee years earlier due to the death of a powerful general, who had taken her as his mistress, while Ifemelu's studies were interrupted because of the military regime in Nigeria. As an African migrant coming from a black majority country, Ifemelu is unable to understand the meanings of the racialized borders in her new country of residence and cannot grasp the significance of skin color in her new environment. David Newman asserts that the impact of the bordering process on our societal norms, even when we do not realize it, affects our daily lives (2006, p. 152). Indeed, linguistic and racialized borders intersect in the episodes in which African migrants change accents in *Americanah*. When watching her aunt in a grocery store Ifemelu cannot help but notice how she not only uses a different accent to speak to white Americans, but also adopts "a new persona, apologetic and self-abasing" (Adichie 2013, p. 108). During her first summer when she babysits for her nephew, Ifemelu thinks that she will see "the real America" when she begins her studies in Philadelphia. In addition to manipulating abrupt shifts in time and place, Adichie's omniscient narrator frequently resorts to irony, humor, and satire, as demonstrated in the depiction of Ifemelu's introductory encounter at her new school with a white woman in the college registrar's office. She speaks so slowly to Ifemelu that she thinks that the woman's speech is impeded by an illness. When it transpires that the woman doubts Ifemelu's knowledge of English, which she has always spoken, the bilingual protagonist promptly crosses a linguistic border herself and starts trying to adopt an American accent in order to avoid further humiliation, although she may not have fully understood the racializing implications of their meeting.

The brightness of Ifemelu's American Dream is tarnished still further in Philadelphia. An epistemological border seems to separate her and other students of African descent from the local insiders and their alien habits. Ifemelu's sense of being barred from understanding America is exacerbated by the fact that American race relations make no sense to her. She, for instance, wonders aloud why it is that Americans do not refer to black and white people on the basis of their skin color. A more experienced Nigerian friend responds: "Because this is America. You're supposed to pretend that you do not notice certain things" (Adichie 2013, p. 127). Gradually, Ifemelu's own colorblindness deepens when she believes that she is finally being offered a chance to taste the American Dream.

As indicated above, upward social mobility is an important strand of the discourse of the dominant white American Dream. Selasi's Kweku hails from humble origins in rural Ghana. No wonder, then, that his trajectory after he received his first scholarship is defined by his inner drive for achievement. Unlike *Americanah*, *Ghana Must Go* is sustained by an "oppressively melancholic mood and nostalgic tone" (Phiri 2017, p. 148). The opening of the novel reinforces this somber tone as it depicts Kweku's slow process of suffering a fatal cardiac arrest in his garden in Ghana. As in *Americanah*, the reader has to wait for the story of the Sai family in the United States to begin: it is introduced as late as chapter ten in part one. By this time, Fola and Kweku, the parent figures, are already married and live in what is called "[a] one bedroom hovel" during the "[h]eartbreaking winter, 1975" (Selasi 2013, p. 53). They wear secondhand clothing, and Kweku hates his overcoat because "it made him look poor" (2013, p. 53). The overcoat encapsulates Kweku's feelings of shame as, for him, it emblematizes how he is occupying the bottom rung in the social hierarchy of the United States.

The myth of the self-made man, also described as the American Dream, is a popular white masculine trope. It promises success and riches through hard work. The myth is a salient part in Kweku's construction of diasporic identity: in a retrospective episode, he remembers how during his medical training, he was "too tired to sleep, too sleepy to stand" (2013, p. 51). One of the memories that flashes through Kweku's mind as he is dying brings him back to the time when the family lived in "the dim, skinnier half of a two-family duplex" on a street where the ghetto began. The sociologist Anssi Paasi explains that "[b]orders are—as expressions of territoriality—normally crucial to what can be called the discursive landscape of social power" (2011, p. 22). In the novel, the overpass under which the house stands separates Boston from Brookline, "the wealth from the want" (Selasi 2013, p. 51). As such, the overpass is redolent of a visible barrier that denotes the historical "color line," which has supposedly been breached in the colorblind United States. Nevertheless, Kweku has to manage to cross this border in order to grasp at his American Dream.

The other side of the divisive border is depicted by Olu, the eldest son in the Sai family, in the last part of Selasi's novel. It takes place in Ghana where the grown-up children reminisce about their life in the duplex. According to Olu, who frequently crossed the border between Boston and

Brookline as a schoolboy, the family's side of this divide was gray and "drained of life," whereas Brookline had "more trees, Carvel Ice Cream, lights hung by the town" (Selasi 2013, p. 220). In reality, the efforts of the Civil Rights Movement contributed to the desegregation of American public schools. One of the measures used to achieve integration was busing children from residentially segregated areas to predominantly white schools (Hewitt 2005, p. 105f.). Olu remembers how he used to hate being bused to Brookline. He resented being "stuck" between his rich classmates in Brookline and the poor ones on the other side of the divide. Olu missed "the comforts of in-group belonging" on either side of the dividing line (Selasi 2013, p. 221). Border scholarship proposes that borders not only separate, but can also be lowered, erased, or even serve as bridges and points of interaction (Newman 2006, p. 150). Olu, as the son of immigrants, negatively compares himself to "an immigrant, a foreigner" (Selasi 2013, p. 221), because, for him, the experience of shuttling across the border provided no communicative bridge. Instead, it imbued a sense of loneliness in him.

Chude-Sokei asserts that there are two Americas—"one white, one black"—that have "their distinct and sometimes irreconcilable demands to African immigrants" (2014, p. 56). This means that African migrants, torn between these two Americas, "are expected to assimilate into either a white American and/or a 'black' social world" (2014, p. 55). Americanness has traditionally implied the need to identify with citizenship ideals that reflected white middle-class hegemony (Carden 2011, p. 131). According to Jim Cullen "[n]o American Dream has broader appeal" than owning a home (2003, p. 136). Brah's use of the term of 'homing desire' refers to both the possibility of migrants' returning to their original home country and to their "declaring a place as home" in their new country (Brah 1996, p. 197). Since Kweku's sense of self-worth stems from exterior factors, his diasporic identity construction is contingent on his professional achievement and wealth. Once he has established himself as a successful surgeon, Kweku plays for high stakes by permanently crossing to the other side of the symbolic border by buying a house in a predominantly white neighborhood in Brookline. The house accords with his lofty social aspirations: it is "a russet brick palace. The grandest thing he'd ever owned" (Selasi 2013, p. 65). Unbeknownst to Kweku, the house that expresses his diasporic homing desire also symbolizes his Colorblind American Dream.

Do Race and Racialization Really Matter?

Like race, gender and sexuality can be considered social borders. Black sexuality has served as a sign of racial difference in the West within hierarchical white/black thinking (Collins 2006, p. 28, p. 44). In historical terms, supposed black promiscuity has been seen as forming a part of this racial difference. Patricia Hill Collins contends that racial difference is still produced in the same manner (2006, p. 36, p. 43). The stereotype of black female promiscuity is perpetuated via a humiliating memory in *Americanah*. When Ifemelu is looking for a job in order to pay the rent, she responds to a newspaper advertisement. After interviewing her, a sly, white American tennis coach explains that he actually advertised for two different jobs: the office position had already been filled, but the other one was still available "for help relaxing" (Adichie 2013, p. 143). Unable to understand exactly what the coach means Ifemelu ends up doing what he wants. This experience crossed the line of Ifemelu's Nigerian principles of sexual behavior and deeply affects her diasporic identity construction. Subsequently, she falls into a depression.

The racial border between white and black women has been discussed by black feminists and scholars of critical whiteness studies. Their critique of white women's gendered racism is also relevant in regard to *Americanah*. Ifemelu is finally employed as a baby-sitter by Kimberly, a wealthy white American woman. The narrator's depiction of Kimberly is of a woman who exudes white privilege: "In her gold sweater belted at an impossibly tiny waist, with her gold hair, in gold flats, she looked improbable, like sunlight" (2013, p. 146). Although Kimberly seems to be unaware of her racial identity, contributors to whiteness studies claim that "white identity is constituted in opposition to the 'not white'" (Lewis/Ramazanoglu 1999, p. 23). Even in this scenario, white women wield power and this also applies to Kimberly.

Patronizing admiration of the racial "other" is one of the strategies a white woman can employ in order to deny her position of power (Brown 1999, p. 5). Kimberly adopts this tactic when praising the beauty of black women during conversations with Ifemelu. Conservative multiculturalism is a form of colorblind thinking. Like its proponents, Kimberly prefers to use the word "culture" when distinguishing human groups instead of referring to ethnic and racial differences.[5] While those who use cultural attrib-

---

5   Cf. Lentin/Titley (2011, p. 62f., p. 68).

utes instead of racial ones normally associate negative characteristics with non-white and non-Western people, Kimberly resorts to flattery. She, for instance, praises Ifemelu's name when they are introduced: "What a beautiful name .... I love multicultural names.... from wonderful rich cultures" (Adichie 2013, p. 146). Kimberly hides the norm of whiteness in her patronizing admiration, but at the same time, she manages to mark an invisible racial boundary between Ifemelu and herself. The narrator satirizes Kimberly by concluding that she would hardly think that Norway had a "rich culture" (2013, p. 146). Yet Ifemelu naively idealizes Kimberly and appears to equate her and what she represents with the "real America" of her American Dream.

Like Ifemelu, once the attainment of his American Dream seems possible, Kweku closes his eyes to the racialization of black people in the United States. As already noted, masculinity plays a central role in Kweku's diasporic identity construction. According to Mary Paniccia Carden, "[t]he father-headed nuclear family occupies a privileged position as representative of the national norm and the outcome of the American Dream" (2011, p. 132). Class is also an important social marker in the black community, and this predominantly white model appeals to upwardly mobile, border-crossing African American men. It not only reinforces "a model of benevolent paternal authority," but is also a black embodiment of an integrationist ideal of masculine sameness. This offers a reassuring, non-threatening image of black masculinity to whites (Collins 2006, p. 166f.; Carden 2011, p. 133). Kweku's diasporic construction of black masculinity fits this description.

Carden connects the black middle-class, father-dominant model of home and family to problems afflicting black American communities in this century. She traces the present crisis in the class-based discourses of blackness to the discourse of the post-Reconstruction racial uplift movement. The educated black leaders of this movement resisted black stereotypes by joining their ideals of masculinity within a class-related hierarchy (Carden 2011, p. 131f.). Perceiving themselves as defenders of the disadvantaged black majority, they nevertheless became alienated from poor black people. A similar tendency can be seen in contemporary debates: a class-based discourse separates exceptional, affluent blacks from the black poor. The latter group are stigmatized as ghetto dwellers and are blamed for their own problems (2011, p. 131, p. 133; Logan 2014, p. 654, p. 670). With his upper-middle-class aspirations, Selasi's Kweku seeks white acceptance in his privileged new neighborhood by committing himself and his family to the American Way of life (Collins 2006, p. 167). Moreover, retreating into his paternal nuclear household, Kweku does not appear to maintain contact with African Americans or any people of African descent outside his family.

Collins uses the term "enlightened racism" when discussing the urban migration of many well-off black Americans to white-dominated neighborhoods in the post-civil rights era in spite of the fact that whites preferred racially homogeneous neighborhoods. She claims that supposedly colorblind white inhabitants would welcome new black neighbors in order to demonstrate that they are not racist (2006, p. 147). This also seems to hold for the Sai family, because there appears to be no resistance to their arrival in Brookline. Although the discourses of race, gender, and class intersect in Kweku's diasporic identity construction, he appears—much to his detriment—to be oblivious to the fact that the racial discourse of his adopted homeland primarily recompenses white men, who represent hegemonic masculinity in the American hierarchy of masculinities. However, the fact that, even as a famous surgeon, Kweku devotes his time to work at the expense of his family can be seen as a sign of his attempt to protect himself from the harsh reality of being cast as black in the United States.

Education forms a social border that divides people into 'us' and 'them.' No wonder, then, that a university education is part and parcel of the contemporary American Dream. Kweku is in possession of strong educational capital and believes that it guarantees his class advantage. Wishing to pass on his class advantage and the realization of his American Dream, he displays benevolent paternalism when expressing his desire to send his children to predominantly white elite schools in the United States. Nevertheless, he does not want his sons to choose their future professions based on talent alone. As I have noted previously, colorblindness is linked to neoliberalism. Neoliberalism advocates the privatization of economic enterprises and personal responsibility, which has a significant impact on family decision-making. This also applies to Kweku's pursuit of his Colorblind American Dream. Towards the end of *Ghana Must Go* Kweku's younger son, a successful artist, reveals that he resented how his father wanted him and his brother to become physicians: "That was the dream, Sai and Sons, family business" (Selasi 2013, p. 242). While this dream never comes true, it is worth keeping Collins's assertion in mind when contemplating black people's economic opportunities in a colorblind society. Collins upholds that black people's total absence in high society would mean that colorblindness had failed, and, therefore their opportunities are contingent on the assumption that racial discrimination has been eliminated (2006, p. 178). The narrator's ironic treatment of Kweku implies that he does not even suspect that a huge network of power relations under-lies colorblind ideology, probably as a result of his immigrant background.

Black and Colorblind in a White World

On the surface, recent approaches to thinking about race and ethnicity fa-vor interaction between different ethnic and racial groups. Thus, mixed marriages can be regarded as a potential means of facilitating the tran-scendence of racial difference and, consequently, assimilation into main-stream American society (Santa Ana 2004, p. 16f.). In *Americanah*, Ifemelu crosses a racial border when she enters into a relationship with Curt, Kimberly's blond and blue-eyed cousin. The ease with which Ifemelu does it proves how unaware she is of the historical intertwining of race, gender, and class in the oppression of black women in the United States. To quote Stephanie Li "[s]he is effectively black without the histo-ry of blackness" (2018, p. 108). In short, Curt, who possesses "the cleft-chinned handsomeness of models in departments store catalogues" (Adichie 2013, p. 192) and whose family had been hoteliers for several generations, represents American hegemonic masculinity and a fictional embodiment of the American Dream.

In the flashbacks relating to Ifemelu and Curt as a couple, there are sev-eral references to the fact that their consumption-centered relationship takes place in a colorblind America. The neoliberal culture of consump-tion is said to use "racial and ethnic minorities to glamorize and commodi-fy diversity" (Santa Ana 2004, p. 15). Curt confides to Ifemelu in his penthouse apartment in Baltimore that he has never been with a black woman. Significantly, his mother confirms the manner in which he glam-orizes and commodifies women of different ethnic and racial backgrounds than his own: [he] "would bring back exotic species—he had dated a Jap-anese girl, a Venezuelan girl" (Adichie 2013, p. 198). Tellingly she adds that with time Curt would "settle down properly" thereby demarcating a clear but invisible boundary between exotic girlfriends like Ifemelu and their upper-class white family.

The manner in which Ifemelu slips into the role of "Curt's Girlfriend" as effortlessly as "into a favorite, flattering dress" (2013, p. 198) suggests that she believes that she can change her diasporic identity at will. How-ever, the ironic narrator remarks that in so doing she has "slipped out of her old skin" (2013, p. 201). Ifemelu's ambivalent feelings towards Curt and his world grow over time. His relentless optimism irritates her, and it does not take long until she associates the sunniness of his white friends with their living "on the glimmering surface of things" (Adichie 2013, p. 207). This privileged world, where other black people are only to be found in the service sector and where racism seems to go unnoticed by whites, is ultimately proven to be far from the space of belonging sought by Ifemelu's homing desire in the United States. Consequently, Ifemelu begins to write an increasingly popular blog while she and Curt are still together, which emphasizes that she only became black when she came to America. The provocative title of one of her posts proclaims: "In America, You Are Black, Baby" (2013, p. 220). As Li argues, the main purpose of the blog posts, which are printed in a different font and with a distinct layout in the novel, is to instruct non-American blacks about the U.S. operations of race (2018, p. 113). However, the blog posts not only contain pieces of advice concerning encounters with whites, but also include Ifemelu's trenchant critique of colorblindness, racism, and the racial border.

In fact, race should not raise institutional barriers in America as the Civil Rights Act of 1964 outlawed discrimination based on race, color, religion, sex, or national origin. In *Ghana Must Go*, Kweku's place of employment, Beth Israel Hospital, appears to have never had previous instances of overt racism and there are no hints that the institution would be guilty of racial discrimination. A pivotal episode takes place in the hospital in the early stages of the novel: Kweku's American Dream turns out to have been his Colorblind American Dream. He initially enjoyed a reputation as being the institution's finest surgeon. Thus, when the fictional Cabot family, who are among wealthy donors to the hospital and part of the local power elite, ask for "a last ditch operation" (Selasi 2013, p. 74) to be performed on an elderly member of the family, the hospital president assigns Kweku to the task.

An ugly incident that takes place before the operation pointedly exposes the underlying racial tensions and the racializing border lurking inside the apparently race-neutral institution. By chance, Kweku happens to overhear a male representative of the white and powerful Cabot family begin to utter a racist remark. Subsequently, when the family physician, a Boston Brahmin, condescendingly asks Kweku: "And where did you do your 'training'?" (2013, p. 74), he cannot help return the racist slight in kind by drawing on the animal stereotypes of colonialist discourse: "'In the jungle, on beasts,' Kweku answered genteelly, 'Chimpanzees taught'" (2013, p. 74). Even though Kweku performs a masterful operation under the watchful eyes of the hospital president, the patient dies. Having ignored racialization and the existence of white privilege, Kweku is shocked that the hospital trustees dismiss him, because the Cabots demanded that someone be held accountable.

The authors of *Whitewashing Race* allege that colorblind ideology no longer challenges institutional practices that sustain racial inequality. According to them, this is true about the U.S. justice system, in particular, because it is permeated by "the experience, perspective and privilege of white Americans" (Brown et al. 2003, p. 59). Kweku's visit to his lawyer's office in order to get help after his wrongful dismissal precedes the hospital scene. Sara Ahmed's explanation about real situations in which institutions are accused of racism fits Kweku's case. Complaints about racist behavior are interpreted as being accusations against white people. Thus, the refusal of an institution to address racism is a way of protecting whiteness from being hurt (Ahmed 2012, p. 147). Kweku's attorney admits that his racist treatment was wrong, yet there is nothing that can be done: "Cause then it becomes: is Beth Israel racist? And this being Boston that question is ... booooom!" (Selasi 2013, p. 70). Kweku pretends for eleven months that he is still employed at the hospital, as he is deeply traumatized and is unable to tell his family that he is unemployed. He even shows up at his former workplace in order to confront the Asian American vice president of the hospital. In "Morphing Race into Ethnicity," previously cited in the introduction, Koshy (2001) pays special attention to wealthy Asian Americans and recent affluent immigrants from Asia as a group in which morphing from race to ethnicity provides access to the American Dream and thereby also to whiteness. It would appear that the hospital vice president belongs to this prosperous group in the racial hierarchy. Nevertheless, Kweku rages against her as lacking solidarity with him. The vice president, who had announced Kweku's dismissal eleven months ago, orders his removal once again. Kweku abandons his family after this incident, as he feels such an acute sense of shame.

When Kweku deserts his family he also leaves behind the house that symbolized his Colorblind American Dream. On a visit to their old neighborhood in Brookline as an adult, Taiwo, the eldest daughter of the family, resents that her father was "straining daily to perform the Provider" and notes that, unlike other houses in the vicinity, their house never possessed "that warm-yellow-glowing-inside-ness of home" (Selasi 2013, p. 123). Instead, there was always the sense of "a thing being built: *A Successful family*" (2013, p. 123). Unlike Kweku, she observes the class boundaries that used to set the Sai family apart from their neighbors. The other houses are larger than their old home, thereby demonstrating the owners' economic capital. Moreover, the successful white families have managed to accumulate their social capital. Thus they have been able to finish "their heavy lifting generations ago" and are now sitting comfortably "at rest and at home" (Selasi 2013, p. 124). Taiwo mourns the fate of Kweku as well as the whole of her dispersed family, but she perceives his desertion as shameful and worse than his dedication to his Colorblind American Dream.

Back to Africa

Recent scholarship has directed attention to the border that both separates and unites African Americans and immigrants of African descent. Chude-Sokei finds complex intra-racial and cross-cultural tensions in the fiction written by "new black Americans" (Chude-Sokei 2014, p. 68). These tensions also occur in *Americanah*. After Ifemelu gives up her white upper-class aspirations, she becomes rich and famous through her provocative blog. A new awakening of her homing desire is brought to the fore when she reconnects with an African American Yale professor called Blaine at a Blogging While Brown convention and begins a relationship with him. While successful black professionals regard it as important to distance themselves from "black issues" in order to win white acceptance in the era of racial colorblindness (Logan 2014, p. 654), Blaine and his racially mixed academic friends are anti-racist liberals and social activists. Racial unity appears to provide a common bond between Ifemelu and Blaine at the beginning of their relationship. Nevertheless, while Blaine keeps preaching the significance of race as the dominant factor in American life to Ifemelu, she, as Li shows, fails to internalize its historical meaning to the African American community. Ifemelu regards race as an important issue in the United States because of racism, but as a Nigerian migrant she also experiences race as a "choice," because it does not define her in her homeland (Li 2018, p. 113).[6] This is illustrated in a retrospective episode in which Ifemelu does not participate in a protest meeting that Blaine organizes on campus. Instead, she attends a farewell lunch. When Blaine accuses her of not being serious enough, Ifemelu discerns a subtle reproach

---

6   For more on the significance of race in Ifemelu and Blaine's relationship, see Li (2018, p. 112–129).

in his voice vis-à-vis her being African and not a responsible African American. This incident contributes to their final break-up.

Significantly Ifemelu's decision to return to Nigeria is made in the aftermath of Obama's re-election. As indicated above, the novel's fragmentary narrative underscores the meaning of her visit to a hair braiding salon. As with many other novels by black women, *Americanah* underlines the political significance of black hair. Ifemelu not only posts blog entries about black hairstyles but also tries to straighten her kinky hair for a job interview in marketing in order to look professional on the advice of her African American career counselor. As a result, the chemicals burn her scalp. On the eve of her departure for Lagos, she has her natural hair braided as it was when she arrived in the United States. Importantly, during this visit, she meets poor, uneducated and illegal African immigrant women, who are separated from her by a social border. Recognizing her own privileged position as a legal immigrant, Ifemelu feels a new bond with the braiders.

In Selasi's novel, Kweku's diasporic identity construction in the United States imaginatively involves his original native county in the form of a home he wants to build there. When he moves back to Ghana, the house, located in a suburb of crumbling colonial mansions, is described as a kind of "rebuttal to the tropics, to home: so a homeland reimagined, all the lines clean and straight" (Selasi 2013, p. 5). The house, as Dustin Crowley puts it, "speaks at once to a global character and to a deep embeddedness in place and culture" (2018, p. 130). Like diasporic identity in Brah's description, the house with its hybrid architecture expresses multi-locality and mutual imbrication between local and global.

The image of slippers is reiterated throughout the course of the novel and is firmly linked to Kweku's border crossings. He used them to hide his soles which are the symbol of his vulnerability. Kweku had gone shoeless as a child in Ghana, and the soles he carefully hides in the slippers are full of bruises. After his funeral in Ghana, Fola receives the slippers, which have been worn to the soles. The metaphorical value of the slippers is accentuated, when she presses them to her cheeks, as she associates them with the scant protection Kweku had against the harshness of his immigrant life. Another image pertaining to Kweku's border crossing also occurs in the last chapter: Fola changes her mind about scattering Kweku's ashes in the ocean: "*We've been scattered enough*, she thinks. Broken pot, fragments. *Keep him inside*, let him stay whole" (Selasi 2013, p. 314, emphasis original). The image reflects the narrator's use of a diasporic aesthetics: at the novel's closure, the fragmented memories can finally come to rest.

It is noteworthy that the last part of *Americanah* depicts the progress of Ifemelu's life back in Lagos in chronological order. Her diasporic identity process continues as an Americanah, that is, a Nigerian who has returned to her homeland. Essential to the development of Ifemelu's diasporic identity is that she maintains her transnational networks, as she had done in the United States, by even keeping in touch with Curt and Blaine. Ifemelu can laugh off her Colorblind American Dream and, at the same time, retain it: "it's a lie but you can buy into it and that's all that matters" (Adichie 2013, p. 434). She feels "shielded from choicelessness" (2013, p. 390) with her new American passport as she can freely travel between the two countries. In contrast to Kweku, Ifemelu has managed to cross challenging borders with greater ease, and her identity is suggestive of a flexible hybridized diasporic identity in which the American and Nigerian elements comport in a propitious manner.

The protagonists' migration processes in the novels by Adichie and Selasi are very different, but the borders that they have to negotiate and cross have much in common. In each novel, the protagonist's journey from Africa to the United States presages the beginning of diasporic identity formation, which is not only linked to the international borders but also involves a number of different kinds of other borders in the diasporic location. What each novel reveals is that the racial border is the crucial boundary that intersects in complicated and limiting ways with a number of other divides, despite discourses of colorblindness and postraciality. It is complicit in a variety of otherizing borders such as those pertaining to language, epistemology, culture, socioeconomic status and education. Furthermore, race intersects with gender, sexuality and class, which not only influences diasporic identity formation but also marks hierarchizing boundaries. Taken together, when the protagonists confront all these borders, it ultimately contributes to the fact that their respective American Dreams turn into Colorblind American Dreams. The diasporic narrative strategy of disturbing the temporal structure of the carefully-crafted novels skillfully captures the ebb and flow of diasporic identity construction. Ultimately, race and racism still matter in the novels' fictional depictions of the United States, which is not removed from the real world.

Works Cited

Adichie, Chimamanda Ngozi (2013): Americanah. London: Fourth Estate.

Ahmed, Sara (2012): On Being Included: Racism and Diversity in Institutional Life. Durham: Duke University Press.

Berlant, Lauren (1997): The Queen of America Goes to Washington: Essays on Sex and Citizenship. Durham: Duke University Press.

Brah, Avtar (1996): Cartographies of Diaspora: Contesting Identities. London: Routledge.

Brown, Heloise. (1999): Introduction. In: Brown, Heloise/Gilkes, Madi/Kaloski-Naylor, Ann (eds.): White? Women. Critical Perspectives on Race and Gender. York: Raw Nerve Books, p. 1–22.

Brown, Michael K./Carnoy, Martin/Currie, Elliott/Duster, Troy/Oppenheimer, David B./Shultz, Marjorie M./Wellman, David (2003): Whitewashing Race: The Myth of a Color-Blind Society (1. ed.). Berkeley: University of California Press.

Budd, Mike/Steinman, Clay (1992): White Racism and The Cosby Show. In: Jump Cut: A Review of Contemporary Media no. 37, p. 5–14.

Burke, Meghan (2019): Colorblind Racism. Cambridge: Polity Press.

Carden, Mary Paniccia (2011): "Trying to find a place when the streets don't go there": Fatherhood, Family, and American Racial Politics in Toni Morrison's "Love". In: African American Review 44, no. 1/2, p. 131–147, www.jstor.org/stable/41328710, 2/1/2021.

Chude-Sokei, Louis (2014): The Newly Black Americans: African Immigrants and Black America. In: Transition no. 113, p. 52–71, DOI:10.2979/transition.113.52.

Collins, Patricia Hill (2006): Black Sexual Politics: African Americans, Gender, and the New Racism. New York: Routledge.

Crowley, Dustin (2018): How Did They Come to This?: Afropolitanism, Migration, and Displacement. In: Research in African Literatures 49, no. 2, p. 125–146, DOI:10.2979/reseafrilite.49.2.08.

Cullen, Jim (2003): The American Dream: A Short History of an Idea that Shaped a Nation. Oxford: Oxford University Press.

Ford, Na'Imah H. (2018): Black Americans and American Blacks: Transnational Identity in Chimamanda Ngozi Adichie's Americanah. In: Fongang, Delphine (ed.): The Postcolonial Subject in Transit. Migration, Borders, and Subjectivity in Contemporary African Diaspora Literature. Lanham, MD: Lexington Books/Fortress Academic, p. 55–70.

Hewitt, Roger (2005): White Backlash and the Politics of Multiculturalism. Cambridge, New York: Cambridge University Press.

Koshy, Susan (2001): Morphing Race into Ethnicity: Asian Americans and Critical Transformations of Whiteness. In: boundary 2 28, no. 1, p. 153–194, DOI:10.1215/01903659-28-1-153.

Lentin, Alana/Titley, Gavan (2011): The Crises of Multiculturalism: Racism in a Neoliberal Age. London: Zed Books, ebookcentral.proquest.com/lib/gbv/detail.action?docID=765179.

Lewis, Brenda/Ramazanoglu, Caroline. (1999): Not Guilty, Not Proud, Just White: Women's Account of Their Whiteness. In: Brown, Heloise/Gilkes, Madi/Kaloski-Naylor, Ann (eds.): White? Women. Critical Perspectives on Race and Gender. York: Raw Nerve Books, p. 23–61.

Li, Stephanie (2018): Pan–African American Literature: Signifying Immigrants in the 21st Century. New Brunswick: Rutgers University Press.

Logan, Enid (2014): Barack Obama, the New Politics of Race, and Classed Constructions of Racial Blackness. In: The Sociological Quarterly 55, no. 4, p. 653–682, DOI:10.1111/tsq.12071.

Newman, David (2006): The lines that continue to separate us: borders in our 'borderless' world. In: Progress in Human Geography 30, no. 2, p. 143–161, DOI:10.1191/0309132506ph599xx.

Nyman, Jopi (2017): Displacement, Memory, and Travel in Contemporary Migrant Writing. Leiden: Brill, booksandjournals.brillonline.com/content/books/9789004342064.

Omi, Michael/Winant, Howard (2015): Racial Formation in the United States (3rd ed.). New York: Routledge.

Paasi, Anssi. (2011): A Border Theory: An Unattainanble Dream or a Realistic Aim for Border Scholars? In: Wastl-Walter, Doris (ed.): The Ashgate Research Companion to Border Studies (1st ed.). Farnham: Ashgate, p. 11–31.

Phiri, Aretha (2017): Lost in translation: re-reading the contemporary Afrodiasporic condition in Taiye Selasi's Ghana Must Go. In: European Journal of English Studies 21, no. 2, p. 144–158, DOI:10.1080/13825577.2017.1344474.

Pinder, Sherrow O. (2015): Colorblindness, Post-raciality, and Whiteness in the United States (1st ed.). New York: Palgrave Macmillan.

Saldívar, Ramón (2011): Historical Fantasy, Speculative Realism, and Postrace Aesthetics in Contemporary American Fiction. In: American Literary History 23, no. 3, p. 574–599, DOI:10.1093/alh/ajr026.

Santa Ana, Jeffrey C. (2004): Affect-Identity: The Emotions of Assimilation, Multiraciality, and Asian American Subjectivity. In: Ty, Eleanor R./Goellnicht, Donald C. (eds.): Asian North American Identities. Beyond the Hyphen. Bloomington: Indiana University Press, p. 15–42.

Selasi, Taiye (2013): Ghana Must Go. London: Viking.

A Haunting Controversy: Yamanaka's Fictionalized Melodramatic Ghost Figures

Janna Odabas

> 'The ghost is not simply a dead or a missing person, but a social figure, and investigating it can lead to that dense site where history and subjectivity make social life.' (Gordon 2004, p. 8)

In her seminal *Ghostly Matters*, Avery Gordon manages to address many concerns relating to ghost figures: their relation to psychology and identity formation, their fictional and narratorial appeal, their relation to history, society, and culture, but also the ways in which the ghosts inherently trouble the neat conceptualizations we try to put them into. In *Cultural Haunting*, Kathleen Brogan establishes the genre of 'stories of cultural haunting' as a pan-ethnic tradition. In her words, the ghosts in these stories "are agents of both cultural memory and cultural renewal: the shape-shifting ghost who transmits erased or threatened group memory represents the creative, on-going process of ethnic redefinition" (Brogan 1998, p. 12). In this conception, the ghost figures serve as connection points to a(n) (ethnic) past that is then re-worked into new conceptions for the future. Following Gordon and Brogan, thus, means to emphasize the importance of recognizing these figures for what they hint at. In Asian American Studies, the ghost figures have mostly been read as ethnic markers, similar to the way Brogan conceives of them. But these figures also challenge such neat classifications in their unruly comings and goings as they occupy the liminal spaces in-between. They serve as references to what is troublesome. This article, therefore, focuses on the ghost figures in Louis-Ann Yamanaka's *Behold the Many* (2006), allowing them to become haunting presences way beyond this one novel.

While some fields belonging to Ethnic Studies have begun the urgently needed discussion about their complicity in essentializing categorizations and their political approach, the field of Asian American Studies seems to me to remain in a general resistance narrative to what is conceived as white America. Even though post-structuralist Asian American Studies scholars like Kandice Chuh are fairly popular at the moment, proposing an anti-essentialist 'subjectless discourse' (2003, p. 9), foregrounding the discursive constructedness of subjectivity and thus allowing for diversity and difference, the discourse often remains stuck in a politicized approach that neglects other aspects. Chuh, for example, reads 'Asian American' as "a representational sign" that becomes a "metaphor for resistance and racism" (2003, p. 27). Although Chuh tries to break with essentializing, she, like many scholars, appears to be clinging to the paradigm of cultural and political resistance that marked the beginnings of Asian American Studies. The ghosts in *Behold the Many* offer a way to think about these questions. They need to be read, though, with a controversy in mind.

The Controversy

In 1997, Lois-Ann Yamanaka published *Blu's Hanging*, a novel which would spark controversy about the very field it was published in. It tells the story of three children whose mother has died and how they cope with their loss and the emotional withdrawal of their grief-stricken father. The debate centered on one of the minor characters named Uncle Paulo, a Filipino American, who is a rapist. When the Association for Asian American Studies committee chose *Blu's Hanging* for the fiction award of 1997, this initiated a huge debate in the field about its self-conception. Ultimately, the award was rescinded due to the controversy surrounding Yamanaka's novel. Critics charged Yamanaka with a racist depiction of Filipino Americans, arguing that this stereotypical representation was causing harmful social reactions. Supporters of Yamanaka claimed the right to freedom of artistic expression. Thus, the debate moved far beyond this single depiction of one Filipino American rapist in one fictional text. Its reception in the secondary literature of the field is, however, rather scant. If the debate is addressed, it causes critics to either call for greater accountability or no representation at all,[1] thus, marking the two opposed reactions to the problem that is at the center of the field of Asian American Studies: is the field driven by political intentions? In essence, the controversy became a fight over the function of literature, over the political or aesthetic orientation of an award given out by an association, and over the role of the author in general, and even more so in the special case of an ethnic author. Do these writers have explicit social responsibilities towards their ethnic groups or

---

1   Kandice Chuh would belong to the latter group of scholars, whereas Viet Nguyen (2002) is but one example of the former approach to the problem of representation within Asian American Studies. Chuh's approach is by far the more popular way out of the paradox that stands at the center of the field.

other Asian American groups? Or are (ethnic) authors free to write whatever they feel like?[2]

My article addresses this debate in relation to a later novel by Yamanaka. Written in 2006, after the controversy, *Behold the Many* takes up such divisive issues as inter-ethnic tensions in the Hawaiian society once again. As Mark Chiang has argued in relation to her earlier work already, Yamanaka's novels can be read as comments or reactions to the ongoing criticism of her books (2009, p. 174). Following such a reading, *Behold the Many* addresses racist stereotypes within the Hawaiian society, albeit consciously further fictionalized than in her earlier texts by means of the constant magical appearances that drive the story.

Haunting and Behold the Many

Yamanaka's *Behold the Many*, set in Hawaii in the early 20th century, revolves around the protagonist Anah, who is being haunted by various ghost figures during her life. The novel is about three sisters of Japanese Portuguese descent, who are infected with tuberculosis and are sent away to a German Catholic orphanage. During their time at the orphanage, each sister makes the acquaintance of Seth, the ghost of a young boy who died before the sisters arrived. One after the other befriends this ghost as they approach their deaths. Leah and Aki, the two younger sisters, die at the orphanage, while the oldest, Anah, survives, only to be haunted by the ghosts of her siblings throughout her life. Anah is also haunted by 'the many' that already appear in the title: these are the ghosts of all the chil-

---

2   These questions have driven the field of Asian American Studies from its conception in the 1970s. They echo some of the fundamental questions that already concerned the first big debate within the field, namely, the Kingston-Chin debate. These questions reflect the renewed tensions between theory and practice twenty years on. The reception of the Yamanaka controversy in academic texts shows how fundamentally these positions still shape the face of Asian American Studies today. According to Mark Chiang in *The Cultural Capital of Asian American Studies* from 2009, this is a crisis of representation that the discipline faces since its institutionalization. One group calls for greater accountability and the other claims a complete break with representation as such. Chiang explains this gap as a result of the institutionalization of Asian American Studies, which was paradoxical because it created the field as a part of the university while the field considered itself as located outside of it (2009, p. 1–5).

dren who died during their time in the orphanage, now looking for a way 'home.' When Anah finally leaves the orphanage to begin her new life as the wife of Ezroh, Seth's brother, she is cursed. Seth's friendship has turned into one-sided love and he cannot accept his brother's engagement to her. This curse follows Anah, complicating her life as a member of Ezroh's family even further, as it adds to his family's suspicions concerning her racial background. Due to the curse, Ezroh and Anah's children are all born with disabilities, and it can only be lifted by the death of Anah's first-born daughter, Hosana. In the final scene of the novel, Hosana, turned into a ghost after being raped and murdered, calls all the ghosts to her—Leah, Aki, Seth, and 'the many'—to take them 'home' with her, to God. The novel thus addresses highly controversial aspects such as the uneasy relationship between efforts of colonization and traditional Hawaiian beliefs or the inter-ethnic tensions that shape everyday life on the islands.

I argue that the ghost figures are troublesome especially because they do not follow a simplified, politicized postcolonial resistance narrative; instead, they expose the paradoxical interconnections that exist between seemingly opposed systems. Therefore, the ghosts function as haunting reminders of the uneasy questions that surround the controversy within the field. Most centrally, the novel emphasizes and stages the overarching '*dis*-ease' of its setting and its characters. This refers to Janice Radway's term as she uses it in the foreword to Avery Gordon's *Ghostly Matters*, stating that some authors "use imaginative fiction [...] to diagnose the political *dis*-ease of our historical moment" (2008, p. xi). Therefore, I read the ghost figures as references that emerge uneasily from the pages of this novel in order to express such *dis*-ease without, however, allowing for a conclusive reading of their function or offering solutions to the problems that they embody.

Following a deconstructive reading of ghosts, I argue that everything is haunted by what it tries to exclude. The ghost's haunting can be examined via Jacques Derrida's concept of hauntology. His concept is not concerned with the ghost's reality status, it rather emphasizes their status as figures that demand recognition. For him, the scholar

> should learn to live by learning not how to make conversation with the ghost but how to talk with him, with her, how to let them speak or how to give them back speech, even if it is in oneself, in the other, in the other in oneself: they are always there, specters, even if they do not exist, even if they are no longer, even if they are not yet. (Derrida 1994, p. 176)

In this ethical approach, the ghosts' presence is accepted, 'even if they do not exist' for they serve a purpose for the one encountering them. They function as reminders that something is amiss, and as such, they need to be taken seriously. Engaging with these figures, then, is necessary "out of a concern for *justice*" (Derrida 1994, p. 175, emphasis original), because inheriting the ghost always means to take on responsibility for a debt. Derrida emphasizes the ghost's status as *revenant*—as a figure that is constantly concerned with temporality: it belongs neither completely to the past, nor the present, nor the future. In Derrida's words, "*it begins by coming back*" (1994, p. 11, emphasis original). It is always already there and it entails both repetition and alterity. As such, it embodies a paradoxical relation to fundamental concepts such as 'time' and 'being' for the ghost itself has no fixed place or time, but constantly refers to its own deferral while at the same time referencing a concrete place and or time with its appearance.

As such, the ghosts are inherently figures of the 'in-between'—to use Homi K. Bhabha's term. In *The Location of Culture* (1994), Bhabha engages with the interconnections that ultimately make up any (post)colonial setting. He troubles the binary and linear conceptions of 'us' versus 'them.' He emphasizes those moments, where these categories break apart, where the boundaries become porous and the borders unrecognizable as spaces where something new can begin to emerge. In Bhabha's words, "[h]ybrid hyphenations emphasize the incommensurable elements—the stubborn chunks—as the basis of cultural identifications"; they are constantly renegotiated and "remaking the boundaries, exposing the limits of any claim to a singular [...] sign of difference" (Bhabha 1994, p. 313). He argues that these social differences "where difference is neither One nor the Other but *something else besides, in-between*—find their agency in a form of the 'future' where the past is not originally, where the present is not simply transitory. It is [...] an interstitial future, that emerges *in-between* the claims of the past and the needs of the present" (1994, p. 313, emphasis original). Both Derrida and Bhabha do not explicitly address the figure of the ghost here. But the ways in which ghost figures challenge conceptions of temporality and spatiality, the ways in which ghosts travel across borders and boundaries, automatically challenges binary constructions. They remain the 'stubborn chunks' that demand recognition of the 'in-between' spaces again and again.

In a novel like *Behold the Many*, the ghost figures play with these categories: where do they belong, which borders or boundaries do they cross, what do they hint at, whose fears do they express, what do they express that a character might not?

Seth and the Dis-*ease of Hawaiian Asian America*

This article highlights the ambiguous, paradoxical status and function of three ghost figures in *Behold the Many*: Seth's, Aki's, and Hosana's. Seth's ghost is the most troublesome of the whole book. Even in reviews, his appearance—although one of the most central characters driving the text—is often ignored. My guess is that this ghost is hard to place within common conceptions of ghost figures: he refers to concepts of a never ending past, guilt, or as a reference to a certain group's memory, but he does not fit entirely into one of these readings. Instead, he emphasizes the unruly and unmanageable aspects of a ghost figure. In this way, he defies attempts at conclusive readings. As already mentioned in the short over-view, Seth curses Anah and his brother for hurting him. During the birth of each of her children, Anah sees Seth, laughing at her and repeating his curse. While some of Anah's children die even during or shortly after their births, all of them have at least some kind of disability or disadvantage due to Seth's curse. This curse is, thus, at the center of the novel, driving the action towards it climactic ending. Uttered by Seth's ghost when Anah leaves the orphanage, it is also a curse that involves every aspect of Anah's life:

> Curse your life for leaving me. Your home is here, turn around, come back. Curse my love for you. How I loved you those many years, passing myself from sister to dying sister. [...] Curse the ground you walk on. [...] Curse the food you cook. [...] Die. Die soon. Curse your womb. [...] Curse what issues forth. [...] Curse the ones you love. [...] There is no light here, dark the tunnel through which we come. [...] I came to you whenever you called, through the dark tunnel, so cold, so scared, I came. [...] Why have you left me here? It is me. Seth. It is cold here, Anah. I want to go home, too. (Yamanaka 2006, p. 212f.)

Therefore, Seth's ghost is depicted as a personal one: his whole life and story is disconnected from the larger colonial setting. He appears as a fig-ure that is rather removed from the general story line. He does not func-tion as a direct critique of the colonial setting; he does not expose guilt. He is simply a boy who died from a tragic accident. But although his curse seems to be a personal revenge on Anah and denies her happiness, it is still linked to the larger community.

The curse enhances the *dis*-ease in Anah's new family. Her in-laws, of course, notice her bad luck and attribute it to her ethnic difference. Even before they get married, Ezroh's Aunty Tova very directly voices her doubts about this interracial marriage. Just as she complains about Japa-nese meals as smelling "horrible" and tasting "so primitive and ghastly" as if they were cooked with dirt in them (2006, p. 240), she also openly states her general attitude towards 'Orientals' as a backward race. Aunty Tova explicitly establishes a hierarchy of ethnic groups in Hawaii, counting the Portuguese among the dominant and well-established groups and denying this position to all 'Orientals.' Her justification indicates her self-serving racist attitudes. Interestingly, Aunty Tova is also the one to raise the possibility of Anah being cursed several times throughout the novel. Talking to her sister, Lydia, she claims to know: "'I tell you, Lydia somebody sure has a curse on her.' [...] 'And she has brought the bad luck here, I just know it. It is so clear that the girl is cursed. Do you think our nephew knows? How can he not know?'" (Yamanaka 2006, p. 248). With regards to her racist hatred being directed at Anah, Aunty Tova functions as the voice of Anah's new extended family and continuously makes Anah's life miserable and the rest of the family suspicious toward her. Because Aunty Tova is, in fact, right in her mad accusations as far as the curse is concerned, Anah is constantly troubled by the possibility that the others might reject her as a member of the family. This prohibits her from sharing her pain and fear about the curse with Ezroh.

Aunty Tova, thus, becomes the living embodiment of Seth's curse: embodying not only the personal disadvantages that Anah must suffer from in her new family, but also exposing the larger interracial conflicts that divide Hawaiian society. In this way, Seth not only haunts Anah's personal happiness but also the inter-ethnic community so typical of Hawaii. Anah's new family might appear at first glance as a happy adoption into an ethnically diverse union of Portuguese, Cape Verdean and Japanese Hawaiians, calling to mind the (tourist) image of Hawaii as an ethnic paradise (Bacchilega 2007, p. 5). However, *Behold the Many*, like Yamanaka's earlier novels, exposes this paradise as haunted by harsh inter-ethnic tensions.[3] Maybe—and this is also what Crystal Parikh argues in relation to the controversy surrounding *Blu's Hanging*—Yamanaka's novels "are interested in countering the exotic/erotic fantasy of Hawaii as Edenic space of escape by figuring the history of traumatic loss that such a fantasy disguises" (Parikh 2002, p. 201) and this is simply not selling well, probing uneasy questions. Parikh also argues that "Hawaii is itself a haunting figure of loss in the American experience" because "the U.S. is haunted [...] by its own imperial and military history" (2002, p. 213). However, I wish to emphasize the internal hauntings of this society and

---

3   For a detailed analysis of the different statuses of various ethnic groups and inter-ethnic conflicts, see Okamura's (2008) *Ethnicity and Inequality in Hawai'i*.

not focus on the ghost figure as simply resisting Western homogenizing tendencies.

This romanticized depiction of Hawaii also appears as a mirror of the Asian American community at large. Usually represented as a harmonious union of different Asian American subgroups, united in their struggles against white oppression, Yamanaka rather paints a picture that reveals internal divisions. Avery Gordon, although a sociologist, concentrates on the functions of haunting in *Ghostly Matters*. In her words, "a postmodern social formation is still haunted by the symptomatic traces of its productions and exclusions" (2004, p. 17). If this is applied to *Behold the Many*, its ghost figures are referents to the larger colonial history, to the interethnic conflicts that divide the Asian American community, and to the somewhat blinded discourse that Asian American Studies has engaged in in the last years. Gordon continues by arguing that to "write ghost stories implies that ghosts are real, that is to say, that they produce material effects" (2004, p. 17). The curse expresses the *dis*-ease that shapes Anah's life afterwards. Read as an allegorical reference to the controversy that surrounds Yamanaka's work in general, the curse functions as a haunting reminder of those aspects that seem unsolvable, a haunting of all offspring that is driven by the wish to 'go home, too'—to arrive at some kind of answer. Seth's curse demands responsibility: a responsibility to also address the haunting and controversial aspects within the field. Being written by a Japanese American, after a controversy over such an author's function within her own community, Seth and especially his curse, therefore serves as a challenge to Asian America from within.

So far, the ghosts—at least in the figure of Seth—seem to function as a way to critique the Asian American self-conception rather openly. The ghosts in the novel, however, also work as a kind of melodramatic gloss to cover the problems that they expose.

Feeling the Melodramatic Ghosts

According to Peter Brooks, being a mode of "excess," (1976, p. xi) the melodramatic mode is associated in general with strong pronunciation of emotions, moral polarization of good and bad, inflated expression, and breathtaking final scenes in which the good wins over the bad (1976, p. 11f.). This seems to suggest immutable value judgments in relation to all moral issues. Although melodrama surely is a mode of exaggeration and has been criticized for its triviality and theatricality, it "has always lent itself to stories of power struggles and to enactments of socio-cultural processes of marginalization or stratification" (Kelleter/Mayer 2007, p. 9). As Linda Williams argues in *Playing the Race Card*, melodrama is a highly popular mode in America for it

> has proven key to understanding the ways in which American mass culture 'talks to itself' about the relations between race and gender. It is through the Manichaean logic of good and evil and of victim and villain that melodrama recognizes virtue, expresses the inexpressible, and reconciles the irreconcilables of American culture. (Williams 2001, p. 299)

This sounds, again, as if the mode of melodrama lends itself to very direct criticism. However, melodrama has its very own, specific way of addressing controversial issues.

Linda Williams focuses on the use of the melodramatic mode in racial conflicts: both whites and blacks frequently use what she calls 'the race card.' So, it is most important to her to recognize any racialized melodrama and "the power of its ability to make us *feel* the aggrieved virtue of racial sufferers, whether as blacks or as whites" (2001, p. 309, my emphasis). With the emphasis of the word 'feel,' I wish to highlight the process in which melodrama works. Melodrama is not only in itself a strong pronunciation of emotions, as Brooks argues, it also creates and enhances emotions in the reader. As Kelleter and Mayer's edited volume *Melodrama* suggests, "the patterns of identification laid out in melodramatic texts are much more ambivalent than their often stereotypically constructed binary structures of evaluation would seem to suggest" (Kelleter/Mayer 2007, p. 12). And this ambivalence of identification also structures *Behold the Many*. Throughout the novel, the reader is constantly torn between different kinds of feelings towards the situation as a whole and characters in particular.

One example of this ambivalent and even paradoxical move is Aki, Anah's sister. In the beginning, the reader feels with her when she is sent away to the orphanage with her diagnosis of tuberculosis, knowing that she is going to die there. During the sisters' time at the orphanage, Aki becomes the troublemaker. Not only does she not obey the rules of the place, she also hurts her younger sister Leah by destroying Leah's hope of being taken home at some point in the future. While one can understand her frustration and empathizes with her grief, Aki begins to appear as somewhat mean-spirited. And, of course, Aki is right in her fear: both Leah and she die at the orphanage and turn into ghosts. Already Aki's death scene produces such torn feelings that shift from one line to the next:

> She took in a final breath, held it, then exhaled one last time. A single tear fell
> from her eye. Anah took her limp hand to her lips and kissed her sister's fingers.
> [...] Anah listened for the holy sister's footsteps, then quickly raised a small par-
> ing knife to cut a strand of Aki's hair. But Aki returned to struggle one last time
> against the threat of knife and the coming of death. She scratched at the air and
> then at Anah's face.
>
> 'Mentirosa,' she hissed at Anah in their father's Portuguese.
>
> And then she left, calling Anah with her last word:
>
> *Liar.*
>
> Her mouth was open, her eyes horrified and stunned. (Yamanaka 2006, p. 91)

The beginning of this quote fits well into the register of the melodramatic:
the typical death scene that is staged in the manner of a tableau, the pronunciation of emotions, the single tear of death, the kisses that seem to
ease the passing. But then, Aki returns one last time and the mood of the
scene changes. Gone is the idea of a peaceful, quiet death; instead, it is replaced by horror and fear. Aki's death no longer indicates a passing from
darkness to light, but rather a passing into an eternal greyness, an in-
between ghostly state. Her joyful passing is replaced by labored breathing,
bloody coughing, and tears. Aki's love for her older sister is darkened by
her anger and frustration because Anah could not keep her promises of finally taking the sisters home.

Not surprisingly, Aki's ghost embodies all of these feelings; and, in turn,
creates various feelings in the readers. This tragic figure remains at Anah's
side, haunting her until the end of the novel, literally hurting her again and
again. This is but one example where Aki's ghost appears in its full force:

> 'Behold the many, Anah.'
>
> But she did not.
>
> 'Mentirosa.'
>
> And for refusing to heed her command, Aki began scratching at Anah's arms, cat-
> like with thin, razored claws, translucent pink, a trinity of talons that pierced her
> flesh again and again, moving under her skin like a reckless trio of maggots. [...]
>
> Aki bit Anah's cheek as she wrangled with air. Aki had no form, she who laughed
> as she bit her sister's neck, back, belly, and then buttocks, leaving the mark of her
> purple teeth all over Anah's body. [...]
>
> And in her vicious, consciousless child's anger, Aki slashed the thin membrane
> over the orb of Anah's eyes, red and blue veins spider-webbing inside, filling her
> eyes with bloody tears. She sliced open the delicate skin of eyelids with the preci-
> sion of light, each cut intended for Anah to see no more what she did not want to
> see until the weight of skin and tears, blood and pus, sealed her eyes shut, blood
> issuing from every hole on her face.

'Behold, mentirosa,' she commanded.

But Anah could not. (Yamanaka 2006, p. 108f.)

The short, repetitive sentences, calling Anah to listen, see, and behold the many, reminding the reader once again of the typical breathless pitch of melodrama, finally turn into the extremely detailed and descriptive narration of violence. Having 'no form,' Aki holds unbelievable powers— especially due to her position in-between life and death, in-between the past and the present. She can cross these borders, but she is also locked in this in-between space. Aki becomes a haunting, frightful presence, but she remains Anah's beloved sister. This ghost figure allows for easier and more established readings than the figure of Seth, for example, with a psychoanalytical take as a figure that embodies Anah's guilty conscience for having survived without being able to protect her younger siblings. With this, Aki's ghost becomes a frightful presence, haunting her sister throughout her life. But she is confined to the spaces of the orphanage, only able to leave these towards the end of the novel, when Anah is about to die and allows all of the ghosts to come close to her again. Thus, Seth is the more puzzling figure. And yet, the way these scenes are being narrated draws a special focus on the ghost Aki. Not only is it hard to place her on either side of a good-bad dichotomy, but moreover, the general layout of the narrative mode establishes her as a figure that needs to be recognized in its full force.

The use of the melodramatic mode in general, and in Aki's character in particular, invites the readers to remain open and flexible in their feelings towards the happenings. *Behold the Many* can thus be read as an invitation to look at everything from various sides and not to identify too easily with the most obvious choice. The novel presents highly charged and emotional settings, and yet, it offers no easy way out of these dilemmas. Instead, it pronounces complexity and invites the readers to think for themselves. By moving its audience, melodrama can express the inexpressible and reconcile the irreconcilables of American culture, as Williams has it. Although this sounds as if melodrama would provide ready answers to unsolvable problems, this is, of course, not the case. Rather, as Kelleter and Mayer argue,

> whenever melodrama takes on ideological issues, it tends to interiorize, personalize, and excessively 'stylize' its subject matter. Thus, social and political issues are almost invariably transferred onto a level of representation where their enactment does not obviously threaten the existing social order. (Kelleter/Mayer 2007, p. 13)

This threat is even further removed by the use of fantastic elements, seemingly referring to any real background only via allegory. Accordingly, the novel does address the complicated situation on Hawaii and highlights the

internal conflicts between ethnic groups, but it does so in a way that focuses on one particular family and the haunting of one girl.

The Haunting Remains

The ending of the novel is also utterly melodramatic, via the ghost of Hosana. Hosana is Anah's and Ezroh's oldest daughter, who dies and becomes a ghost in order to take all the other lost souls home to God.

> The dark sky opens up with the first rays of this dawn. Anah sees Hosana in the
> threshold of that light, standing before her in a kind of indomitable radiance.
>
> 'Come,' she says to the many around them, 'I know the way home.'
>
> There is rustling in the flower and herb beds, a trembling in the trees, the sound of
> little feet, many feet running on the gravel road. She turns away from Anah and
> heads into the light, the children in the wind following her.
>
> […]
>
> Seth lingers in the shadows of a mountain apple tree. Anah stands up and walks
> toward him, he who never aged, little towheaded boy, the quiet one who followed
> Leah, then Aki, then her, a loyal friend who never complained, his calm but sad
> presence in her most agonizing and unbearable moments. An angry wraith who
> believed she had betrayed him. 'Seth, my friend and brother in marriage.' Anah
> holds out her hands to him.
>
> 'I want to hear and I want to be heard.'
>
> 'Love—is—sweet,' he says, not moving.
>
> 'Remember always, brother,' says a voice behind her. Anah turns. It is Ezroh, who
> falls to his knees before the little boy who fell from the big tree all those years
> ago. Seth walks toward him and places both hands on his brother's head. His eyes
> survey the panorama of the valley as if placing the horses in the pastures, the
> green hills, his childhood home, a father, a brother, and a once beloved friend in
> the sweep of his memory. When fades the light behind an errant cloud, so fades
> he. (Yamanaka 2006, p. 335ff.)

With only a few sentences, enhanced by the repeated quoting from scripture, Yamanaka creates an atmosphere of highly charged emotion and a
scene so rich in its stereotypical images of light and darkness that it appears almost involuntarily as part of a film or theater scene that absolutely
absorbs its viewer. This theatricality is furthered by the narrative representation of a tableau: the final scene of the novel is compositionally arranged;
the images described not only absorb the viewers but lure and force them to

envision the characters as if on stage. They appear as frozen for a moment, a visual representation of the emotional ending of the novel.[4]

In their final disappearance, the ghosts are taken home by one ghost that is not directly connected to the postcolonial history during which almost all the others came into being. This ending seemingly creates a Hawaii that is rid of its ghosts. Finally, everything and everyone is at peace. But only seemingly, because this is of course only the short ending to a novel that revolves around the most troublesome aspects of Hawaiian history and the internal (mis)representations of Asian America as part of an ethnic paradise. Thus, interestingly, the ghosts function as both a way to address problematical aspects and a way to gloss them over. I hesitate to do so un-questioningly, but the ending can be read as a possible healing for the community. Certainly, it leaves room for hope. And yet, the novel as well as its reader remains haunted by what has been tried to exclude. In Janice Radway's words, "being haunted draws us affectively, sometimes against our will and always a bit magically, into the structure of feeling of a reality we come to experience, not as cold knowledge, but as a transformative recognition" (Radway 2008, p. viii). For what remains after closing the novel is the haunting, the vivid images of the ghosts: of the curse, of Seth's and Aki's painful presence, and of the many ghosts who simply wish to go home. The reader becomes haunted by these images and is invited or maybe even forced to feel their presence.

I would like to end by coming back to the beginning and the controversy that haunts this novel. Yamanaka offers a way to address highly controversial aspects in her writing, without giving a final solution for these problems. Still, she manages to expose harsh living conditions and internal conflicts in a society that is often constructed as harmonious. Yamanaka uses fictionalized ghost figures that highlight the *dis*-ease on which the seemingly ethnic paradise Hawaii has been built and by which it is still haunted. And yet, the ghosts also expose the internal conflicts of the ethnic groups in this multiracial society, not only blaming a white American presence that tries to impose its culture and belief systems but facing the troubled conception of Hawaii's Asian American society. Read this way, the specters embody the *dis*-ease at the center of the field of Asian American Studies and its self-conception as a politically motivated discourse. The representation of an internally divided Asian American community as

---

4   This is following Brooks' analysis of the use of a tableau in melodramatic representations (1976, p. 36–48).

part of the Hawaiian society simply does not fit a black and white painting of a unified Asian America that resists an oppressive white dominance. Taken in their full complexity, the ghosts never resolve their own ambiguous position and function within this novel. They remain haunting presences, reminders of those unresolved questions that have driven the field of Asian American Studies since its very beginnings. Following Kathleen Brogan's approach, they refer to questions of identity, tradition, and origins, but they also help to re-think and especially re-*feel* what it means to be Asian American. They do not exist to solve the question, not to offer easy answers, but to at least address what might be troublesome or unresolved. For, in Derrida's words, specters "are always *there* […]. They give us to rethink the 'there'" (1994, p. 176, emphasis original).

Works Cited

Bacchilega, Cristina (2007): Legendary Hawai'i and the Politics of Place: Tradition, Translation, and Tourism. Philadelphia: University of Pennsylvania Press.

Bhabha, Homi K. (1994): The Location of Culture. London: Routledge.

Brogan, Kathleen (1998): Cultural Haunting: Ghosts and Ethnicity in Recent American Literature. Charlottesville: University Press of Virginia.

Brooks, Peter Preston (1976): The Melodramatic Imagination: Balzac, Henry James, Melodrama, and the Mode of Excess. New Haven, London: Yale University Press.

Chiang, Mark (2009): The Cultural Capital of Asian American Studies: Autonomy and Representation in the University. New York: New York University Press.

Chuh, Kandice (2003): Imagine Otherwise: On Asian Americanist Critique. Durham: Duke University Press.

Derrida, Jacques (1994): Specters of Marx: The State of the Debt, the Work of Mourning, and the New International. New York: Routledge.

Gordon, Avery F. (2004): Ghostly Matters: Haunting and the Sociological Imagination. Minneapolis: University of Minnesota Press.

Kelleter, Frank/Mayer, Ruth (2007): The Melodramatic Mode Revisited: An Introduction. In: Kelleter, Frank/Krah, Barbara/Mayer, Ruth (eds.): Melodrama! The Mode of Excess from Early America to Hollywood. Heidelberg: Winter, p. 7–17.

Nguyen, Viet Thanh (2002): Race and Resistance: Literature and Politics in Asian America. New York: Oxford University Press.

Okamura, Jonathan Y. (2008): Ethnicity and Inequality in Hawai'i. Philadelphia: Temple University Press.

Parikh, Crystal (2002): Blue Hawaii: Asian Hawaiian Cultural Production and Racial Melancholia. In: Journal of Asian American Studies 5, no. 3, p. 199–216.

Radway, Janice (2008): Foreword. In: Gordon, Avery F. (ed.): Ghostly Matters. Haunting and the Sociological Imagination (2. ed.). Minneapolis, London: University of Minnesota Press, p. vii–xiii.

Williams, Linda (2001): Playing the Race Card: Melodramas of Black and White From Uncle Tom to O.J. Simpson. Princeton: Princeton University Press.

Yamanaka, Lois-Ann (1997): Blu's Hanging. New York: Avon Books.

Yamanaka, Lois-Ann (2006): Behold the Many. New York: Picador.

Post-Ethnic Virtual Reality in William Gibson's *Burning Chrome*: Savage Hybrids Wandering Cyber-Borderlands

Aikaterini Delikonstantinidou

Introduction: Ethnicity and Post-ethnicity in Cyberspace

As the western world rode the crest of the neoliberal wave, William Gibson's fiction of the 1980s responded to the urgent shifts brought about by the new global order that came into being at the time. The emerging political and economic regime, hinging on the notion that "the economic world" of late capitalism is "a pure and perfect order" (Bourdieu 1998, p. 3) and attended by new social formations brought about by globalized capitalism, cannot be thought of separately from the technological revolutions that enabled, empowered, and sustained it. Novel information and communication technologies, more and more cyber-inflected, contributed instrumentally to the rise of a world "so fluidly interconnected" that "identitarian sedimentations organized in more or less stable historical groups (ethnicities, nations, classes)" had to "restructure themselves in the midst of interethnic, transclass, and transnational groupings" (García Canclini 1995, p. xxviii). Collective subjectivities and manners of subaltern identification based on ethnicity, *inter alia*, had to be radically reconceptualized and reconfigured if they were not to be rendered moot within the context of the neoliberalism and globalization.

Under these incipient conditions, ethnicity could no longer be considered as an unmediated, experiential given, or expressed in terms of individuality and separatism, with one ethnicity pitted against another. Rather, the new state of affairs sweeping across the globe precipitated a reading of ethnicity as a political, social, and cultural construct in constant dialogue and interaction with other histories and forms of connectedness. It also launched articulations of ethnicity in terms of cross- or trans-ethnic collectivism, association, or affiliation, traversing or transcending national borders; articulations of ethnicity anticipating the emergence of post-ethnicity. In light of these developments, then, the post-ethnic emerges as "a radical and necessary extension of the 'ethnic'" (Radhakrishnan 1987, p. 202). To put it more clearly, the terms and conditions of ethnic being, becoming, and belonging must be expressed and negotiated differently in a technology-saturated present where cyberculture impinges on every domain of the lifeworld.

Although often depicted as an environment where the most problematic "real world" social issues and phenomena do not apply as such, cyberspace does not constitute a *de facto* realm of escapism or a less problematic heterotopia. One cannot but consider the profound and, to some extent, covert connections between offline and online sociocultural representations of race and ethnicity. New digital technologies, generally, and new media, particularly, are unmistakably involved in practices of ethnic and post-ethnic profiling and othering. In various technological manifestations of the cyberspace—such as interactive media, virtual technologies, simulated art, cyber fiction and non-fiction—ethnicity, even as post-ethnicity, plays a determinative role when it comes to matters of inclusion and exclusion.

Not only is the cyberspace swarmed with negative figurations of (post)ethnicity, as well as with new "insiders" and "outsiders," but also it retains a white, western, male, privileged profile, despite current attempts at an inclusive and intensified cyberspace activity on the part of ethnoracial minorities. Questions including the so-called digital divide, the provision of computing resources to people in the Global South, racial ideologies, and technoscientific progressivism are not to be unproblematically brushed off. Even though the public conversation on cyberculture is often directed away from questions of race and ethnicity, we should recognize "the continued importance of looking carefully at 'the specific and ineluctable issue of representation in cross-ethnic situations' which arise out of postmodern paradigms," among which the cyber one is perhaps paramount (Sanders 2008, p. v). Specifically, we should pay attention to the reexamination of the notions of racial and ethnic difference "reinscribed as cultural diversity and pluralism," as well as to the "cultural commodification of Otherness" within the cyber context (2008, p. v). Gibson's *Burning Chrome* (1986a) will be examined precisely for the light it sheds on how post-ethnic identities and their alternative, border epistemologies are or can be articulated within cyberspace and cyber-inflected contemporary societies in (thought) provoking ways.

Post-(Cyber)Body Matters

The question of identity, (post)ethnic and otherwise, has become pervasive and urgent in critical discourses surrounding our new techno-reality. Many thinkers of cyberculture(s) have discussed the composability of identities within cyberspace and virtual reality in terms of transcendence of the material world, suggesting that, given the human-machine interface, identity needs to be reconceptualized as other than embodied. Indeed, the growing intimacy between human and machine in digital culture has generated speculations about the present state and the "fate of the body," that "resound throughout cyberculture" and post-humanist strands of thought (Dery 1996, p. 292). Yet, here, we suggest that the issue of individual and collective identities in cyberculture be approached in terms of prosthesis rather than transcendence, with identity reconceptualized not as "other than" embodied but as "more than" embodied; extended and enhanced.

The rendering of the body as a "hybrid/machinic assemblage of nature/culture/technology," and the attendant inability to maintain a strict binary opposition and fixed borders between wired corporeality and organic corporeality within techno-digital post-humanism[1] (Kennedy 2000, p. 473), compels us to "reassess the concept of embodiment" (Cavallaro 2000, p. xvi). However, it does not permit us to altogether abandon it. As Dani Cavallaro pointedly observes:

> immersion in the virtual environments produced by technoscience does not automatically amount to an experience of disembodiment, for it is grounded in ritual/ceremonial experiences of an eminently material nature. The body is extended by technology, as its sensory faculties are stretched beyond familiar territories, and at the same time it is humbled into a recognition of its limitations. (2000, p. 79)

The human body has fused with technology, crossing over to the domain of the hybrid. The interpenetration of the organic and the inorganic within it has fundamentally disrupted any sense of a seamless, stable, and bounded subjectivity, raising the need for imagining new modes of subjectivity. Identity itself has been foregrounded as contextual, fluid, permeable, and fragmented as the body in which it is anchored, or rather, from which it

---

1   'Post-humanism' is used here in the sense of a lived reality that necessitates radical redefinitions of the nature of humanity, insofar as it witnesses the increasing transformation of human bodies "into cyborged hybrids of technology and biology through our ever-more-frequent interactions with machines, or with one another *through* technological interface" (Dery 1993, p. 564).

derives. Nevertheless, neither the human body nor subjectivity, nor embodied identity have ceased to matter—at least not yet.

On Identity (and) Crisis

The four short stories from Gibson's *Burning Chrome* collection that will be examined in this paper, namely "Johnny Mnemonic" (1986c), "Burning Chrome" (1986b), "The Winter Market" (1986e), and "New Rose Hotel" (1986d), bear testament to the fact that technophilic bodies, however aesthetically and functionally transformed in terms of their surface, organic, and sensorial architecture, do not function in ways that produce convenient solutions to the difficult questions of embodied identity, whether individual or collective. Neither, in fact, does cyberspace: a late capitalist technoscape structured as a global information matrix and presenting itself as a virtual bodiless reality.

Gibson construes cyberspace as a collective "consensual hallucination" (1984, p. 51), existing in conjunction with an irreducibly material post-industrial urban ecosystem. It is a space "as permeable to disparate [political and] economic activities as any other geopolitical space" (Tomas 2000, p. 186). Moreover, Gibson constructs the technophilic bodies jacking into this cyberspace as extreme reconfigurations of the human realm, which, however, do not conclusively articulate cyborg identity in bodiless terms. In this sense, then, his cyberpunk imaginary, as exemplified by the *Burning Chrome* corpus, does not release its moorings into material, bodily reality. Gibson's cyberpunk stories do not wallow in solipsistic fantasies about the substitution of the physical self with a disembodied, virtual surrogate and of real-world communities and their "agonistic pluralism" (Mouffe 1993, p. 6) with a neutralized, virtual "nonspace" of consensus and synthesis (Gibson 1986b, p. 170). Instead, they repeatedly remind us of "the reality of our embodied and embedded existence in the real world, and of the ethical disposition necessary for coexistence to be possible in that world" (Robins 2000, p. 85). Any resistance or liberatory possibilities harbored by his fiction issue neither from a vision of social harmony, nor from a dystopic surrender to "the sensorial order of a collective cyberpsychic non-space," within which individual and group heterogeneity is cancelled via corporate-authored homogenization (Tomas 2000, p. 186). On the contrary, they derive from a compelling, embattled "future-is-now" vision that embraces crisis in the sense of interminable struggle between different orders of existence—and their constituent political and economic expediencies—within which Gibson's hybrids are caught.

With regard to (post)ethnicity, more particularly, *Burning Chrome* brings forth a form of savage hybridity, on the basis of Alberto Moreiras's (1999, p. 395) elaboration on Homi Bhabha's concept, precisely in as far as it involves a particular kind of deconstruction of 'pure' ethnic identity contingent on crisis. The said crisis emanates from the very "aporetic relationship between the negative presentation of the subaltern as such and the political need for hegemonic action," on which we will touch upon in later sections of this paper (Moreiras 1999, p. 393). In other words, the *Burning Chrome* stories that will be discussed spell out the idea of identity as always already hybridized, referring to a hybridity that becomes 'savage' in its reiterated relation to crisis, chaos, catastrophe; conditions that push against and rupture previously established borders, identitarian and other, to create transgressive zones as sites of emergent (alternative) cyborg collective identities.

Within this web of border-troubling transgressive zones constituting Gibson's "contestatory and disruptive" version of a cyborg culture, the body's social and cultural form is rewritten in ways directly related to a (potentially liberating) revision of social and, particularly, of post-ethnic identities (Tomas 2000, p. 177, p. 185). Indeed, the body is rewritten as a hybrid entity, a bio-techno-political compound that articulates both cultural diversity and cultural difference with (a) radical ambivalence placed at the crux of this articulation. It is in this sense, as we shall further see, that Gibson's cyber-inflected culturescapes can be said to be populated by savage hybrids: by technophilic bodies that articulate subaltern narratives of resistance and represent new subaltern positionalities with respect to dominant trans- or supranational culture, as well as a refusal to merge into static hybrids developed in hegemonic discourses.

Burning Chrome's *Hybrids*

One of the most representative short stories in the *Burning Chrome* collection, which exhibits radical reconfigurations of (post)ethnic identity composition due to profound cyborg transformations, in bodily reality and in conceptions/structures of collectivity, is "Johnny Mnemonic." Johnny's technophilic body is a product of both aesthetic and functional operations upon his body's surface and basic organic/sensorial constitution. His face has been cosmetically redesigned in the model of a 'normal' Sony Mao face—the visible index of belonging to a specific (sub)cultural collectivi-ty—so that Johnny can disguise his true identity as an eponymous data trafficker. His 'true' identity, however, involves his having a data storage system implanted in his head, rendering him the sophisticated extension of a hardware/software infrastructure. Literally "a very technical boy," John-ny has been enhanced by a "modified series of microsurgical contraautism prosthesis," allowing him to store digital data too sensitive to risk transmis-sion via computer networks (Gibson 1986c, p. 1, p. 9), yet without being aware of the contents of the data and without being able to retrieve them.

The other principal character in "Johnny Mnemonic" is the 'razorgirl,' Molly Millions, who is hired by Johnny as a bodyguard in order to protect him from the Yakuza assassin. She is also a cyborg, as she has undergone extensive functional modifications, including prosthetic additions and re-designed upgraded senses. Johnny, Molly, as well as the Yakuza assassin, a "factory custom" figure (1986c, p. 8), emerge as "customized functional products of a cyborg culture" (Tomas 2000, p. 178). This is a culture reg-imented and controlled by criminal supranational corporations, (in-ter)governmental agendas, and military projects, and one "that serves as a genetic context for the implosion and mutation of biological organisms, bio-technology and advanced information systems" (2000, p. 178). The same can be said to apply in the case of Jones, the cybernetically enhanced dolphin (and heroin addict), who helps Johnny and Molly retrieve the in-formation stored in the protagonist's head by means of the SQUID and other sensors implanted in his skull. Similar to the 'tribal' group of the Lo Teks, within whose dwellings Molly harbors Johnny, Jones unsettles defi-nitions of organisms in terms of species classifications, as he appears to interact and communicate with other cyborgs in an unmistakably—albeit technologically multimediated—humanly manner. Quite revealingly, the story's Lo Teks go as far as to celebrate the body "as trans-species hetero-topic site" (2000, p. 177) by extensively manipulating their body surface with technologies involving animal-like muscle grafts and the use of ani-mal transplants, such as fangs.

The massive intersections of information technologies and biotechnolo-gies upon and within the body, human and non-human, in "Johnny Mne-monic" challenge conventional conceptualizations of embodied identity. The body is not dematerialized but, inasmuch as its architecture is con-stantly de-assembled and re-assembled with organic and synthetic parts of various origins continually added and abstracted, it becomes thoroughly hybridized. This technologically derived hybridization has profound im-plications for ethnic identity, since it generates major transformations in the way characters conceive of their culture of origin, or, rather, of origins as such, as well as in the way they interact with and negotiate their place within cyborg cyberculture.

What Gibson's main characters in "Johnny Mnemonic" have in common with characters in both "Burning Chrome" and "The Winter Market" is that they all negotiate and adapt into the zones of shifting meanings across which they move, simultaneously upholding and resisting the latter's constituent structures of power, representation, and knowledge, through the very technologies of prosthetic and genetic enhancement they assimilate. More than that, aesthetic and functional manipulations of bodies create multiple signifying patterns and alternative body ecosystems that are used both for the conditional disassembling and reassembling of individual and social identities—sometimes at will and others in accordance with external pressures. Cyborg bodies, ephemeral, protean, and ambiguous, become the signifiers of hybrid subjectivities that challenge conventional assumptions about (post)ethnicity.

Jacked into the "crowed matrix" of cyberspace, "where the only stars are dense concentrations of information, and high above it all burn corporate galaxies and the cold spiral arms of military systems" (Gibson 1986b, p. 170), the characters of "Burning Chrome," the eponymous short story of the collection, take a step closer towards a dematerialized existence. They too, however, do not achieve a state of bodiless-ness. Instead of negating bodily reality, "Burning Chrome" rather dramatizes "the ambiguous character of the relationship between the body and technology" (Cavallaro 2000, p. 94). The story "highlights certain structural analogies between the physical organism and computer technology" (2000, p. 99), as in "Bobby's software and Jack's hard" (Gibson 1986b, p. 170), yet, it does not prioritize the latter to the former.

Notwithstanding the story's emphasis on Jack's prosthesis (his myoelectric arm) and on his sensorial relocation during his temporary absorption into cyberspace, the protagonist's corporeal self remains forestaged throughout, especially by way of thoughts and actions expressing his ambivalent relation to his prosthesis. The story further foregrounds the ambiguous character of the relationship between the body and technology by means of Rikki's character. Rikki has to sell her natural body for the dubious delight of "closet necrophiliacs" in order to purchase the "Zeiss Ikon Eyes" prosthetic adjunct that will allow her to edit her body and become a simulated simulation star (1986b, p. 183) that is, a virtual public persona who packages and transmits her fantasies for mass consumption. By means of her persona,

> 'Burning Chrome' typifies cyberpunk's paradoxical configuration of the body by simultaneously presenting the natural body as an incomplete entity, wholly dependent on the possibility of prosthetic enhancement, and highlighting the central role played by that body in the acquisition of the valuable prosthesis. (Cavallaro 2000, p. 99)

In effect, Jack, Rikki, and Bobby, no more than Chrome—an actual person metonymized as the database she owns and manages—are all occupying the space where material and virtual worlds meet; an evanescent borderland where, at times, they clash and collide.

The main characters' enhanced bodies become the bridge that connects the natural and the factitious, the sensory and the transcendental. Cyborgs in "Burning Chrome" have one foot planted in the material sediment of empirical objective reality and the other in the virtual architecture of cyberspace, and thus they upset the longstanding border between the two realms. At the same time, the non-materiality of cyberspace itself is undercut and its supposedly borderless internal state is belied by the fact that ICE can literally kill intruders traversing the virtual world and seeking to smuggle information. Indeed, the story fleshes out an extraordinary paradox that gets further accentuated by the short story of "The Winter Market," in which the *mise en oeuvre* of cyber-inflected technofetishism is evolving precisely because the residual resistance of materiality keeps it going through the very fact of resistance.

"The Winter Market" brings us even closer to the extremities of the technocultural hybridization of the human body. In fact, with "The Winter Market" we move all the way from the extensive technological enhancements and the temporary marginalization of bodies when "jacked in," in "Johnny Mnemonic" and "Burning Chrome," to a body thoroughly interfaced with hardware/software technology. Within this story, central aspects constituting "human-ness," such as memory, imagination, and the senses, are "relocated and rewritten through a wide variety of hardware-based software personality constructs" (Tomas 2000, p. 178). The rapidly degenerating state of Lise's, the protagonist's, organic body, partly due to her self-destructive massive drug abuse, results in the permanent donning of an exoskeleton that ultimately functions to "accentuate the character's bodiliness by mapping the body's inside on the outside, thereby *doubling* her materiality" (Cavallaro 2000, p. 97). At the same time, Lise's extreme desire to escape "hated flesh" results in a sharp foregrounding of her corporeality *via negativa* (Gibson 1986e, p. 139). The overlapping discourses on cybernetics, technologification, and disembodiment, on which the story rests, serve to render Lise's diseased, suffering body and her longing for human physical contact strikingly pronounced. More than that, the tragedy of not being able to feel another's touch, not even as a final act of self-corporeal affirmation before completely fusing with technology, under-mines the supposed liberatory possibilities that a merging with the net provides.

Eventually, Lise does become a bodiless cyborg, her disembodied con-sciousness accessible in marketable digital packages by "computer users longing to see their deepest fantasies embodied in visible shapes" (Cavallaro 2000, p. 98), while her rare ability to "dive down deep, down and out, out into Jung's sea, and bring back [...] dreams" (Gibson 1986e, p. 123) makes her a successful dream artist. However, Lise's post-human cyber-self remains clad in ambiguity until the very end of the story. Nei-ther dead nor alive, less dis-embodied than anti-embodied, and as such af-firming embodiment, Lise operates as the source of a strange tension be-tween agency *and* dehumanization, transcendence *and* decadence, opposi-tional *and* reactionary forces enmeshed with the commodification of every aspect of human existence, from fashion to body parts. In that respect, as we shall see further down, Lise can be said to emblematize savage hy-bridity as the site of a new subaltern consciousness: "a place for the desta-bilization of all ontopologies, for a critique of totality" (Moreiras 1999, p. 399). It is as savage hybrid that she dwells in an atopic site of ambiva-lence, at once transgressive and reticent, beyond identity and difference as conventionally conceived.

Complicating (Postmodern) Orientalism

Since its inception, cyberspace has been often presented, as we have seen, as "a transcendental signified, a grand unifying agent" (Cavallaro 2000, p. 30), which subsumes difference and dissolves the boundaries distin-guishing one collective—in our case, (post)ethnic—identity from another. Yet, differences between individuals and groups, differences inscribed in (post)human bodies, even when these are jacked-in, and manifest by their sociocultural groupings, complicate assumptions about the erasure of questions of ethnic identity in cyberspace. Whereas territorial identities cannot function in the conventional ways they do outside cyberspace, new ethnoracial hierarchies and new subalterns are constructed inside it, along new and old lines of conquest, thus reconfiguring ethnicity as post-ethnicity. Certain theorists and cultural critics have even talked about cy-berspace as a Brave New World; a world first explored by white male Euro American pioneers, the people who had and have the greatest access to the emergent cyberculture, as well as the means for acquiring the skills needed to fully participate in that culture. Indeed, cyberspace has been conceptualized "as some kind of electronic equivalent of the American West," and a "vista of a new frontier," predicated upon the "myth" of "white male Americans" as the quintessential colonizers (Chesher 1997, p. 82).

This old conquest *topos* is echoed in the *Burning Chrome* collection, particularly to the extent that Gibson's stories exhibit traces of an orientalized postmodernism, which can be also construed as postmodern orientalism. As we will see though, Gibson's visual and stylistic tropes in *Burning Chrome* may partially rely on eastern iconographies, typologies, and cultural narratives, yet they cannot be said to conclusively uphold the frontier between East and West, or American white supremacy for that matter. Gibson's nomadic hybrids can be approached neither as 'different,' nor as 'same'; they are neither conquerors nor conquered. Rather, they are strategically rendered both familiar and other, while their savage hybridity complicates the very notion of postmodern orientalism.

Gibson's cyberpunk stories invest in cultural transactions between West (notably America) and East (predominantly Japan). They contain many references to 'oriental' cultures and borrow heavily from their cultural lexicon. Expounding on cyberpunk's relation to orientalist discourses, Leonard Patrich Sanders argues that Gibson's cyberpunk "exhibits the characteristics of an orientalised postmodernism as it imagines a world in which multinational corporations characterized as Japanese *zaibatsu* control global economies, and the excess of accumulated garbage is figured in the trope of *gomi*[2]" (2008, p. ii). It is important to note that Gibson often refers to the characters that populate his stories as *gomi:* "things that fit some strange design […] Some of it still operative. Some of it, like Lise, human." (Gibson 1986e, p. 120). In effect, most of his characters are presented as people whose economic activities and very existence are dependent upon, if not parasitic on, omniscient military and supranational corporate or aristocratic formations (Tomas 2000, p. 184), like Yakuza—"the world's wealthiest criminal order" (Gibson 1986c, p. 8)—or the *zaibatsu.*

Moreover, according to Sanders, oriental postmodernism in Gibson's stories can also be thought of as postmodern orientalism[3] "in its nostalgic

---

2   'Gomi' is the Japanese word for 'junk.'
3   Postmodern orientalism can be described as a more recent variant of orientalism characterized "uneven, paradoxical, interconnected and mutually implicated cultural transactions at the threshold of East-West relations" (Sanders 2008, p. ii).

reconstruction of scenes from the residue of imperialism, its deployment of figures of 'cross-ethic representation' […] like the Eurasian, and its expressions of a purely fantasmatic experience of the Orient, as in the evocation of cyberspace" (2008, p. ii). For the scholar, Gibson's short stories reflect a vision of the Far East informed by imperial and colonial discourses, specifically by post-war, post-Vietnam American orientalism and techno-orientalism. Thus, they exhibit, however subtly, an insidious form of ethnic/racial stereotyping. His cyberpunk stories are interspersed with Japanese products (*gomi*), sites (Chiba City), cultural figures (ninjas, samurai warriors), and peoples (the Eurasian), despite the fact that, at least in the 1980s, the writer lacked first-hand experience of the culture to which he referred and which he imaginatively reconstructed. Within this context, Sanders raises several issues and addresses a number of textual instances which beg further discussion.

Interestingly, Sanders employs Gibson's "New Rose Hotel" short story as an illustrative example of Gibson's postmodern orientalism. The story, written in 1981, is primarily set in near-future Japan. It revolves around the activities of two corporate extraction agents, the unnamed narrator and Fox, who are betrayed by their female partner and the narrator's lover, Sandii, after a successful operation that would have secured the services of a valuable Japanese genetics scientist to the protagonists' employer, mega-corporation Hosaka. In view of Sander's analysis, Gibson's delineation of the figure of Sandii and of the story's eastern settings confers an orientalist import on the story, given that both are marked as ethnoracially 'other.'

Sandii, the "Eurasian, half gaijin," with the "dark European eyes" and "Asian cheekbones," clad in a Chinese-knockoff dress from Tokyo, is both exoticised and eroticized by means of the author's description and by the *femme fatale* function he ascribes to her in the story (Gibson 1986d, p. 104). She is constructed as the quintessential alluring, hyperse(x/)nsual, yet dangerous female and ethnic 'other.' At the same time, Morocco, and, specifically, the marketplace at Djemaa el Fna is presented in typical orientalist fashion as "thick with jugglers, dancers, storytellers, small boys turning lathes with their feet, legless beggars with wooden bowls under animated holograms advertising French software […] bales of raw wool and plastic tubs of Chinese microchips" (1986d, p. 108). Gibson offers us a vision of Marrakech as an exotic realm, manifesting vestiges of the 1960s counterculture and playing host to "the interfusion of crowds among a high technological bazaar representative of late capitalism" (Sanders 2008, p. 90). The character of Sandii, resonantly patterned on the

old oriental figure of the geisha; the exoticization of Marrakech; the dislo-
cation and depersonalization to which eastern places/spaces are subjected
contribute, in Sander's reading, to the construction of the Orient as an
"imaginative geography" (Said 1978, p. 58), cut to the measure of postmodern orientalist fantasies and desires. The same holds for the estrange-
ment and (self)alienation experienced by the protagonist in "the land of his
exile" that is the New Rose Hotel (Gibson 1986d, p. 109).

If the fictional character of Sandii is patterned upon the ethnoracial and
gender stereotype of the geisha, thus pointing to certain affinities between
Gibsonian cyberpunk and orientalist discourses, the Yakuza assassin and
Molly Millions of Gibson's "Johnny Mnemonic" draw directly from the
orientalist cultural imaginary, as they constitute updated versions of the
Japanese cultural figures of the ninja and the street samurai. Employed by
Japan's Yakuza crime syndicate, which resembles the *zaibatsu* industrial
conglomerates, the assassin partakes of the syndicate's "rituals and proto-
col designed to reinforce group identity, mostly derived from the samurai
ethos" (Sanders 2008, p. 212). The unnamed assassin with the amputated
left thumb that conceals a piece of sophisticated weaponry "amalgamates
aspects of Oriental otherness and Asian power," Sanders claims and goes
on to explain based on Gibson's text: he moves "like a man stepping from
a flat stone to another in an ornamental garden" (imagery conspicuously
deriving from Japanese culture); his keen sense of smell links him to the
ninja (from the Japanese *hinin*, 'not human'); he is described as a "tourist
tech," (Gibson 1986c, p. 17) in an explicit reference to the stereotypical
figure of the Japanese tourist; and when he dies, he does so with "the dignity of silence" in "a graceful curve," like a "diver," offering a compelling
image allusive of the kamikaze figure—the Japanese pilots on suicide
missions at the end of the Second World War (Sanders 2008, p. 213f.).
The Yakuza assassin thus plays into a modernized samurai warrior fantasy, which, according to Lisa Nakamura, permits one "to perform a notion
of the oriental warrior adopted from popular media," an "orientalized male
persona, complete with sword, [which] confirms the idea of the Asian man
as potent, antique, exotic, and anachronistic" (Nakamura 2002, p. 39); a
persona all too familiar.

Similarly, Molly, the Yakuza assassin's foe, is a figure who also draws
from the Japanese warrior tradition. The prosthetically enhanced agent and
cyborg street warrior explicitly refers to herself as a "street samurai" when
she first appears in Gibson's *Neuromancer* (Gibson 1984, p. 41). Molly,
through her identification as a samurai warrior, similarly to Sandii in her
resemblance to the geisha figure and Lise in her description as *gomi,* can

be said to partake of an orientalized version of the Japanese culture. Nevertheless, as we will argue further below, she, no less than Lise and Sandii, occupies, or rather embodies (however ambiguously) a space of undecidability from which she neither altogether subverts nor upholds gender and ethnoracial norms and dichotomies between western and eastern cultures. Rather, she displaces such dichotomies in a third space of post-ethnic subaltern experience that complicates the notion of postmodern orientalism.

The notion of postmodern orientalism is also dramatically complicated by the very existence and experience of cyberspace in Gibson's stories. The post-urban, post-industrial, even post-human world of Gibsonian cyberspace, in which heteroclite networks of data have replaced communities of the past and the virtual has prevailed as *the* scene of (de/re)territorialization, precipitates reconsideration of the aforementioned norms and dichotomies and, by extension, of our conventional assumptions about ethnicity.

His cyberspace constitutes both a rational space, "created and mediated by machines and mathematics," and a dreamland or otherworld, a fantasmatic space that is "irrational," as well as "mystical, performative, and cognitively dissonant" (Sanders 2008, p. 233). According to Sanders, cyberspace can be understood "as enabling/being enabled by Orientalism," inasmuch as Gibson has employed the representation of cyberspace "as a means of expressing or exploring the non-existence or purely mental, fantasmatic experience of 'the Orient'" (2008, p. 234). Further, in his view, Gibsonian cyberspace can be regarded as an example of postmodern orientalism, firstly, because "it exhibits the spaces and forces of multinational capitalism, as per Jameson's definition of postmodernism"; secondly, because "it developed from Asian cities, in terms of aesthetic and geographical influences on Gibson's imagination"; and, thirdly, because, "like the Orient, cyberspace is the space of fantasy" (2008, p. 234f.). The spatial metaphors Gibson mobilizes within his cyberpunk fiction, in order to help his readers make sense of the nonspace of cyberspace, allow readers to "create imagined geographies of the Internet and other dataspaces" (Kneale 1999, p. 207), which, as has been shown above, are in certain ways implicated in the "imaginative geographies" of orientalist discourse.

However, one finds it difficult to corroborate the argument that the stories of the *Burning Chrome* corpus seek "to orient the reader to a technologically-overloaded present/future (which is portrayed as belonging to the Japanese or other Far Eastern countries) through the promise of readable *difference*" (Chun 2002, p. 250). And this is because difference itself, as a concept with which one can cognitively map reality and as lived reality, is complicated and even radically revised in *Burning Chrome*. Thus, by implication, an imperialist/colonialist discourse predicated on difference, the kind of discourse orientalism sets up, is rendered highly problematic in the stories under consideration.

Difference is premised on a metaphysics of subjectivity and on a particular understanding of the subject; an understanding unsettled in Gibson's stories within which the subject is fundamentally reconfigured. The nomadic, hybrid subjectivity that Gibson's characters represent, "through its very undecidability *qua* hybrid, pre-empts the closure of any discursive position around either identity or difference" (Moreiras 1999, p. 396). Furthermore, although Gibson has bestowed certain distinctively Asian features to descriptions of the cyberspace and of the cyberspace experience in other works, the limited presence of such features in *Burning Chrome* makes it hard to sustain Sanders's argument that cyberspace "is most clearly signaled to be 'oriental' in nature" (2008, p. 263). Additionally, the absence of exploration rhetoric by Gibson when it comes to the narrativization of the cyberspace experience in *Burning Chrome* further undercuts the argument that cyberspace incorporates and offers an "otherized" virtual Orient to be explored, conquered, and possessed by both characters and readers.

Instead of narratives of the "other," an other which, either as space or subject, is marked by cultural, specifically ethnic, difference(s), Gibson's stories in *Burning Chrome* provide subaltern narratives of resistance, particularly through the major characters of the short stories already touched upon: resistance against co-optation by dominant power structures and the ideological discourses (such as orientalism) underpinning them, *and* resistance against extreme insularity, which threatens both individual and collective with an impending collapse at its very center—a possibility inherent in insular entities.

Savage Hybrids Negotiating (Hyper)Reality

Gibson's major characters, in the short stories we have discussed above, wander through a 'savage space,' at once outside and inside of culturescapes upon which hegemonic forces (corporations, governments, the military, and other) exercise their power. They are nomadic subjects, inhabiting diverse subject positions at once, simultaneously within and without dominant cultural structures: straddling virtual reality and material reality, working for and against corporate agendas, playing over and over against late capitalist commodification projects. Therefore, they allow for the conceptualization of plural, albeit fragmented, identities and of dispersed subjectivity bearing liberatory potential.

Gibson stages vertiginous transcultural negotiations between embodiment and disembodiment, virtual and material, diaspora and utopia, Occident(alism) and Orient(alism), and has his characters perform these negotiations as nomadic hybrids. Hybrids that exemplify an individualized, heterogeneous, and ambivalent difference that rejects all totalizing identity positions and that preserves the "outside" of post-ethnic alterity while, simultaneously, tactically embracing the "inside" of hegemony. In a manner surprisingly similar to that of theorist García Canclini, albeit, unlike him in fictional terms, Gibson subsumes hybridity within artifice, recognizing the omnipresence (although not absolute reign) of simulation, as he dystopically charts the impossibility of identity as pure ontology. His articulations of individual and collective identities—the subcultural cyborg identities of Lise, Johnny, Molly, the assassin, the Lo Teks, Automatic Jack, as well as Sandii—are premised on a deconstruction of an unadulterated essence. Rather than privileging individual and collective/communal "pure" identities, Gibson shifts his focus to post-urban, post-human, technology-inflected hybridization.

The heteroclite networks through which his nomadic hybrids wander, these transgressive borderzones formed at the interstices of hegemonic and subaltern, urban and cybernetic, communion and disruption, replace sociocultural communities of the past, displace traditional notions of ethnicity, call into question neoliberal notions of subjectivity and individuality, and foreground the effects of the constant disintegration of secured truths. His hybrids bear witness to, as well as perform themselves, the (up)mapping of cultural space in terms of a chaotic "renegotiation of the characters of knowledge, technology, economics and geographical landscape, where the chief organizing system is a virtual symbolic" (McCarthy 2006, p. 155). The hybridity that is thematized and dramatized in *Burning Chrome*'s short stories becomes "savage," as we have seen, precisely in its reiterated relation to crisis, chaos, catastrophe, and the virtual; it is a hybridity that "foments chaos in the fractal and random distribution of sites of cultural meaning that it promotes" (2006, p. 155). It manifests as a slippery object whose very impermanent, diasporic, and liminal nature allows for the imagining of a post-ethnic politics that would get beyond the dominant concern with identity and difference to focus, in an alternative manner, on social inequality and on possible ways of amending it.

In many ways, the radical transgressions Gibson's nomadic hybrids perform in the *Burning Chrome* stories correspond to Bhabha's "savage hybridity," which Alberto Moreiras defines the "the radicalization of the ret-icent version of cultural hybridity on the basis of its constitutive negativi-ty" (2001, p. 296). It is a hybridity defined along the lines of the notion of double articulation, which "turns a reticent understanding of cultural change into a principle of counterhegemonic praxis, and it places it at the service of the subaltern position in the constitution of the hegemonic sys-tem" (2001, p. 296). Gibson's hybrids traverse back and forth constantly the "frontier" between radical negativity and tactical positivity. They pre-serve a "residual outside" as "the other side of the popular," what can be conceived as the "negative articulation" of the subaltern, or that which is excluded from any (counter)hegemonic system of meaning (Williams 2002, p. 19), while they simultaneously engage in a tactical essentialism, occupying a provisional positive subject-position on the 'inside' of the labor of hegemony, or within the hegemonic game of knowledge and power; a tactical suspension of heterogeneity conducive to determinate identification.

The most representative instantiation of savage or nomadic post-ethnic hybridity based on double articulation that can be identified within the *Burning Chrome* corpus is Lise. Her character sheds lurid light on the fact that cyberculture is productive of new hierarchies and subalterns "peculiar to the global machinic apparatus" that "put into question territorial identi-ties [...] and all previous configurations of identity" (Poster 2002, p. 30). As we have seen, the main character of "The Winter Market" translates her self to a mainframe computer in order to escape from a body that con-demns her to a liminal existence, to a *gomi* status, by manipulating the high technology that initially trapped her in the exoskeleton. As a posthu-man, she exploits and at the same time is exploited by the structures of disempowerment and commodification that first marginalized her and then de-humanized her, fully conscious of the implications.

She chooses to be rendered marketable and essentially "other," her in-dividual consciousness subsumed by the collective consciousness of the matrix, and as such she remains within the hegemonic relations that har-ness her consciousness and profit from it. At the same time, as irreducibly heterogeneous and abject, she performs a negation of the game of power and knowledge that sustains hegemony, actively resisting what destroys her (Moreiras 1999, p. 399), and as such she challenges hegemonic rela-tions. In the end of the story, Lise's digitalized self occupies a new subal-ternity as the site, "not just *of* negated identity, but also *for* a constant ne-gation of identity positions" (1999, p. 377). As a post-ethnic, subaltern subject, Lise provides an alternative instrumentalization of self that is re-sistant to the dominant rational(izing) order. She becomes that which is left outside of hegemonic cultural relations, *and* that which tactically presents itself as essentially other in the terms that hegemony posits. As savage hybrid, Lise occupies both 'positions' simultaneously and distinctly.

In their radically ambivalent relation to the hegemonic forces that govern the culturescapes within which they wander, other major characters also exhibit this savage hybridity as cultural diversity and cultural difference. In "Johnny Mnemonic," we witnessed Johnny, Molly, and the Lo Teks operating in "the abyssal yet constitutive locus of the 'in-between'" (Syrotinski 2007, p. 37): in-between dominant culture and sub-culture, hegemonic structures and liminal (infra)structures, human and posthuman, even trans-species, identities. The story's hybrids exemplify savage hybridity in as far as they constitute radically split subjects, neither grounded in a synergistic nor in an antagonistic relation to hegemonic domination, but materially and socially ungrounded "vis-à-vis any conceivable operation of state or social regime constitution" (Moreiras 1999, p. 396).

The same can be said to be true for Automatic Jack in "Burning Chrome," insofar as he both dwells in and transgresses dominant power structures, namely, transnational information economies and their (il)legal matrixial branches in their own terms (jacking into cyberspace, hacking information); terms that, ultimately become his own. By jacking into simulated stimulation rigs and cyberspace decks, by becoming "uprooted from a fixed location and projected on to constant interfaces with other bodies and sensoria, with other data bases, memory banks, and information systems" (Suárez 2000, p. 183). Jack exemplifies a deterritorialized, indeed nomadic, body, subject, and identity.

Similarly, Sandii in "the New Rose Hotel," albeit neither a cyborg nor a body jacked in cyberspace, is constructed as a transitional figure, embodying a nomadic identity that is "contradictory, partial, and strategic" (Haraway 1999, p. 276). A transcultural reconfiguration of the female subject as a plural self immune to state, national, sociocultural particularisms and yet manipulating them to her personal advantage, Sandii exhibits nomadic hybridity in the terms set by Moreiras. Her past(s) is as mutable as the identity/ies she wears like garments; her identities are fluid, undetermined, contextual and positional; her embodied self constitutes a site at once ethnically marked and post-ethnically allowing the coexistence of multiple allegiances that vie with each other. Sandii is as elusive to the hegemonic forces trying to control her as to her heartbroken lover.

Gibson's characters represent hybrid subjectivity at its limit; that is, occupying the "diasporic ground or abyssal foundation" of savage hybridity as one that does not sometimes allow for identity and sometimes for difference but rather simultaneously undermines both identitarian and differential positions, which are driven into aporia. It is therefore not a place for subjective conciliation [...] On the contrary, it points to the conditions of possibility for the constitution of the socio-political subject as at the same time conditions of impossibility: because the subject, through its constitutive, hybrid undecidability, is always already split. (Moreiras 1999, p. 396)

His characters embody "edge identities" subject to dual articulations of identity and difference, upon a patchwork of intersections and fractal expressions of subaltern subjectivity (Bersten 2004, p. 12). These edge identities are not simple hybrids along a single axis; rather, they exist in the spaces between categories, where diverse axes intersect, to paraphrase Roxanne Bersten's words (2004, p. 12). In that respect they instantiate a movement beyond collective subjectivities/institutions, such as ethnicity, and their residual resistance, and towards a rhizomatic network of alternative, fundamentally interrelated collectivities allowing for subversive political engagement.

Towards a Politics of Transfigurative Subversion

Savage hybridity mobilizes a "politics of transfiguration," a politics "emphasizing the emergence of qualitatively new needs and modes of association that burst open the utopian possibilities of existing society" (Gilroy 1993, p. 37), and "in which accepted notions of language, history, the real, and the possible are thrown open to question and found wanting" (Benhabib 2003, p. xxvi; Lock 1999, p. 2). Its implications in view of our discussion so far are worth considering.

In its preservation of a savage outside and its appeal to an "otherwise" understood as the negation of what hegemony negates, such a politics of transfiguration enables the "*affirmative* site of subaltern politics, which thus appears as a site beyond hegemony: the non-site that [...] affirms the radical ambivalence of historical subjectivation and drives any politics of fulfillment against their own limit" (Moreiras 1999, p. 403). Indeed, within the context offered by Moreiras, hybridity thinking is no longer circumscribed to the terrain of a politics of the subject that limits both its theoretical and practical effectiveness (allowing hybridity to be co-opted by the forces of hegemony). Instead, it "allows space for a new understanding" (1999, p. 396) beyond ideological reappropriation or domestication and beyond "Jacobin dreams of revolutionary terror" (1999, 394). As the theorist construes it, savage hybridity is the very site of the aporetic relationship that emerges when a system of difference(s) lacks a systemic or foundational ground that would give it a principle of constitution, and thus becomes "a ground that does not ground, a principle of reason upon the abyss" (Moreiras 1999, p. 398). It is this political ir-resolution on which savage hybridity dwells and in doing that it embraces "a remainder within and beyond all hegemonic closures" (1999, p. 398). This remainder or reserve "is beyond all difference and all identity, and it is at the same time the condition of (im)possibility of both" (1999, p. 398f.), and of a politics resting on the latter.

By interweaving in his futuristic vision the strand of savage hybridity, Gibson has his post-ethnic savage hybrids enact a transfigurative politics, which, with its attendant commitment to the process of constant renewal, brings into being new vocabularies and vantage points whence to reimagine dominant models of being. Thus, he not only presents to his readers "a figure of the need to preserve, critically speaking, the excessive outside of subalternity," but also provides novel ways of radicalizing subaltern resistance "against the terror of dominant identities more effectively" within the larger commitment to social justice (1999, p. 373). It is in this regard, then, that we might consider his vision as permeated by a dynamic subversive in its operation. This is a dynamic that makes possible the imagining, articulation, and enactment of ways to counteract the hegemony of global capitalism and neoliberalism; a dynamic that carries the promise of emancipation outside of the confines of identitarian politics, within which identity is open to commodification.

Conclusion; or Savagely Hybridizing the Reader

In resetting the parameters of hybridization by means of his vision of a 'then and there' post-ethnic, hybrid cultural space/state, within which new contestatory and disruptive forms of integration and heterogeneity emerge, Gibson's stories tranformatively impact on the 'here and now.' The writer's reconfigurations of difference(s) among individuals and collectivities evolve in a spirit of continuity and of a break with the past. They operate to fundamentally dissolve conventional notions of corporeality and embodied identity, as well as inaugurate novel forms of intersubjectivity and alternative forms of figuring social cohesion. They do so without subsuming diversity into identity and interpolating alterity into ulterior sameness, and without utopically exaggerating the liberatory potential of permeable boundaries, fragmented identities, and the loss of unitary subjectivity.

Gibson has his savage/nomadic hybrids perform an attempt to navigate through both humanist values and post-humanist visions, in order to offer readers a glimpse of new ways to cope with a (hyper)reality that changes faster than people can rearrange their thinking patterns, attitudes, and values. He has strategically inscribed in his texts partial affinities with antagonistic, even incompatible discourses in, what can be read as, an effort to move the reader (herself a post-ethnic subject) beyond categorical gridding altogether; to lend her a critical lens with which she can recognize his savage hybrids as part of culture and as agents of change within it. Infinitely adaptable, his savage hybrids become subversion embodied and while in his stories allow the reader to partake of that subversion.

In his stories we become the savage hybrid: the undecideable, the perpetual, and the plural. As such we can counteract the imposing of a segregative binary logic and of closure and enjoy, instead, an irreversibly open system providing infinite degrees of freedom. We learn to move through a variety of strategies to negotiate spaces and states of being while oppressive systems continue to demand conformity. We consider tactical alliances for the formation of networks of resistance opening potential escape routes that may eventually render even these alliances unnecessary. Ultimately, we are both encouraged and enabled to envisage a move beyond all kinds of limits and an embrace of life in a chaotic vortex.

Works Cited

Benhabib, Seyla (2003): The Reluctant Modernism of Hannah Arendt (2 ed. ed.). Lanham, Md: Rowman & Littlefield.

Bersten, Rosanne (2004): Marginalia Edge Identities and Virtual Communities. RMIT University of Melbourne, Melbourne: Dissertation.

Bourdieu, Pierre (1998): Utopia of Endless Exploitation: The Essence of Neoliberalism, 22/1/2014.

Cavallaro, Dani (2000): Cyberpunk and Cyberculture: Science Fiction and the Work of William Gibson. London: Athlone.

Chesher, Chris (1997): The ontology of digital domains. In: Holmes, David (ed.): Virtual Politics. Identity and Community in Cyberspace. London: Sage, p. 79–92.

Chun, Wendy Hui Kyong (2002): Othering Space. In: Mirzoeff, Nicholas (ed.): The Visual Culture Reader (2. ed.). London: Routledge, p. 243–254.

Dery, Mark (1996): Escape Velocity: Cyberculture at the End of the Century. New York: Grove Press.

García Canclini, Néstor (1995): Hybrid Cultures: Strategies for Entering and Leaving Modernity. Minneapolis: University of Minnesota Press.

Gibson, William (1984): Neuromancer. New York, NY: Ace Books.

Gibson, William (ed.): (1986a). Burning Chrome. New York: Ace Books.

Gibson, William (1986b): Burning Chrome. In: Gibson, William (ed.): Burning Chrome. New York: Ace Books, p. 168–191.

Gibson, William (1986c): Johnny Mnemonic. In: Gibson, William (ed.): Burning Chrome. New York: Ace Books, p. 1–22.

Gibson, William (1986d): The New Rose Hotel. In: Gibson, William (ed.): Burning Chrome. New York: Ace Books, p. 103–116.

Gibson, William (1986e): The Winter Market. In: Gibson, William (ed.): Burning Chrome. New York: Ace Books, p. 117–141.

Gilroy, Paul (1993): The Black Atlantic: Modernity and Double Consciousness. Cambridge: Harvard University Press.

Haraway, Donna (1999): A Cyborg Manifesto. In: During, Simon (ed.): The Cultural Studies Reader (2. ed.). London: Routledge, p. 271–291.

Kennedy, Barbara M. (2000): Introduction. In: Kennedy, Barbara M./Bell, David (eds.): The Cybercultures Reader. London: Routledge, p. 471–476.

Kneale, James (1999): The Virtual Realities of Technology and Fiction: Reading William Gibson's Cyberspace. In: Crang, Mike/Crang, Phil/May, Jon (eds.): Virtual Geographies. Bodies, Space, and Relations. London: Routledge, p. 205–221.

Lock, Graham (1999): Blutopia: Visions of the Future and Revisions of the Past in the Work of Sun Ra, Duke Ellington, and Anthony Braxton. Durham: Duke University Press.

McCarthy, Bridie (2006): At the Limits: Postcolonial and Hyperreal Translations of Australian Poetry. Deakin University: Dissertation.

Moreiras, Alberto (1999): Hybridity and Double Consciousness. In: Cultural Studies 13, no. 3, p. 373–407, DOI:10.1080/095023899335149.

Moreiras, Alberto (2001): The exhaustion of difference: The Politics of Latin American Cultural Studies. Durham, NC: Duke University Press.

Mouffe, Chantal (1993): The Return of the Political. London: Verso.

Nakamura, Lisa (2002): Cybertypes: Race, Ethnicity and Identity on the Internet. New York: Routledge.

Poster, Mark (2002): High-Tech Frankenstein, or Heidegger Meets Stelarc. In: Zylinska, Joanna (ed.): The Cyborg Experiments. The Extensions of the Body in the Media Age. London: Continuum, p. 15–32.

Radhakrishnan, R. (1987): Ethnic Identity and Post-Structuralist Differance. In: Cultural Critique 6, p. 199–220, DOI:10.2307/1354262.

Robins, Kevin (2000): Cyberspace and the World We Live In. In: Kennedy, Barbara M./Bell, David (eds.): The Cybercultures Reader. London: Routledge, p. 77–95.

Said, Edward (1978): Orientalism. Harmondsworth: Penguin.

Sanders, Leonard Patrick (2008): Postmodern Orientalism: William Gibson, Cyberpunk and Japan. Massey University Albany, New Zealand: Dissertation.

Suárez, Juan A. (2000): Exotica in Cyberspace: The Geographies of Hybridity in William Gibson's Neuromancer. In: Santaolalla, Isabel (ed.): "New" Exoticisms:. Changing Patterns in the Construction of Otherness. Amsterdam: Rodopi, p. 177–196.

Syrotinski, Michael (2007): Deconstruction and the Postcolonial: At the Limits of Theory. Liverpool: Liverpool University Press.

Tomas, David (2000): The Technophilic Body: On Technicity in William Gibson's Cyborg Culture. In: Kennedy, Barbara M./Bell, David (eds.): The Cybercultures Reader. London: Routledge, p. 175–189.

Williams, Gareth (2002): The Other Side of the Popular: Neoliberalism and Subalternity in Latin America. Durham: Duke University Press.

Crossing the Boundaries of Decency? *12 Years a Slave* and the Pornography of Pain

Page R. Laws

> For there are some things that distress us when we see them in reality, but the most accurate representations of these same things we view with pleasure—as, for example, the forms of the most despised animals and of corpses.[1]

> Only more obscene than the brutality unleashed at the whipping post is the demand that this suffering be materialized and evidenced by the display of the tortured body or endless recitations of the ghastly and the terrible. In light of this, how does one give expression to these outrages without exacerbating the indifference to suffering that is the consequence of the benumbing spectacle or contend with the narcissistic identification that obliterates the other or the prurience that too often is the response to such displays?[2]

Spectator theory—the concern for the soul of the audience witnessing and aesthetically 'enjoying' horrible scenes in a work of art—is as old as Aristotle's *Poetics,* and as new as the critical reactions to the 2013 Academy Award-winning Best Picture *12 Years a Slave* (directed by British *auteur* Steve McQueen) or Barry Jenkins' gut-wrenching TV adaptation of Colson Whitehead's *The Underground Railroad* (2021). The paradox inherent in movie-goers' paying steep ticket prices to see the feigned rape, torture, and bloody flaying of Patsey (Yale School of Drama-trained actress Lupita Nyong'o) was perhaps only increased by seeing her 'heal up' fast enough to wear gorgeous designer gowns to the awards shows and be declared by *People Magazine* 'The Most Beautiful Woman in the World' (Jordan/Coulton 2014). Though Nyong'o and McQueen certainly deserve their respective acting and directing accolades, and though I certainly understand that no actor was really harmed in the making of this film, the problem of sadism and erotic exploitation is virtually built into the slave narrative genre in both its written and cinematic form. This is, in fact, the second film adaptation of Solomon Northup's hard-hitting 1853 slave narrative, the first adaptation—*Solomon Northup's Odyssey*—having been di-

---

1   Aristotle/Hardison/Golden (1968, p. 7).
2   Hartman (1997, p. 4).

rected for television's American Playhouse by famous African American photographer and director Gordon Parks. It was broadcast in 1984.

Even for an as-told-to tale, Northup's narrative comes to us through an exceptionally complex series of possibly adulterating filters. It was originally told by Northup after his rescue to a white lawyer named David Wilson who wrote it in what we suspect to be Wilson's rather than Northup's own style. Wilson's style has been denigrated as full of "stale, genteel diction and images" (Worley 1997, p. 243). But, even in the eyes of the previously quoted Sam Worley, the book deserves attention because of its "amazing attention to empirical detail and unwillingness to reduce the complexity of Northup's experience to a stark moral allegory" (1997, p. 244). Wilson and Northup dedicated their book to Harriett Beecher Stowe, author of the most famous fictionalized slave narrative, *Uncle Tom's Cabin,* so her godmotherly presence likewise infuses and filters the narrative.

Gordon Parks' screenwriters were Lou Potter and Samm-Art Williams. Parks' Solomon was played by the charismatic, exceptionally virile Avery Brooks in a performance that, as Chad Williams has pointed out, very much reflects the actor and the director's activist aesthetic as shaped by the 1960s and 70s (cf. Williams 2014, p. 16ff.). Parks somewhat de-emphasizes the violence in the story, perhaps because it was destined for a 1980s TV audience.

With no such compunctions, McQueen and his screenwriter John Ridley go back to the original book and decide to fully articulate—one might even say accentuate—its violence by their interpretation of certain key scenes and their interpolation of others. They also cast as Northup an actor with a more introspective persona—Chiwetel Ejiofor—who, at age 19, played a role in Spielberg's *Amistad* (1997). Ejiofor's rather passive performance traps us right alongside him in a state of mostly helpless victimization and forced spectatorship/voyeurism. These decisions on Ridley and McQueen's parts make it especially important to consider the risk of the film's becoming, at moments, unintentionally pornographic. As critic Karen Halttunen has written about certain sentimental works of 18th-century literature and art, "There seems to be a very thin line separating spectatorial sympathy for the established culture from the sadistic gaze of the pornographic [...] It is a very small step from sentimental spectatorship to sadistic pleasures" (qtd. in Klarer 2005, p. 580). Scholars of the Holocaust have likewise been long aware of this problem of 'decently' depicting the indecency of mass murder, with a number of essays having been inspired by the 1993 opening of the National Holocaust Museum in Washington, DC.

This paper considers McQueen's film as a work reflecting recent cinematic and cultural aesthetics, but to do so one must discuss the source book and its place among slave narratives—especially Frederick Douglass' *Narrative of the Life of a Slave* (1845) and Stowe's *Uncle Tom's Cabin* (1851). I shall briefly discuss Gordon Parks' much milder TV adaptation and situate McQueen's film among its other important TV and cinematic forebears, especially *Roots* and its sequels (1977, 1979, 1988, 2016), *Amistad* (1997), and *Beloved* (1998), plus the ludic takes on slavery in Rainer Werner Fassbinder's *Whity* (1971) and Quentin Tarantino's *Django Unchained* (2012). In a close reading of three key violent scenes in *12 Years a Slave,* the focus will shift to 'shifting focus' itself, one of McQueen and cinematographer Sean Bobbitt's signature moves in key scenes. Their often ironic use of sharper and blurred focus within a given shot, along with their penchant for head and bust 'cut-off' close-ups keeps us feeling utterly trapped, right along with their focal character Northup, within the frame with whatever horror we are witnessing.

Ironically, the public was also introduced to McQueen's film via a controversy not of the director's making but also involving who or what the movie's 'true focus' or center is supposed to be. Rothman of *Time.com* reported on January 2, 2014, that in Italy posters were issued that placed either Brad Pitt or Michael Fassbender (both white, of course) in the center of the poster frame, and placed Chewitel Ejiofor (the film's actual Black lead) in a smaller image over to the side. The Italian distributer BiM's racialist redaction of the film's content was fortunately exposed, and an apology issued.

A 'Second-Rank Slave Narrative'?[3] The Literary Merits of Northup's Book

> The passage through the blood-stained gate is an inaugural moment in the formation of the enslaved. In this regard, it is a primal scene.[4]

In the epigraph just above, Saidiya Hartman, (whose theory infuses this article), is referring to the beating of Aunt Hester as a formative moment for the very young Frederick Douglass' in *Narrative of the Life of a Slave.* Sam Worley has pointed out salient differences between Douglass and

---

3   Sam Worley uses this expression in "Solomon Northup and the Sly Philosophy of the Slave Pen" (1997), but mostly to be provocative. He goes on to praise the book.

4   Hartman (1997, p. 3).

Northup's narratives: "Douglass works to create his own identity; Northup must be brutally trained to deny his" (1997, p. 244).

Douglass' *Narrative* is an Enlightenment tract appealing to righteous people's reason, while Stowe's *Uncle Tom's Cabin* aims right at their hearts. Marianne Noble entitles her article on the subject, "The Ecstasies of Sentimental Wounding in *Uncle Tom's Cabin*" (1997). Though Noble sees Stowe as shifting the gender of the brutalized Black body from female to male, the problem of eroticism is by no means reduced. Now the slave's suffering becomes 'tainted' (my word) by masochism, and we, as witnesses, are concomitantly tainted by sadism. Noble's term, "sentimental wounding," refers to "a rhetorical effect [in which a] bodily experience of anguish [is] caused by identification with the pain of another" (1997, p. 295) Noble cogently describes the "trap" into which "the sentimental wound" can lead us:

> [T]he effort to provoke in readers [and, in this case, viewers] an experience of intersubjective connectedness at the level of the body has the unanticipated effect of eroticizing the reading [viewing] experience, and in so doing, it undermined its own effort to humanize the slaves, who were positioned as erotic objects of sympathy rather than subjects in their own right. (1997, p. 296)

Noble even summons Sigmund Freud to corroborate her claim clinically. In "A Child is Being Beaten," Freud claimed that "many patients used *Uncle Tom's Cabin* for 'onanistic gratification'" (1997, p. 296). One hopes they locked their library doors for privacy.

It is difficult to imagine Solomon Northup's book, *12 Years a Slave,* being used for similar pornographic purposes, mostly because of its formal, rather distant tone. While it is impossible to separate Northup and his 'white amanuensis' David Wilson, one does come to trust that Wilson is being fairly true to Northup (in contrast, say, to the white official who took down the original *Confessions of Nat Turner* from Turner himself in jail).

For instance, Northup and Wilson begin their narrative with what will soon be understood as a characteristic tone of caution and veneration for eyewitness detail: "I can speak of slavery only so far as it came under my own observation—only so far as I have known and experienced it in my own person" (Northup 1853/2013, p. 15). This establishes the vital premise that we are hearing testimony from a careful, competent eyewitness. Northup and Wilson then go on to give the backstory of the Northup family, acknowledging, right from the start, the good deeds of Henry B. Northup, Solomon's white benefactor and eventual rescuer. Solomon's pride in his own father's role as an independent Black farmer (once he was manumitted by Henry Northup's father) comes through quite clearly.

Solomon seems to have limited but affectionate recollections of his mixed-race mother (Black, white and Indian). More space is given to his own career as a repairer of canals and transporter of lumber. Northup (with co-author Wilson hereafter understood) refers to this experience as something that will later "astonish the simple-witted lumbermen on the banks of the Bayou Boeuf" (Northup 1853/2013, p. 17). The note of condescension is unmistakable. Solomon speaks with confidence of his prowess on the violin but is also honest enough to admit that moving his family to Saratoga Springs was probably a mistake. He says his own habits started "tending to shiftlessness and extravagance" (1853/2013, p. 18). Neither adaptation mentions this surprising confession. On the contrary, screenwriter Ridley and director McQueen make Northup's life in Saratoga Springs seem an unlikely idyll of middle-class comfort and respectability.

In the original book, Solomon has three children on whom he dotes: "Their presence," says Northup, "was my delight; and I clasped them to my bosom with as warm and tender love as if their clouded skins had been as white as snow" (1853/2013, p. 19). One is reminded of William Blake's poem "The Little Black Boy," in which a Black mother promises her son that God will make him white up in Heaven. Both utterances are clearly from a white perspective. Perhaps we are hearing from Wilson, white amanuensis, rather than Northup. It is more difficult to distinguish which man is the source of the keen, even dripping irony in the following passage where Northup is being spirited away from Washington DC at the beginning of his captivity:

> So we passed, hand-cuffed in silence, through the streets of Washington through the Capital of a nation whose theory of government, we are told, rests on the foundation of man's inalienable right to life, LIBERTY, and the pursuit of happiness! Hail! Columbia, happy land, indeed. (1853/2013, p. 32)

Ridley and McQueen recognize this prize passage and adapt it cinematically by a slow zoom out from the window of the secret slave-holding pen where Solomon is confined and has received his first brutal beating for insisting on his proper name and identity. That shot is followed by a crawling pan up the exterior wall and then, finally, by a scene-culminating shot of the Capitol building, still under construction, on the close horizon. Both adaptation teams likewise choose to include Northup's disgust at first seeing his fellow Blacks—untrained in the social graces he has enjoyed—eating a meal. "The use of plates was dispensed with and their sable fingers took the place of knives and forks" (1853/2013, p. 37), writes the original Northup.

The 1853 source book contains praise of Northup's white patrons—both in the North and the South—that neither film director can bear to include. Says Northup, for instance, in the original, about Master Ford, "Were all men such as he, slavery would be deprived of more than half its bitterness" (1853/2013, p. 47). He continues, even speaking of the "bright side of slavery" (1853/2013, p. 53). Northup says of Ford that he could have "borne his gentle servitude, without murmuring, all my days" (1853/2013, p. 53). This sentiment is unpalatable to a post-Civil Rights Movement film audience, be it 1984 or 2013. And yet it is true to the spirit of the 19th century and both films' common source: the book.

As much as Northup reveres William Ford (played by a beloved TV actor Mason Adams in Gordon Parks' film and a rather mild Benedict Cumberbatch in McQueen's film), he despises Ford's "po' white trash" carpenter Tibeats for whom he must work: "I despised both his disposition and his intellect" (1853/2013, p. 55). The loathing is mutual. Tibeats (played wonderfully in McQueen's version by Paul Dano, a specialist in sadistic characters since his role in the 2007 *There Will Be Blood*) hates Northup for his obviously superior intellect, as demonstrated by Northup's engineering a clever way to float Master Ford's lumber rather than carry it overland. Dano's Tibeats says twice to Northup, "Are you an engineer or are you a nigger?" (McQueen 2013). In all versions, Northup eventually literally strikes back at Tibeats. Parks, almost inexplicably, omits the whole follow-up scene where Tibeats and others then try to hang Northup. Perhaps it would have been just too gruesome for an American Playhouse TV audience. In any case, this brings us to our first close reading of a scene in McQueen's film: the harrowing scene of 'lynching interruptus.'

The Ridley/McQueen adaptation, as noted at the start of this article, features, as all adaptations do, omissions of source material; changes (for instance McQueen gives Northup two children instead of three, thereby saving on casting costs); and interpolations (for instance the early scene when Solomon is lying among a crowd of sleeping slaves and a strange woman rolls over next to him and initiates sex). In the original book, Northup has no sex (at least that he tells about) for 12 years. Gordon Parks (1984) found that unlikely and gave Northup (Avery Brooks) an interpolated girlfriend, Jenny, who is made, oddly enough, to take the place of Patsey (whom Parks decides to completely omit from his version).

The original version of the scene in Northup's book mentions a near-lynching but by no means the partial asphyxiation that McQueen depicts. In the book, Northup is bound and left at least partly immobilized in the burning sun. The heat and his bindings are, however, the chief source of his pain. He wears a noose, but there is no mention of his having been left in a hanging position. The evidence for that conclusion is the following passage from the book: "I wanted to lie down, but knew I could not rise again. The ground was so parched and boiling hot I was aware it would add to the discomfort of my situation" (Northup 1853/2013, p. 60). If Northup, again in the original text, were able to lie down but decided not to, the noose could not have been restraining him tightly from above. Here are some points to consider in Ridley and McQueen's version.

First note the dream-like speed at which we go from the men's approaching Solomon on horseback to their dragging him, already bound, to a tree right near the Big House. The quick cuts with no transition seem to emphasize the sudden, inexorable nature of Solomon's impending doom. In another moment—we are seeing the scene in very matter-of-fact middle-and long-distance shots—the rope is over the limb and the men are hoisting Northup upward off of his feet—gasping and gurgling as the noose tightens. His body convulses and twitches, just as the bodies of the lynched slaves in one of the film's parallel scenes.

It is at this point that Chapin, the overseer (J.D. Evermore), interrupts the hoisting and the quick-paced progress of the scene so far. He dramatically warns the would-be lynchers that they are, in effect, breaking the law, not because they are killing another human being but because they are about to destroy a valuable piece of property that does not belong to them. They are, in effect, vandals—not murderers (though neither term is used in the dialogue). As the lynchers digest this, the rope slips back far enough to put Northup—still gurgling and gasping—on his feet, but only on his tiptoes. This sets up the strange, almost delicate *danse macabre sur les pointes* that Solomon will perform—his toes just barely touching the ground—for the rest of that day. We have a few quick close up shots of his toes just touching the earth, and perilously sliding in the mud, to make the situation even worse. The toes are taking just barely enough of his body weight to prevent total asphyxiation.

The realization that partial asphyxiation is a sexual practice used by some to enhance pleasure will probably not occur to the horrified viewer on a first viewing of the scene, but the thought may well occur later. This is perhaps the most thoroughly sadistic scene in the film. McQueen prolongs it in a series of masterful (given his intent) zoom outs and mixed-(soft and sharp) focus shots. Solomon is made to stand there, still choking, toes reaching frantically for the ground, as his tormentors are grandly dismissed by Chapin, the overseer ("'Be gone, I say!'") (McQueen 2013), and another slave is dispatched on mule back to quickly fetch Master Ford from what must have been a distant location. It must have been a distant spot because the unseen mule trip takes forever—trapped as we are in the hanging scenario—both inside and outside of our focal character's head. We see him from the outside and hear him choke and then grow strangely silent. We see other characters in the film, from his POV, just looking at him squirm and dangle. In fact, a whole parade of onlookers comes by. There are slaves, down on Solomon's same level, going calmly about their chores. No one dares do anything to help him, save one woman, Rachel (Nicole Collins), who finally brings him a cup of water. It is a crucifixion of sorts. All look on, but only one thief has a kind word to spare.

The overseer watches from the Big House's lower porch, its lovely ironwork, likely crafted by slaves, reminiscent of Bourbon Street in New Orleans. Time passes. The Mistress (Liza J. Bennett) appears on the upper porch, gazes down at Solomon, still standing, still choking. She simply turns and walks away. Time passes. Perhaps the most wrenching moment is a shot done over Northup/Ejiofor's shoulder that pulls into focus children playing in the background of the same frame in which Solomon is hanging. The next generation is being indoctrinated into both fear and callous disregard for one another. More time passes. During the lynching act itself, a kind of low rasping instrumental moan, reminiscent of the sound of an Australian didgeridoo, has been heard on the soundtrack. But now, during the slow dying process, we hear the sounds of a summer day: birds, insects, children laughing at play. We have one super-long shot that shows Northup—still dangling from his tree like the Spanish moss—away off in the distance. His torture and his agony have become simply part of the scenery. He hangs there just as the moss hangs, with both man, nature, and the forcibly complicit movie audience, all apparently indifferent to his plight.

In the last part of the scene, time starts up again. We see and hear the master's horse galloping up. The master (Benedict Cumberbatch) leaps from his horse and pulls a sword or machete from his saddle. Finally, someone is taking urgent action to save Solomon's life—or is it to save a valuable piece of property? We next cut to a low-angle shot of Solomon lying in the elegant foyer of the Big House, having been dumped (albeit with a pillow for his head) on the hard wooden floor. At least he is inside, his body curled into a fetal position.

Though the source material—Northup standing bound in the sun with a noose around his neck—is disturbing in and of itself, McQueen clearly accentuates the sadism of the scene, spreading the guilt to people as unlikely as Mrs. Ford whom Northup in the source book adores: "It was a great pleasure to work for so good a mistress" (Northup 1853/2013, p. 73). He speaks of the "gentle and generous hand of my protectress" and calls the Fords' plantation "that little paradise in the Great Pine Woods" (1853/2013, p. 73). This is a far cry from the mistress in McQueen's adaptation who peers down disdainfully from the upper porch on the dying Northup and does nothing.

And then, having barely survived Tibeats, we (still locked into Northup's POV and fate) are almost immediately introduced to Edwin Epps, played in the McQueen film with convincing menace by Michael Fassbender, as the very incarnation of sadism. In the original book, Northup and Wilson describe the cultivation of cotton and later sugar cane with great thoroughness and exactitude, perhaps because eyewitness veracity in one area lends credence to the incredible depredations they are describing in another area, namely the habits and disposition of Epps. Epps' use of terror, torture, and nasty nocturnal surprises such as forced dancing for the exhausted slaves truly strains credulity. But chief among his deplorable habits is his abuse of Patsey, his best cotton picker and preferred sexual victim. In a 19th century book, one is not surprised to hear Patsey's sexual torture summed up in euphemisms. She is said to be, for example, "the slave of a licentious master and a jealous mistress" (1853/2013, p. 90). Northup continues, "The enslaved victim of lust and hate, Patsey had no comfort of her life" (1853/2013, p. 90).

McQueen's depiction of one of Patsey's routine rapes not only shows us what the book only implies of their relationship, but it accentuates what McQueen must see as the real nature of Epps' lust. Unfortunately, in order to understand Epps' nature, we as audience members are trapped, again, into witnessing it along with our hapless protagonist.

The prelude-to-a-rape scene begins in nearly total darkness. We realize it must be late at night in some communal space where the slaves sleep. Someone can be heard entering the space. The intruder passes a makeshift cot, moving left of frame to right. On the cot lies a horizontal figure we recognize—again with difficulty—as Northup. We get a shot of Northup at the camera level of his cot with special focus on Ejiofor's eyes. They are wide open—whites gleaming—in the darkness. Once we see them, we are astonished that the intruder has not also seen them. Or, we surmise, perhaps he has seen that Northup is wide awake, and he just does not care. After all, a Black man is invisible in all ways that matter, thoroughly useless as a witness in that he cannot testify against a white man. Northup is relegated to helpless voyeur. We clearly recognize the intruder is Epps when we cut to a shot of his laying Patsey (Lupita Nyong'o) on some hard wooden surface in order to rape her. There's an odd, almost tender gesture of his pulling her head up and touching it to his. But the gesture, we quickly understand, is not tender. It ends in a head butt that is part of his positioning of her body beneath him. Patsey lies back with a look of both sorrow and pathetic resignation. Restrained as she is by her rapist's grasp, Nyong'o is acting almost exclusively with her eyes. McQueen's shot of the copulating couple is chaste by current standards —he only shows them from their waists up. Yet the violence of Epps' thrusts is unmistakable. Fassbender acts with his whole face, effectively suggesting the sex act with his grunts and upper body movements. Epps pushes Patsey's head downward into her neck, with no care for what pain that must cause her. He seems to be reaching a climax when suddenly he hesitates and calls out her name—again almost tenderly—as if seeking her attention.

But we soon realize what he is doing. Having fallen short of his climax, he is forcing her to help him. She raises up slightly to receive a vicious blow across the face. Fassbender feigns, very realistically, the climax he had been seeking, having achieved it by the direct act of inflicting pain. We infer he has become dependent on such measures to achieve sexual satisfaction. Elsewhere his jealous wife taunts him with the epithet "Eunuch!" Epps quickly climbs off of Patsey's body and leaves the frame. We are left with the sight of her still sprawled on the wooden platform, her eyes staring upward, whites gleaming, just as Northup's had.

Our third scene for analysis from McQueen's film, the whipping of Patsey near the swine pen (a heavily symbolic feature of the Epps family's front yard), depicts a *locus classicus* of every slavery film, even the parodic ones.[5] As noted earlier, Gordon Parks rather inexplicably omits Patsey

---

5   The best known slavery films, *Roots* and its sequels (1977, 1979, 1988, 2016), *Amistad* (1997), and *Beloved* (1998) all have memorable whipping scenes. Such scenes have become so identified with slave narratives, that film-makers such as Rainer Werner Fassbinder and Quentin Tarantino do 'send-ups' of whipping scenes in *Whity* (1971) and Tarantino's *Django Unchained* (2012) respectively. For an analysis of the scene in *Whity*, please see my chapter "Rainer and *Der weise Neger*: Fassbinder's and Kaufmann's On and Off Screen Affair as German Racial Allegory," in *From Black to Schwarz: Cultural Crossovers between African America and Germany,* (2011) especially p. 251–254. For discussion of Tarantino's *Django Unchained,* see the special June 2013 issue of *Transition* journal, with an interview of Tarantino by Henry Louis Gates, JR. and other articles. Tarantino has never, to my knowledge, credited the Fassbinder film as an inspiration for his own dubious, hyperviolent, and self-indulgent 'revenge fantasy/ Western.'

from his whole 1984 adaptation, preferring to create a 'girlfriend' for Solomon (Avery Brooks) named Jenny (Rhetta Greene), whom he is, however, also forced to whip. Parks set the scene at first off-screen, with plenteous, very realistic cracks and thuds of the whip and howls of pain emanating from the unseen victim. The TV viewers were soon allowed to see, however, that Northup was only pretending to whip his girlfriend, a practice at which the real Northup boasts of being skilled. In the Parks version, Northup does, however, eventually lose his girlfriend to the sexual overtures of her master.

In the McQueen adaptation, Northup and Patsey are friends but not lovers. Patsey trusts Northup enough to ask him to drown her and end the torture of her life with Epps. Northup refuses in a gesture we eventually may judge as weakness on his part. The reproachful, already dead eyes of Patsey are the last thing he appears to notice as he drives away in the carriage with his Northern rescuers near the end of the film, leaving her behind in hell.

The scene in which Patsey is whipped, however, serves as a culminating example of McQueen's hyper-violent, 21st-century take on Northup's narrative. Northup's book does admittedly provide suggestive source material. The original Epps orders Patsey staked out on the ground (not at a whipping post, where McQueen places her). Epps in the book shouts to Northup, "Strike harder or your turn will come next, you scoundrel" (Northup 2013, p. 119). That such a man would ever have been fooled by Gordon Parks' ploy of off-screen yelling remains very doubtful. Northup and Wilson write of Patsey's "flesh quivering at every stroke" (2013, p. 119). McQueen has his Northup striking, but without full force—wounding but not lacerating. It is Mrs. Epps (Sarah Paulson), standing close at hand to enjoy her rival's come-uppance, who says in disgust at Northup's weak lashing, "He pantomimes" (McQueen 2013). The reference to theatrical spectacle (though the invention of screenwriter Ridley) is spot on for the spectatorial nature of the whipping event—virtually all the whipping events in slave movies. They are the public aspect of private sadism—intended to instill fear into other slaves as much as enjoyment for sadistic overseers and masters.

McQueen's (2013) whipping scene is shot with as much emphasis on the faces of the whippers as the whipped. Northup increases the severity of his blows once Epps very convincingly screams a threat in his ear that he will kill *all* his negroes if Northup does not strike harder. There is an occasional quick close-up reverse shot to catch a spray comprised of flying blood and bits of flesh coming off of the victim's back, especially once

Epps himself takes over the whipping from Northup. Epps first gives Northup a stroke of the lash to show his disgust at his ineptitude, and then takes over flogging Patsey with fresh passion. He establishes a lashing rhythm reminiscent of the sex scene. Northup implores Epps to stop by citing some hard-to-discern Scripture about sin. Epps finally stops to rebut Northup's accusation, claiming there is no sin when a man destroys his own property.

Though McQueen has been liberal (overly so) in his showing of nude Black bodies at the slave pens and markets and (unbelievably) inside a slave dealer's home, he does not show Patsey's full nude body in this scene until one quick shot at the end, followed by an equally fast reverse angle of her falling backwards onto her opened-up back when she is cut down from the whipping post. Her legs partly straddle the obscenely phallic whipping post as she falls. There follows another brief scene that seems *de rigeur* in cinematic slave narratives—namely the tending of the horribly wounded flesh on the victim's back, shown first with a high angle shot looking down on the bloody pulp and then in a shot including the slave women nursing Patsey. They are torturing her further, albeit for the purpose of healing. Rarely are pity and terror so effectively combined, except perhaps in Greek tragedies.

Though certain other key elements of tragedy are missing from slave narratives—written or filmed—Aristotle's theory of the way horrible events can have a salutary, cathartic effect on their witnesses remains at the heart of this paper's concerns. Have we as spectators been cleansed, ennobled, or really just degraded by the spectacle of Patsey's whipping? Or perhaps, in more modern post-Brechtian terms, have we been politicized into an urge to take corrective action—perhaps for the victims' heirs? Many believe reparations and other corrections would be just and very appropriate, even 150 years post-Emancipation.

12 Years: Directorial Intent

[W]riting about whipping and whipping itself both participate in a staging of the body—whether that body is 'real' or 'fantastic'—before the eyes of captivated spectators.[6]

---

6   Mills (2012, p. 176–179).

> The double meaning of witnessing—*eyewitness* testimony based on first-hand knowledge, on the one hand, and *bearing witness* to something beyond recognition that can't be seen, on the other—is the heart of subjectivity. The tension between eyewitness testimony and bearing witness both positions the subject in finite history and necessitates the infinite response-ability [sic] of subjectivity.[7]

British Director Steven McQueen's conscious intent in making *12 Years* (2013) is clearly not to titillate but rather to infuriate us—the spectators—at the unspeakable evils perpetrated under the once legal system of chattel slavery. As Luc Boltanski says in his book *Distant Suffering: Morality, Media and Politics* (1999, p. 57), "But pity is transformed by indignation. It is no longer disarmed and powerless, but acquires the weapons of anger [...] The speech act which expresses it is an accusation." Boltanski continues with a categorization of various types of provocation artists may employ to reach an audience. The first type, denunciation, gives rise to a feeling of 'indignation.' Here one might place Frederick Douglass' abolitionist *Narrative of the Life of a Slave* and Northup and Wilson's original book *12 Years a Slave.* The second type, 'sentiment'—and here one would have to place *Uncle Tom's Cabin*—gives rise to 'tender-heartedness' in the reader or audience. Boltanski's third category 'aesthetics' gives rise to and awareness of the Sublime in its technical, literary meaning, including horrors. Had Steve McQueen's film been around in 1999, surely Boltanski would have placed it in that third, roiling pot of mixed, elevated emotions.

Avoiding Pornography? The Future of Cinematic Slave Narratives

> [P]ornography is invariably degrading to anyone who looks at or reads it; it creates 'incurable distance' and betrays those with whom we are trying to identify.[8]

> We wanted to come as close as possible to desecration without re-desecrating.[9]

In his interview with Quentin Tarantino about *Django Unchained*, Henry Louis Gates, Jr. —also a consultant on McQueen's film—asked Tarantino why he thought slavery has become such a hot topic in movies. As evidence, Gates cited the recent release of *Lincoln*, the then-impending release of McQueen's *12 Years* and a project he himself is co-producing on

---

7 Oliver (2001, p. 16).
8 James Agee, discussing graphic newsreels of the Battle of Iwo Jima qtd. in Dean (2003, p. 98).
9 Michael Berenbaum, Project Director of the US Holocaust Memorial Museum qtd. in Dean (2003, p. 101).

Frederick Douglass. Tarantino, whose send-up of slave films also featured horrifically violent scenes such as dogs disemboweling slaves, answered that he did not know why slavery is in 'the air' as a theme, but that he (Tarantino) found it exciting "from an American storytelling perspective and an American healing perspective" (Gates, JR. 2013, n.p.).

Tarantino makes the point often made in such discussions—that re-experiencing a horror can be a salutary part of the healing process.[10] This is certainly a truism and keeps psychiatrists in business. But do we really need Tarantino as a guide through such a process? Do we really need a violent video game (*Assassin's Creed: Liberation*) in which slavery is the theme? (Suellentrop 2014, p. 3). What price do we pay for what Edmund Burke called way back in the 18th century a "license to look" (cf. Klarer 2005, p. 574)? Is the erotic charge associated with sadism cancelled out by good intentions? Director Steve McQueen is a Black British artist. Do we grant him extra leeway to explore these issues because of his race and his clear intention to incite righteous anger rather than titillate?

Critic Carolyn Dean, in discussing ideas of Fredric Jameson, says, "pornography does not encourage but freezes discussion" (2003, p. 93). Though there is potential danger in the graphic violence used in McQueen's film, it seems to, on the whole, stimulate rather than freeze analysis (e.g. this very study). In that sense, the film places us on a razor's edge of complex sensations which demand further discussion. It should therefore *not* be labeled as pornographic, but certainly *should* be considered as a difficult, even slightly dangerous work of art.

---

10   *Miami Herald* journalist Leonard Pitts, writing a March 2014 column in response to *12 Years* said: "If reconciliation is truly what black and white Americans seek in the great chimera called 'race,' then the pathway to that lies not in going around, but together, through that which brings us heartache and sorrow and makes us weep" (2014, n.p.).

Works Cited

Aristotle/Hardison, O. B./Golden, L. (1968): Aristotle's Poetics: A Translation and Commentary for Students of Literature. Englewood Cliffs, NJ: Prentice-Hall.

Boltanski, Luc (1999): Distant Suffering: Morality, Media and Politics. Cambridge: Cambridge University Press.

Dean, Carolyn J. (2003): Empathy, Pornography, and Suffering. In: differences: A Journal of Feminist Cultural Studies 14, no. 1, p. 88–124.

Gates, Henry Louis, JR. (2013): 'An Unfathomable Place': a conversation with Quentin Tarantino about Django Unchained. In: Transition no. 112, p. 47–66, muse.jhu.edu/article/523345, 30/12/2020.

Hartman, Saidiya V. (1997): Scenes of Subjection: Terror, Slavery, and Self-Making in Nineteenth Century America. New York, NY: Oxford University Press.

Jordan, Julie/Coulton, Antoinette Y. (2014). Lupita Nyong'o Is PEOPLE's Most Beautiful. In: PEOPLE.com of 23/04/2014, people.com/celebrity/lupita-nyongo-is-peoples-most-beautiful-2/, 2/1/2021.

Klarer, Mario (2005): Humanitarian Pornography: John Gabriel Stedman's 'Narrative of a Five Years Expedition against the Revolted Negroes of Suriname' (1796). In: New Literary History 36, no. 4, p. 559–587.

Laws, Page R. (2011): Rainer and Der weisse Neger: Fassbinder's and Kaufmann's On and Off Screen Affair as German Racial Allegory. In: Diedrich, Maria/Heinrichs, Jürgen (eds.): From Black to Schwarz: Cultural crossovers between African America and Germany. Michigan: Michigan State University Press, p. 245–265.

Mills, Robert (2012): In Praise of the Whip: A Cultural History of Arousal (review). In: Journal of the History of Sexuality 21, no. 1, p. 176–179, DOI:10.1353/sex.2012.0009, 30/12/2020.

Noble, Marianne (1997): The Ecstasies of Sentimental Wounding in Uncle Tom's Cabin. In: The Yale Journal of Criticism 10, no. 2, p. 295–320, DOI:10.1353/yale.1997.0024, 30/12/2020.

Northup, Solomon (2013): Twelve Years a Slave: Narrative of Solomon Northup, a Citizen of New York, Kidnapped in Washington City in 1841, and Rescued in 1853: Seven Treasures Publications (Original work published 1853).

Oliver, Kelly (2001): Witnessing: Beyond Recognition. Minneapolis, London: University of Minnesota Press.

Parks, Gordon (Director): (1984). Solomon Northup's Odyssey. American Playhouse, Season 4, Episode 3 [Television broadcast]. PBS.

Pitts, Leonard (2014). A healing Movie. In: The Virginian-Pilot of 09/03/2014.

Regency Enterprises, River Road Entertainment, Plan B Entertainment (Producer). & McQueen, S. (Director): (2013). 12 Years a Slave: Fox Searchlight Pictures, Entertainment One Films, Summit Entertainment.

Rothman, Lily (2013). Controversial Italian 12 Years a Slave Poster Stirs Debate Over Movies and Race. In: Time.com of 27/12/2013, entertainment.time.com/2013/12/

27/controversial-italian-12-years-a-slave-poster-stirs-debate-over-movies-and-race/, 30/12/2020.

Suellentrop, Chris (2014). Slavery as New Focus for a Game — Assassin's Creed: Liberation Examines Colonial Blacks. In: The New York Times of 27/01/2014.

Williams, Chad L. (2014): Solomon Northup's Odyssey: From American Playhouse to 12 Years a Slave. In: Humanities 35, no. 1, p. 16–18.

Worley, Sam (1997): Solomon Northup and the Sly Philosophy of the Slave Pen. In: Callaloo 20, no. 1, p. 243–259.

List of Contributors

Pirjo Ahokas is Professor emerita of Comparative Literature at the University of Turku, Finland. She is the author of *Forging a New Self*, a monograph on Bernard Malamud's novels and co-editor (with Martine Chard-Hutchinson) of *Reclaiming Memory: American Representations of the Holocaust*. Pirjo Ahokas's subsequent research deals with works by authors of Asian American, African American and Native American descent. She has also concentrated on new writing by Black British women authors. Pirjo Ahokas was a Fulbright visiting scholar at Yale University and an ACLS grantee at Harvard University. She is the former president and vice president of the Finnish American Studies Association. Pirjo Ahokas was a member of the steering board of the national Finnish Graduate School in American Studies. She is the co-editor of several collections of essays in Finnish and has been active in organizing international conferences at the University of Turku.

Aikaterini Delikonstantinidou (MA, MEd, PhD) is adjunct professor in the Department of Museum Studies, University of Patras, and postdoctoral fellow in the Department of Theatre Studies, National and Kapodistrian University of Athens. She works for the editorial team of *Critical Stages*, the journal of the International Association of Theatre Critics. As of May 2019, she is also the Young Scholar Representative of the Hellenic Association for American Studies (HELAAS). Her first monograph, titled *Latinx Reception of Greek Tragic Myth: Healing and Radical Politics* was released by Peter Lang in the summer of 2020 (Dramaturgy Series). Her research interests include theatre and the performing arts, myth's multi/transmedia reception, education, and the digital paradigm.

Astrid M. Fellner is Chair of North American Literary and Cultural Studies at Saarland University, Germany. She is Co-Speaker in the German Research foundation and Canadian Social Science Foundation-funded interdisciplinary International Graduate Research Training Program "Diversity: Mediating Difference in Transcultural Space" that Saarland University and University of Trier are conducting with the Université de Montréal. She is also Project Leader of the EU-funded INTERREG Großregion VA-Project "University of the Greater Region Center for Border Studies" at Saarland U and is Action Coordinator of a trilingual Border Glossary, a handbook of 40 key terms in Border Studies. She is also a member of the interdisciplinary BMBF-project "Linking Borderlands," in which she studies border films and industrial culture of the Greater Region in comparison with the German/Polish border. Her publications include *Articulating Selves: Contemporary Chicana Self-Representation* (2002) and several edited volumes and articles in the fields of Border Studies, U.S. Latino/a literature, Post-Revolutionary American Literature, Canadian literature, Indigenous Studies, Gender/Queer Studies, and Cultural Studies.

Dorothea Fischer-Hornung is a retired Senior Lecturer in the English Department at the University of Heidelberg, Germany, and faculty member of the Heidelberg Center for American Studies. Among her publications are the co-edited volumes *Aesthetic Practices and Politics in Media, Music, and Art: Performing Migration* (with Rocío G. Davis and Johanna C. Kardux; Routledge) and *Vampires and Zombies: Transnational Transformations* (with Monika Mueller; University Press of Mississippi). She is the author of numerous publications in the field of African and Native American literature and culture, with an emphasis on dance and performance studies. She was a founding member and executive officer of MESEA, The Society for Multi-Ethnic Studies: Europe and the Americas. And since 2004 she has been founding co-editor of the interdisciplinary journal *Atlantic Studies: Global Currents* (Routledge).

Bettina Hofmann teaches American Studies at the University of Wuppertal. She studied American literature and Jewish Studies at Heidelberg University, the Hochschule für Jüdische Studien, Heidelberg and at Brandeis University. Among her most recent publications are the volume *Translated Memories: Transgenerational Perspectives on the Holocaust*. Ed. Bettina Hofmann together with Ursula Reuter. Lanham, MD: Lexington, 2020 and "Transatlantische Perspektiven: Jüdisch-amerikanische Schriftsteller blicken auf die Ukraine." *Blondzende Stern: Jüdische Schriftstellerinnen und Schriftsteller aus der Ukraine als Grenzgänger zwischen den Kulturen in Ost und West*. Eds. Kerstin Schoor, Ievgeniia Voloshchuk and Borys Bigum. Göttingen: Wallstein, 2020, p. 338–355 and "Approaches to Teaching 'Goodbye, Columbus,'" together with Josh Lambert, Rachel Gordan, Benjamin Schreier, and Julian Levinson. *Teaching Jewish American Literature*. Eds. Roberta Rosenberg and Rachel Rubinstein. New York: MLA, 2020, p. 317–27.

Nadine M. Knight is an associate professor of English, affiliate of Africana Studies, and current Director of Interdisciplinary Studies at College of the Holy Cross in Worcester, Massachusetts, USA. Her research interests include African American representation and the relationship between war, race, and place in American literature, film, and television. She has published on militancy in Black American feminist literature of the 1970s, on the struggles for emancipation, security, and freedom in Colson White-head's novels, and on the Civil War plays of Suzan-Lori Parks, among other works.

Page Laws is Professor of English and founding Dean (now Emerita) of the Robert C Nusbaum Honors College at Norfolk State University in Virginia. Laws received her BA from Wellesley College and her MPhil and PhD in Comparative Literature from Yale University. She is an avid book, theater and film critic whose reviews have appeared in national and local newspapers and publications such as *Cineaste* and Brightlights-film.com. Her most recent academic essays are "Turning the Tide for African Literary Criticism: Achebe's 'An Image of Africa' as a Founding Text of Africana Studies," *Celebrating the 60th Anniversary of 'Things Fall Apart.'* Eds. Désiré Baloubi and Christina R Pinkston. Palgrave Macmillan, 2021, p. 169–178; and "Littoral/Literal Watermarks: Layers of Signification in Maritime Marseille," *Palimpsests in Ethnic and Postcolonial Literature and Culture.* Eds. Y. D. Kalogeras (et al.) Palgrave Macmillan, 2021, p. 81–98.

Francesca de Lucia holds a master's degree from the University of Geneva and a PhD from the University of Oxford. She taught at Minzu University in Beijing from 2016 to 2020 and has previously worked as an associate professor at Zhejiang Normal University of China in Jinhua. Her book *Italian American Cultural Fictions: From Diaspora to Globalization* was published by Peter Lang in 2017. The main focus of her research is on ethnic identity in literature and film. Her articles include "'An Abrupt Impression of Familiarity': Ethnic Projection in Arthur Miller's Work" (2012), "Founding Chinese America in Louis Chu's *Eat a Bowl of Tea*" (2017), "Looking for an Invisible Enemy in Israeli Film" (2018), "Gender, Generations and Ethnicity in Louise DeSalvo's *Crazy in the Kitchen*" (2019) and "L''Errand into the Wilderness' di Anthony Giardina" (2020).

Ludmila Martanovschi currently coordinates the American Studies BA Program at the Faculty of Letters, Ovidius University, Constanța, Romania. She received a PhD in Contemporary American Indian Literature from the University of Bucharest in 2008. As Fulbright grantee, she did research at the University of Nevada, Las Vegas, in 2003-2004, and at the Theater Program, the Graduate Center, City University of New York, in 2011. Having been an active member of the Society for Multi-Ethnic Studies: Europe and the Americas (MESEA) for fifteen years, she has published book chapters and journal articles in the field. Co-edited with Tatiani G. Rapatzikou, the recent collection of essays *Ethnicity and Gender Deba-*

tes. Cross-Readings of American Literature and Culture in the New Millennium (Peter Lang, 2020) proves her commitment to interdisciplinary scholarship and academic collaboration. Also, at present, she conducts research on the contemporary connections between migration, mobility, social justice and environmentalism.

Janna Odabas has completed the program of American Studies at the Graduate School of North American Studies at the John-F-Kennedy Institute of the Free University, Berlin. She earned her PhD in 2017 and her dissertation is published under the title *The Ghosts Within: Literary Imaginations of Asian America* (transcript, 2018). She earned her BA and MA degree with honors at Leibniz University Hannover, where she also worked as a research assistant. She published the articles "Ghostly Presences in *The Gangster We Are All Looking For* by Lê Thi Diem Thuy" (*Migration and Exile,* Ada Savin), "Do Ghosts Grow Up? Ghostliness in Maxine Hong Kingston's *The Woman Warrior* and *China Men*" (*On the Legacy of Maxine Hong Kingston*, Sämi Ludwig/Nicoleta Alexoae-Zagni), "Gespenstisches Amerika: Geister als Figuren der Selbstdarstellung und die Heimsuchung des 'Weißen Amerikas' in Louis Erdreichs *Tracks*" (*Ordnungen des Unheimlichen*, Florian Lehmann).

Silvia Schultermandl is Chair of American Studies at the University of Münster. She is the author of *Unlinear Matrilineage: Mother-Daughter Conflicts in Asian American Literature* (2009) and *Ambivalent Transnational Belonging in American Literature* (2021) and co-editor of seven collections of essays which explore various themes in transnational studies, American literature and culture, as well as family and kinship studies. Her articles have appeared in the following journals, among others: *Meridians*, *Atlantic Studies*, *Interactions*, *Journal of Transnational American Studies*, and *Journal of American Culture*. She is currently developing the *Palgrave Series in Kinship, Representation, and Difference* and is embarking on a new project on kinship and social media. Her areas of interest include affect theory, literary theory, critical race theory, queer theory, visual culture, and transnational feminism.

Elke Sturm-Trigonakis received her PhD in Spanish and Portuguese Philology and General Linguistics from the University of Heidelberg in 1993, and since 2001 has been Professor of Comparative Literature at the Aristotle University of Thessaloniki. Her main research field are multilingual and hybrid (New) World Literature, the picaresque novel, crime fiction, and postcolonial literature. Her books include *Barcelona in der Literatur* (1994), *Barcelona. La Novel.la Urbana* (1996), *Global playing in der Lit-*

eratur (2007), *Comparative Cultural Studies and the New Weltliteratur* (2013), *Το πικαρικό μυθιστόρημα. Εισαγωγή σε ένα αειφόρο λογοτεχνικό είδος* [The Picaresque Novel. Introduction to a Sustainable Literary Genre], 2020), *Sprachen und Kulturen in (Inter)Aktion* (ed., with S. Delianidou, 2013), *Turns und kein Ende? Aktuelle Tendenzen in Germanistik und Komparatistik* (ed., with O. Laskaridou, E. Petropoulou, K. Karakassi, 2017) and *World Literature and the Postcolonial. Narratives of (Neo) Colonization in a Globalized World*, 2020. She coordinates the Mediterranean-South European network of German Studies (MSEG).